SOCIALISM IS DEAD! LONG LIVE SOCIALISM!

The Marx Code—Socialism with a Human Face

(A New World Order)

By
Todor Bombov

Strategic Book Publishing and Rights Co.

I dedicate this work to my cherished parents, Boris and Nadezhda—pure and holy Bulgarians, great martyrs.

I dedicate this work to my uncle, too—Zdravko Bombov—who not only believed in the great idea but offered himself as a sacrifice to it when only twenty years old.

Table of Contents

Preface for the US Readers

Dear reader,

This book was under arrest, along with its author. This event occurred on March 27, 1986. During that time, the totalitarian system in East Europe was called *socialism* and even by the scientific nonsense and absurd names of *communism* and *communist system*. In this system, the official ideology was allegedly Marxism, but really it could not endure any Marxist criticism. Since this "socialist" system was afraid of the weapon of criticism, it applied criticism of the weapon against its own citizens, as Marx would have said. I had already written the first twenty odd pages when the "communist" State Security put me under arrest. After that, I had to reconstruct from memory all these pages. And I did. Then I continued writing the book. In 1993, when the "communist" regime toppled down, I succeeded in publishing the first edition of this book, and in 2002, I published the second edition. Now, in 2016, just thirty years after this arrest, I suggest to the US audience (as well as the world's), a new edition.

Why?

Because the United States, Europe, and the whole world, in the beginning of the twenty-first century, are in need of a new fundamental alternative! All of us saw the two dazzling explosions of the rebels/romanticists, Julian Assange and Edward Snowden, who like fireworks illuminated the dusky night of the life of servitude of seven billion people, penned into the Matrix, and strangling in the noose of the contemporary world totalitarianism. All of us saw what happened a few years ago in New York, London, and other cities. Occupy Wall Street, Occupy London, Blockupy, Zeitgeist, and Thrive—these are movements against the arbitrariness of the banks and monopolies, i.e., against the contemporary world order. The movements, Zeitgeist and Thrive, have brilliant criticism on the now existing World Bank system, but they have no idea how to change it and what to replace it with! They give a vision of a wonderful future world, but the way to reach it is sheer utopia! These two movements do not suggest any practically possible solution and the contemporary world order remains as if forever! In this connection, The Rebellion of the Indignant was the new global outcry, which wished a New World Order in reply to that imposed by George H. W. Bush's circles of a serial imperialist New World Order after the crash of the "communist" system! But today, a quarter of a century later, people all over the world are desperately looking for the Exodus again! And just here, in the heart of the problem, I propound to the audience, my work for a FULL solution of the problem, the problem being CAPITALISM! It's clear to me that only Marx's socialism could settle this New World Order! The only possible way to lead us to this order (and to the future) is through science, and this science is Marxism!

So, what does this work represent?

It is a book of Marxism. It suggests a New World Order of social equality and social justice. But along with that, it is also a political and economic dissection of the ex-society in all of East Europe by the lancet of Marx! It is an analysis from inside—an analysis made on the reality of my country, Bulgaria, the most devoted satellite of the ex-Soviet Union and its nearly full copy of political and economic systems.

The former name of this book was *Socialism—Lie of the Century or Century of the Lie*. It was topical to the end of the bygone twentieth century, but the new conditions force new steps. This is why for the US audience I did a new editing and new title of the book.

This work of mine is divided into two autonomous books.

The first book, *The State*, represents a radically new political system of the society, which is the most democratic system ever possible! This is completely new society, a real civil society, which otherwise in the capitalist system is only a utopia!

The second book, *The Economic Theory of Socialism*, is a sequel, and as far as I know, the only sequel of the greatest work by Marx—*Capital*! The economics of socialism makes Marx's socialism already completely possible. That's why, this very fact should provoke the curiosity of the readers, I hope.

This third edition was also processed and much expanded concerning the previous two and was prepared in its English version for three whole years. I hope it was worth the endeavors.

As it turns out, American people are increasingly interested in socialism! "Socialism" was the most looked-up word of 2015 on Merriam-Webster! It will be the most looked-up word in every next year, too! That is why, nowadays, a pressing need for Marxism is already felt everywhere! Let us return Marx to the studies and among the multitude! Let us return Marx among the scientists and among the workers! Return Marx—the greatest scientist of the second millennium!

- Todor Bombov

Preface to the First Edition

Dear reader,

The book, *Socialism—Lie of the Century or Century of the Lie,* was written about four or five years after 1985 and completed in February to March 1990. That is why, it has been written in the present tense—to be a criticism of the regime that existed until recently, and under another title—*What Is Socialism and Does It Have Any Ground at Our Side*? However, unfortunately, it could not be published for three years, which forced the author to enter some changes—passing it into past tense and canceling some out-of-date texts. No good words may be said about a democracy which, due to various reasons (and ways), does not admit another, different viewpoint both regarding totalitarianism and democracy.

The purpose of the book is to represent the historical truth about Marxism, explaining in this way the nature of the "socialist" system that existed until recently.

Under the common title of this work, the two books are actually put together.

In book one—*The State*—I scrutinize the principles of scientific socialism, i.e., all of those principles of Marxism concerning the state that build socialism as a political system. These are principles that have been rudely crushed and "forgotten" from Lenin's death to our days.

The book reveals the scientific untenable nature of the so-called "people's state"—the touchstone of the real acknowledgment of Marxism. Marx, Engels, and Lenin had always been the most irreconcilable opponents of the "people's state" whose petty bourgeois ideology was due to Lassalle and Proudhon, but not to the communist prime teachers.

In book two—*Theory of Wage*—I scrutinize the economic laws that build socialism as a more effective economic system than capitalism. These laws are extracted from Marx's main work –*Capital*. Such a production process is possible, in which the wage as a social relation represents a self-expanding value. This, on its part, does not allow the phenomenon of inflation to exist. This production process represents a repeating Carnot's cycle, which, on its part, allows social property of the means of production to be established that has been considered absurdity under the commodity production; to reject the exploitation and the unemployment in society, as well as to point out what is social equality and social justice with their concrete, but not abstract meaning.

The commodity of labor power is scrutinized—when and how it ceases being a commodity under socialism. The act of wage leveling is scrutinized, too—immanent not to socialism, but to equalitarian capitalism. Besides that, the subject matter of rent and of land under social property is examined. The book ends with the withering away of the commodity—according to its two conditions—and the transition from commodity to non-commodity, communist production relations.

- Todor Bombov

Preface to the Second Edition

Dear reader,

The book, *Socialism—Lie of the Century or Century of the Lie,* was written with big interruptions. The first ideas and flashes date from 1982, but the first summarized assembly into an integrated, orderly built system was made in the winters of 1988/89 and 1989/90. That is why it was written under another title—*What Is Socialism and Does It Have Any Ground at Our Side?* Dimitar Blagoev's title was not borrowed occasionally, nor was it a freak, but it expressed in the most exact way the content of the book if it would have been printed until 1990. Unfortunately, this was not made until 1993 when its first edition appeared. My publishing woes were not able to stop the creative writing process and finally, the book became a real fact, in spite of its modest printing and marketing. Therefore, this first edition became the skeleton around which the wholly revised and completed book was built later with its two autonomous parts; especially in the economic theory where three new chapters were added and there was a range of changes and additions to the other ones. This process of remaking the first edition and the preparation of a new edition of this work began mainly in the beginning of 1997 and went on until and including the year 2000. I consider that all disparities and mistakes in the first edition were removed, even in details.

I admit that the book, *The Socialism,* will be more accessible in its first part for a wider range of readers while reading the second one will need some preliminary theoretical preparation—general (macro-economics) and special (after *Capital* of Marx). The special preparation is particularly needed.

- **Todor Bombov**

"The classics should not only be respected but, from time to time, a bit perused."[1]

It was said—the scientists in the world are many, but the clever men are few.

Nowadays, a real invasion of heads of science has appeared, and they have forgotten "that socialism, having become a science, demands the same treatment as every other science—it must be studied."[2]

The trouble, however, comes not so much that it was "applied" without being studied, but rather from being studied with the purpose of not applied.

[1] Emile Korotki, *Fragments by the Unwritten*, 18
[2] Friedrich Engels, *The Peasant War in Germany*, 4:26

BOOK ONE

The State

Principles of Scientific Socialism

Chapter One

Origin and Nature of State

As the basic question of philosophy is the question of being-consciousness correlation, so the basic question in scientific socialism is that one about the state. Since its very beginning, battles have been carried on for the state using both weapon and criticism, both gunpowder and pen.

About one hundred thousand years ago on earth, there appeared a new qualitative state of the animate nature; a new form of organization and of movement of matter, quite unknown until those times appeared—the social form. **Society** appeared whose constructive unit was the separate man, the individual. The same way that substances crystallize in given conditions, i.e., it is "more profitable," or "more useful" for molecules to be bound in a crystal lattice rather than to exist "alone for themselves," under determined conditions, primitive men understood that it would be more advantageous to be bound into a kind of "crystal lattice"—the society. Just the society transmuted the monkey into a human by imposing labor to him, which developed his mental activity, his "Capacity to Judge." So, the adaptation of the individual to live within a society was a great step ahead of the development of the animate nature. Only society enabled species to communicate at a higher level through speech, which precisely forwarded, along with releasing the arms, the transformation of the livelihood activity into labor activity. Labor is an expedient activity of the human just because it is applied in a society. Labor outside of society is unthinkable. Indeed, Robinson Crusoe survived by his labor alone, but it was only because, before that, he was accustomed to work within the society. This is why a man placed early under inhuman conditions, say out of, or isolated from society, usually goes back to his primitive state, to his animal appearance and instincts (Kaspar Hauser, Rudyard Kipling's Mowgli, etc.).

Man's brain, which is the source of his conscious activity, can be developed only in one continuous flow of information with the exchange and processing of this information. And that is possible only within the combined work, i.e., work within society. During the continuous mingling with its like animal, the monkey's brain develops while fighting to survive, until arriving at the joint man.

From its first appearance to our days, society has been unceasingly developed thanks to the different abilities of each one of its members. Each man is strictly individual, single, and unique by its possibilities—physical and intellectual, as well as by its necessities—material and spiritual. The possibilities represent that whole amount of intellectual and physical energy, emanated by a given social unit—man, group, society—which is applied as a purposeful activity, i.e., as a labor. The possibilities are an aggregate of all the physical and intellectual forces of this unit spent during the process of its reproduction. While the necessities yet, as Marx says, are a historical product, they are such a material and spiritual indispensability, which is already realized by this same social unit. That is why freedom is also a necessity, even a higher necessity!

The necessities are immanent to the human only, but not "any living being's property,"[3] as a contemporary theory had taught us. They are not a property, but a quality. Furthermore, they do not relate to any living being, but to the human only and to his society. Such a property is the need—this is just the need, which is related to any living being.

There are multiple reasons, but mostly the need expressed in the fight for existence and survival have been the main reasons, which have forced particular individuals to form a society. The possibilities of the individual prove to be insufficient to satisfy his own unceasingly growing necessities. That is why, in order to satisfy the necessities of each individual, it necessitated the use of the possibilities of the society. Society may be developed without the possibilities of some individuals, but no individual may be developed without the possibilities of the society. This means that the individual depends on society and he must be subordinated to that society. This individual's subordination originates the question about the liberty of this individual with its concomitant dependence on the society. A question is known to us in the newer times as human liberty and rights—when and how may the particular person be free and may his or her liberty be compatible with the liberty of all the others?

The answer to these questions cannot be found if society is not

---

[3]. Andrei G. Zdravomyslov, *Necessities, Interests, Values*, 18 .

considered along its development—when and why the monolithic entity of the society became divided into hostile camps and how long it will be divided in this way.

The entire vital activity of the individual as well as of society represents an unceasing satisfaction of various necessities with the purpose to grow given possibilities. Some necessities remain permanent over the course of time while others change according to the level of society's possibilities at any given moment. So, in order to evaluate the real quantity of these necessities, they should be contrasted to their opposites—the possibilities. There is a mutual connection between possibilities and necessities, individual and social; they are narrowly interlaced. The possibilities determine the level of the necessities, but in their turn, necessities influence the development of possibilities, too. In an antagonistic world, possibilities are not always necessary, and necessities are not always possible!

Taken as a whole unit, possibilities and necessities frame the **interests**. These interests are halfway considered now—being related to the necessities only, i.e., identified with them solely. In fact, the interest is a necessity with a deprived possibility. Interest is the possibility to satisfy one's own necessity through the satisfaction of another's necessity, which is deprived of such possibility. Interests have always been and will always be "the economic relations of a given society,"[4] which governs this society—relations between the possibilities and the necessities within it.

In a certain stage of the development of society, in the contradictions and fights between possibilities and necessities, this leads to **social inequality**.

What is the reason for this and how did it arrive?

It's an economic reason, i.e., sheer material—as a "result of altered relations of production and exchange, in the interest of increased production and in furtherance of intercourse."[5]

Thanks to the intensifying division of labor, generating growth of the possibilities of the productive forces, more and more products meant for the satisfaction of the necessities of the tribal society are produced for **exchange** and less for personal use of the individual. In the tribal society, "the gentile constitution was finished. It had been shattered by

---

[4]. Karl Marx, *Capital*, 1:781
[5]. Friedrich Engels, *Anti-Dühring*, 8:183.

the division of labor and its result, the cleavage of society into classes. It was replaced by the *state*."[6] Still, Plato wrote about the division of labor and the origin of the exchange, and on their basis, the origin of the state. "A State," Socrates says, "arises, as I conceive, out of the needs of mankind; no one is self-sufficing, but all of us have many wants. Can any other origin of a State be imagined?"

"There can I be no other,"[7] answers Adeimantus.

This was barely with the participation of the individual in the social division of labor, which appears "caused by differences of sex and age"[8] that the different possibilities of different individuals start to get distinguished as a natural difference or a natural inequality. The division of labor is the basis of their manifestation. "It is, therefore, the law of division of labor that lies at the basis of the division into classes."[9]

The changed conditions of production and the originated on this basis exchange in the tribal society gradually decomposed this society and it formed different layers—an unimportant part became dominating over the other enormous mass not by another thing, but by its better ability to satisfy necessities. This quantitative difference of possessions has led to a qualitative difference of property—it was transformed into **private**! When the equilibrium between the social possibilities and the individual necessities was broken and degenerated into a conflict, then the entity of society was broken, too. Society was divided into groups having different social interests. Already the social interests entered into contradiction with the individual ones and vice versa.

When the possibilities of the society are in harmony with the necessities of the individual and vice versa, then we can speak of social equality, regardless of the extant natural inequality in the possibilities of the individual. Natural inequality in the possibilities has led to a **social inequality** in the necessities! Or, if the natural inequality represents inequality in realizing the possibilities, the social inequality is inequality in satisfaction of the necessities, i.e., if the natural inequality is innate, the social inequality is acquired.

Social inequality—this is the estate inequality within the society,

---

[6]. Friedrich Engels, *The Origin of the Family, Private Property and the State*, 5:176.
[7]. Plato, *The Republic*, 67
[8]. Marx, *Capital*, 1:393
[9]. Friedrich Engels, *Socialism: Utopian and Scientific*, 1:147

when any unimportant part of it, thanks to its dominant position towards the means of production, in satisfaction of its necessities, dominates with its property status over the other underlying parts, whose status is a result of the realization not so much of its own individual possibilities, but mostly of the social ones. Social inequality arises in an elemental, unconscious way, "based ... on voluntariness and custom"[10], like a blind homage of the authority. The existence of private property is the economic basis of the existence of social inequality. In other words, social inequality is an indicator of the existence of private property, which "by no means makes its appearance in history as the result of robbery or force."[11] We cannot still speak about force, here. Force comes later when the utilization of another's labor is done already in a conscious, premeditated, purposeful way, when another's labor commences to be appropriated, i.e., when the social inequality develops into **social injustice**.

Of course, during the centuries, justice was always a rather elastic term, but always until now and "everywhere there is one principle of justice, which is the interest of the stronger."[12] First, if we actually consider justice as dressed in a black legal toga only, then much of justice is abstract and hazy. But it obtains a quite concrete and clear appearance when it is landed to its economic nature, i.e., when it refers to the **labor**.

And second, when justice refers not so much to the separate individual's labor, but rather to large social groups' labor, i.e., we speak not of individual justice, but of social justice. I cannot give another name, but social injustice, to indicate the appropriation of another's labor of large groups of people by an organized minority via the conscious and systematic activity of plundering called exploitation.

Social injustice represents an infringement of the social distribution of the products of labor, received when the possibilities of the entire society are consciously used to satisfy the necessities of an unimportant part of it. There is injustice in the distribution processes only as a result of extant already social inequality. Social injustice appears when the common individual interests are differentiated as disparate social interests.

---

[10]. Engels, *Anti-Dühring*, 8:183.
[11]. Ibid.
[12]. Plato, *The Republic*, 25.

The exchange transformed the products into commodities, which, in their turn, imposed the need for a universal commodity—money. And if commodity created the social inequality and private property, money created **the power**! The law comes with the exchange, the same way the appetite comes while eating. In order to be established as a normal social system, private property legalized social injustice through the **force**, i.e., the power was constituted in a special machinery of compulsion with interior functions—for repressions, and exterior functions—for armed intervention. In this manner, the social groups, resulting from the estate differentiation, accepted the name of **classes**, and the shell locking them up in the joint for life was called a **State**.

So, if social inequality is an expression of private property, social injustice and force are respectively a synthetic expression of the state. Social injustice in the distribution processes is a result of the exchange, having been imposed in the society through private property. That's why the state is a reflection of the exchange. There is a state only where and when the exchange is extant. There cannot be an exchange without its legislative regulation by the state. As for it, the state cannot function without commodity and money, i.e., without the exchange, simply because any force is measured and paid out with gold. Force, says Marx, "is itself an economic power."[13]

The force within the state is manifested with the power of one class over the entire society, whose power results from its dominating position in the production. The state was always represented not by all constitutive classes, but by only one—that one which was in power. Yet, in order to be in power, this class carries out injustice and violence against its subordinate classes. Injustice and violence are both features determining the state because all phenomena of the social life in it are finally reduced to them.

The state is a power of one class, which, based on its dominating position in the production carries out an unjust social distribution of the products of labor by using violence.

State's power represents "the concentrated and organized social force"[14]. Until nowadays, the state has always been the animal-trainer who formed public opinion by cracking a whip. Every state exists only through injustice and force, and vice versa, injustice and force in the society can exist only within the state. The state exists just because

---

[13]. Marx, *Capital*, 1:819.
[14]. Ibid., 693

injustice and force exist in the society, i.e., the state is their protective cover. As Lenin writes, the state exists because of the irreconcilability of the contradictions between the classes from which it is constituted. The state exists just because these contradictions are irreconcilable and lead to injustice and force.

The possibilities of every individual are, by their nature related to the necessities for their satisfaction. This situation, however, changes with the intervention of the state—the possibilities are separated, detached from the necessities of a significant part of the society, which is subordinated to other class interests. Then, many necessities become impossible as well as many possibilities become unnecessary. The antagonistic state oppresses the other class interests in a way that the oppressed cannot use the full possibilities but only minimum possibilities of the society. Such a state restricts the possibilities and denatures the necessities for its own profit and according to its own model.

Every class carries out its power only by force, by dictate, no matter that the form of doing this is rough or soft (through "the stick or carrot"). However, this class calls its own dictate and represents it in the whole society as a democracy. That's why any class state proves to be a democracy of that class, i.e., the **class** democracy represents the **contents** of the state. A few such types of the state have been known until now, according to the mode of production: a slave-owning democracy—in the slave-owning state; a democracy of the landed aristocracy—in the feudal state; a democracy of the bourgeois—in the capitalist state. That's why the democracy of the working class represents the contents of the socialist state.

Just the class division of society creates two different, two parallel worlds/antipodes in this very society. And this means yet two polar models of behavior in the political life of the society—the democracy of the rich class is, in fact, a dictatorship for the poor one! In other words, the state is not of people and democracy is not for all.

However, these are elementary to the point of being naïve, and childishly simple truths are not acceptable for this caste, whichever was called opportunism. Since their appearance, until reaching today's higher phase, the representatives of this confraternity have always dreamed of their so-called "people's state," i.e., a state of the entire people and a common democracy for the entire people. According to Marxism, democracy is not and cannot be common to the entire people; it can be a class democracy only.

It is our duty to remind the wide audience of the authentic Marxism, i.e., Marx's truth about society.

So, now the matter is, according to the *science* of Marxism, what is a socialist state and what is its nature?

Chapter Two

The Socialist State

The truth and the lie are always lying one next to the other—just as Marx and Spenser were lying one next to the other in Highgate. However, it does not mean that along with the truth is buried the lie, too.

In difference of opportunistic rebuses, quibbles, and tangles, Lenin determines in only a few lines quite briefly and in a very simple and clear way, what the socialist state must be, on the grounds of the historical experience of the Paris Commune and of Marx's critical analyses.

> In this connection, the following measures of the Commune, emphasized by Marx, are particularly noteworthy: the abolition of all representation allowances, and of all monetary privileges to officials, the reduction of the remuneration of *all* servants of the state to the level of "*workmen's wages*". This shows more clearly than anything else *the turn* from bourgeois to proletarian democracy . . .[15]

And more:

> All officials, without exception, elected and subject to recall *at any time*, their salaries reduced to the level of ordinary "workmen's wages"—these simple and "self-evident" democratic measures, while completely uniting the interests of the workers and the majority of the peasants, at the same time serve as a bridge leading from capitalism to socialism.[16]

These are namely the measures taken by the Commune that Marx stops his attention on by particularly stressing their importance.

> The Commune was formed of the municipal councilors, chosen by universal suffrage in the various wards of the town, responsible and revocable at short terms . . .

---

[15]. Vladimir Illyich Lenin, *The State and Revolution*, 33:41-42.
[16]. Ibid.,43.

From the members of the Commune downwards, the public service had to be done at *workman's wage*. The vested interests and the representation allowances of the high dignitaries of state disappeared along with the high dignitaries themselves.[17]

In fact, out of the thirty most significant measures undertaken by the Paris Commune, we can extract five of them to which all the change of one society is reduced, while destroying the old state and at the same time, creating the new one. By their nature, these measures represent five principles, which are **universal** for every state, pretending to be called a socialist state. This is the reason that they are principles—to be universal, despite national differences. They are principles that fill and give contents of the socialist state as a power of the working class. To be clear, I will arrange them like that:

1. The salary of **all** high state officials **without any exception** must be equal to the wage of the ordinary worker, i.e., to the average worker's wage.

2. Abolition of monetary and any other privileges in general of the state employees and particularly of the high officers.

3. Abolition of any representation allowances and the whole state entertainment in general.

4. Full eligibility of every major with civic rights to all positions.

5. Removability **at any time** of all state officials **without any exception**.

This is socialism! This is Marx's socialism! And nothing else!

Here is your "holy and clear republic," dear Apostle Levski!

And whether socialism had its ground in the former so-called "socialist" system will become clear to us if we scrutinize each principle separately. Because the natural question appears—was that system socialism in the twentieth century? Was that socialism in fact?

As for the first principle, this was the greatest sacrilege done of Marxism, leading to a monstrous distortion of socialism. This was the most discussed matter, the most sensational and for this reason, the most "forgotten" by the academicians of Marxism and the matter that was most kept in silence in front of the masses; a matter kept in greater secrecy to them both before and after the "reconstruction" (perestroika).

---

[17]. Karl Marx, *The Civil War in France*, 3:308.

It's a **principle**, stigmatized as dogma! It's a subject matter of vital importance for each socialist society, always rejected for being "obsolete" and "naïve" and which could not be implemented into "contemporary" conditions. However, the aim hidden behind these subterfuges is, by using different methods and means, to move away in the course of time this principle and, if not forgotten, to become it void by "prescription" and to get the "legal" reason to declare it "obsolete" under the new "contemporary" conditions. So, this measure of the Paris Commune was adopted by the various "pettifogging ideologists"[18] like an expression of vulgarity, humiliation, or atavism. Unless it is attacked as wage leveling, too, this principle is conceived by them nearly like an April Fool's Day joke, born from the communards' sense of humor.

Is this principle really a wage leveling, though? Is it really a dogma? Is this survival or anachronism?

Let's remember that some time ago Lenin was a dogmatist for the opportunists, defending firmly and in full this underlying principle. If it meant wage leveling, then this was going to say that the founders of scientific socialism, who have raised this measure into principle, i.e., Marx, Engels, and Lenin, should be arranged among the ideologists of petite bourgeoisie socialism! That, too, could turn into a scientific truth as these things run today!

That is why we should more closely examine the nature of this principle. For this purpose, we have to search the connection between worker's labor and high officer's work.

Worker's labor, i.e., the productive labor, is that one which creates a value, while high officer's work, i.e., the management work, is that one which does not create any value. Two different forms of concrete labor, both producing value, can be compared. However, the difficulty comes here from how the two forms of labor may be compared if one of them does not produce any value.

"There are, however, states of society in which ... these two forms of labor are mere modifications of the labor of the same individual, and not special and fixed functions of different persons."[19]

Marx gives us the cue that this comparison can be made only through abstract labor, i.e., through spending human energy in general. The comparison can be made only according to the **quantity** of labor,

---

[18]. Marx, *Capital*, 1:671.
[19]. Ibid., 60-61.

spent for a unit of labor time. But that cannot be done through the exchange value, as in comparing the productive labor of two different workers. So, in order to be able to compare the two forms of labor of quite different qualities, we have to express the abstract labor not in exchange value, but in **responsibility**. The two forms of labor can be placed under equal conditions only when they are measured through responsibility and more precisely, through **equal** responsibility. Only then the two forms of different quality of labor can be compared, despite all kinds of specified differences of each particular form of concrete labor. In other words, independently of the different qualities, worker's labor and high officer's work are placed under equal conditions only if the equal responsibility regarding the final results from their work is established, only if the accomplishment of their professional obligations is available.

Nowadays, just as before, everywhere the responsibility is mingled in a disordered and comic manner with the intensity of work. The tension, the intensity of work is represented as . . . responsibility! Starting from here, from the different tension of work, taxed as a different responsibility, it has emitted the understanding of "high," and following this logic, "low" responsibility, and respectively "great" and "little" responsibility. This is nonsense. For a long time in the "socialist" states, the conception was imposed that the official position created the so-called "responsible comrades." From time to time, they themselves proved the absurdity of this title, when being blamed for corruption—they proved that they were ever neither responsible nor comrades!

When the stupidities come in from a high place, they are accepted as proven theorems. Even something more, this conception existed not only like a theoretic formula but as its practical basis, too. In our state, picked people were overpaid for their "responsible work," for "responsibility and quality," i.e., they were paid the same way that usually a privilege was paid—without reason. But responsibility cannot be a privilege. Just the contrary—the privilege had to pass for responsibility!

Only if the responsibility is equal for all the members of the society, can we say that there is a responsibility in practice in the entire society for all. This means that a *mutual control* is carried out in such a society, i.e., acting in it both in direct relation and feedback in a simplified management structure without useless functions. Mutual control is the most sure control, which rejects the need for a special monitoring network. This equal responsibility wants to say that the worker must

28

respond to the minister the same way the minister must respond to the worker, i.e., the officers are responsible to the workers as well as the workers to the officers. The very participation of the workmen in the rule of the state is not an abstracted concept, as it was in the utopia in the near past, but has its concrete expression in the fact that all state officials are elected and removable **at any time**, i.e., responsible to the workmen and to all citizens, too. Just now, once placed under the control of the working class and the whole society, the officers and particularly the great officers would do real work, not just imitate an activity. Control upward, from workers' side (and from the citizens in general,) does not indicate an intervention in the employees' work, but a report for this work; this is not anarchy, but an order and even the best order. Upward control is necessary for purifying and non-admission of the social infirmities, for both treating and preventing the cankers of the top and vice versa. This mutual control is not an "intervention in the internal affairs," because it means a responsibility according to the final result, at the exit of the "black box." Only in the last resort is the responsibility in capitalism expressed as forensic responsibility, i.e., as a state-imposed constraint, while the responsibility of which we speak, is a conscious practice, i.e., grown into a habit, created as a **social attitude**, as a given mode of life.

Thus, once placed under equal conditions—the equal responsibility—the two types of labor of different quality can be commensurable. As the work of the minister (deputy, magistrate, and suchlike) is sophisticated and highly intellectual, requiring a larger tension, higher education, and greater expenditure of mental energy than the labor of the average worker and citizen, his salary would have to be higher. But, if the salary of the minister, according to the principle of the Paris Commune, is equal to an average worker's one, that would mean that the minister's higher qualification work would be paid less, i.e., the salary will not answer the individual quantity of work, spent by the minister, but would be lower. This is an injustice! Yes! But with a reversed sign yet! It would be an injustice for a small part of the society—the high officers, but justice for the other enormous part. It is just here that the social injustice of socialism is present. But because of that any state is a state—because there is social injustice there. Otherwise, it would not be a state. There is social injustice in the socialist state, too, but it faces an opposite direction. And this social injustice will exist as long as the path of the withering away of the state is longer, i.e., as on a lower level of development of the productive forces is located the beginning of the socialist mode of production.

Exploitation always means social injustice, although social injustice does not always mean exploitation. Social injustice cannot be rejected at once by a magic rod, by a king's scepter, or by decree, because it has existed for millennia as an immanent characteristic of the state. And because this is a condition that the working class finds in the beginning of socialism, the social injustice in the state must be assumed by somebody and this should be the most conscious part of this class—its vanguard, its workers' party.

A fact moreover, when minister's salary corresponds to the average wage, it does not mean that the minister is paid less than the value of labor power. Contrariwise, this means that the minister is paid precisely at the value of labor power. For the value of labor power is established not by the individual differences of any particular worker, but by the value of labor power of the **average** worker. Thus, minister's salary will precisely correspond to the value of labor power; it will be determined directly by the value of labor power. In this way, the salary of the minister will be an indicator of the value of labor power, its equivalence, and measure. Through minister's salary, the living standard of the society may be judged. This is the only way that the appeal for responsibility will not only be a *sense* of responsibility but an *attitude* of responsibility yet. Responsibility means a subordination of the personal possibilities to the social necessities.

What was the practice in such a "socialist" state like Bulgaria, for example?

This guiding, underlying principle was the target of mockery without any shame. To the end of the 1980s, the highest salary of a high state or party functionary nominally was 2500 levs per month, while the average wage was 200 to 220 levs! In other words, a high state officer received ten to twelve times more than the average worker; a large employee pocketed monthly the year's wage of a worker or the monthly wages of a dozen workers! The same was true in the Soviet Union. For protocol only: in the hardest times of the Bolshevik Revolution, Lenin's monthly salary was 500 rubles, and it was approximately equal to the average one in Russia. Then when two high functionaries raised his salary from 500 to 800 rubles, Lenin was seriously angry and imposed on them a severe party penalty after which his salary remained unaltered. In this manner, I would like to recall that Lenin carried on the relentless fight for defending this principle and this fight was especially practical. These two guys were Vladimir Bonch-Bruevich, the head of the Sovnarcom chancellery, and Lenin's closest friend, and Nikolay Gorbunov, a Sovnarcom's secretary. (Sovnarcom was the Soviet government during the Revolution times.) In Lenin's eyes, this was a heavy offense, arbitrariness, equal to a crime![20]

But for the fathers of our homeland, the average wage would have been a humiliation; for them, "the reduction of the remuneration of high state officials seem 'simply' a demand of naïve, primitive democracy,"[21] just like Bernstein accepted this before. This was just Bernstein, who called this simple and great measure of the Commune, primitive and dogma. Lenin proved a half-century later that it was neither primitive nor dogma. Unfortunately, for seventy-five years after the October Revolution, the same version was repeated after the old Bernstein's model.

It is true that during the Leninist Soviet power, there were people who were receiving monthly salaries of 1500 to 2000 rubles, i.e., three or four times more than the average wage. But:

1. They were scientific specialists, i.e., **scientists,** but not **employees**, involved at state positions;

2. They were **foreign,** but not Soviet-owned staff and the Soviet power allotted much more money for involving, for **purchasing** them—a practice that is nowadays known as a *purchase of brains*;

3. They were **bourgeois** specialists, but not **communists,** which "justified" their purchase;

4. This was a **short-term** measure, but not a permanent **practice,** an exception, but not a rule, intended for coming out more quickly of the ruins after the war and the revolution;

5. In the final reckoning, Lenin himself recognized in an honest and clear manner how such a measure is called, *despite all above reasons:*

Clearly, this measure is a **compromise**, a **departure** from the principles of the Paris Commune and of every proletarian power, which call for the reduction of all salaries to the level of

---

[20]. Vladimir Illyich Lenin, *Letters*, 50:78.
[21]. Lenin, *The State and Revolution*, 33:42.

the wages of the average worker, which urge that careerism be fought not merely in words but in deeds.

Moreover, it is clear that this measure not only implies the cessation—in a certain field and to a certain degree—of the offensive against capital . . . ; it is also *a step backward* on the part of our socialist Soviet state power, which from the very outset proclaimed and pursued the policy of reducing high salaries to the level of the wages of the average worker.[22]

This subject-matter—of high officials' salaries—was intentionally and jealously hidden by our friends of the people in front of the large workers' masses the same way as the priests of the tribe were hiding their sacraments and mysteries from the eyes of people uninitiated into their trade. Everything about socialism was expounded, except this "simple" but essential rule only. Theories, systems, and models were developed in whole; futuristic images were constructed; "conceptions" were built with professor's learning, but did not touch this subject that was vitally important and easily understandable by the working class.

"To conceal from the people the fact that the enlistment of bourgeois experts by means of extremely high salaries is a retreat from the principles of the Paris Commune would be sinking to the level of bourgeois politicians and deceiving the people."[23]

That is what it means to conceal from the masses the high payment of the state high officials—**bourgeois scheming** and **deceit** to the working class! By this very party that was blowing its own trumpet and called itself **communist** and **Leninist**! The more is that no "reconstructions" had changed anything in this respect!

Separate phrases of Lenin, Marx, and Engels were attentively selected to defend the existing disgrace and outrage against socialism. For this purpose, there were entire teams of well-paid academicians who specialized in Marxist-Leninist equilibristic. That disfiguration of Marxism was maybe the top of human demagogy in general. In the unprecedented deluge of literature about communism, there was no word to mention the nature, the purpose, and the importance of this simple, i.e., understandable by everyone, principle that represents one of the necessary conditions for the **practical** realization of socialism. The

---

[22]. Vladimir Illyich Lenin, *The Immediate Tasks of the Soviet Government*, 36:166-167, (bolded is mine—T.B.).

[23]. Ibid.,167.

reason—to keep enormous masses of wretches in uncomplaining subordination, to make them become masochists!

"And it is on this particularly striking point, perhaps the most important as far as the problem of the state is concerned, that the ideas of Marx have been most completely ignored! In popular commentaries, the number of which is legion, this is not mentioned. The thing done is to keep silent about it as if it were a piece of old-fashioned 'naiveté'. . ."[24]

Lenin wrote these words as if a minute before "socialism" had been crushed and the ink was not yet dried up! We should say that at this point the ideas of Lenin were most completely ignored, as well! The striving of our "communists," otherwise faithful to the Leninist ideology, was to rate this principle as survival and through different methods (including police ones) to have it far away during the time and thus to make it start at least resembling an anachronism. It was "accepted" for a long time to be silent at this point on our side, too. Thus, it was begun where later we kept silent on many other subjects, too.

The main principle of socialism is a **law** for socialism. *Dura lex, sed lex!*[25]

Of course, we don't speak here of Christian asceticism or of Puritanism of higher officials. But of normal, ordinary, socially approved necessities as the average workman has, i.e., the average citizen—that is a legal requirement yet. And isn't it true that higher officials were once low officials before! In this way, the minister will better understand an average workman's necessities, because of experiencing them through his own pocket. All the same, minister means servant in Latin!

This social injustice is inevitable since the society is closed in a state. Beyond dispute, however, it is only through this social injustice that it is possible to raise the social conscience, but not only the individual one, on the level of the most conscious part of the working class—its party. It is only through this social injustice that the union between party and class is established and practiced in times of peace when all the other revolutionary means are covered with rust. This is a revolutionary measure of a revolutionary party under the conditions of the state but not of the revolution. Just because of that this social injustice is necessary—because after the socialist revolution, the fight

---

[24]. Lenin, *The State and Revolution,* 33:42.
[25]. Hard law, but law (Latin).

for socialism must go on, already starting from the positions of being in power in the state. The former communists/revolutionists, while continuing to be workers' leaders, all the same, they are already state employees. It is impossible to ask the employees to become revolutionists, but the inverse is possible. For this reason, the fight against the bureaucracy and careerism starts from this social injustice— that's why the high official in socialism is paid not like a **specialist** of high qualifications, nor like a **scientist**, but like a state **employee**, which the official actually is. Really, with this social injustice, and this underlying principle, there is set up "an effective barrier to place-hunting and careerism."[26] In this social injustice, the closest connection between party and class is expressed during the building of the new society. Their material unity is a prerequisite to their ideological unity, too. Economic equality between the minister and the workman cannot be a sufficient, but it is a necessary condition to their juridical equality, too, to their equality in the eyes of the law! Otherwise, equality and law are empty words!

How much Anatole France apprehended that one of the largest barriers to the realization of socialism, a tumor for the society, is "the great Services of the State."[27]

For this reason, the observation of this "out-of-date" principle of the Paris Commune and the early Soviet power is not a dogma. This measure means to defend the interests of the working class, but not the own proper employee's interests, a really communist party, but not a party's coterie. Even the "reconstruction" (perestroika) which collected so many hopes by preaching a renewal of socialism had not restored this **fundamental** principle of socialism. Except generally democratic changes, obligatory in such a case, with the overthrow of the totalitarian dictatorship, no principle of socialism was introduced. The generally democratic changes were represented as socialist ones! A lie substituted another!

This is why the demand that the Commune was raised for a cheap government was not accidental. A cheap government—a small number of higher employees for a small charge and respectively allotted fewer resources to the state and more to the society. Only by introducing this principle is a real war declared of the bureaucracy instead of holding

---

[26]. Marx, *The Civil War in France*, 3:281.
[27] Anatole France, *The White Stone*, 125.

diplomatic negotiations with it. This is the only way of destroying the so-called "high-handed machinery" without giving it any chance of restoration.

The "reconstruction" (perestroika) stigmatized the cropped up *high-handed machinery*, the bureaucracy in general, shook a finger at it, and it lurked down, expecting the wind to pass. One way or another, the enormous army of officials remained on the battlefield for a long time, accepting the circle defense. Bureaucracy always seems to show an astonishing vitality and incredible adaptability, thanks to the wonderful system of the ties that imposed the meanness and led to the absence of professionalism, to the domination of the want of talent in any areas of social life. And yet Plato, 2,500 years ago, rejected the "great connections in the State!"[28]

The second principle is only a continuation of the first one. Our glorious people's pirates were directly ashamed to increase ad infinitum their salaries and because of that, they did it indirectly, through their various privileges, accepting an additional dose of monetary narcotic. And the same way as in using any narcotic, the next dose could not be smaller. Until the effect was lasting, i.e., until the crisis that imposed the "reconstruction," because the opium was strong enough, everything looked pink, i.e., socialist, in the eyes of those gentlemen who were falling down in the habitual euphoria in such case—the sick imagination paints beautiful pictures, but illusions only, far from reality. Through such mighty injections, such mighty sybarites maintained the good taste, the good tone, the good digestion, and the friendliness towards the simple people. "Formerly the wealth of individuals constituted the public treasure; but now this has become the patrimony of private persons,"[29] recalled Montesquieu in vain.

The privileges started with raising the former revolutionaries as well-paid "active combatants against fascism and capitalism." It was so stupid title! The former combatants for freedom became "applicants for state's table, suppliants for a post,"[30] forgetting two things—the first, that the fight never stops, but gets another form; that's why this scientific degree was simply unsuitable. The second was that life is never measured in money, although money serves for measuring in life. The ex-heroes represent a miserable view when they shelve their principles!

---

[28]. Plato, *The Republic*, 241.

[29]. Montesquieu, *The Spirit of Laws,* 75.

[30]. Ivan Vazov, *Place-hunters*, 4:489.

So, these fat "people's pensions" actually represented pensions for revolutionary invalidity. Then the acquired privileges became inherited— for children, grandchildren, and the large kin, there were established priorities to enter educational, state, and night establishments.

These privileges are good evidence that the so-called "socialist revolution" in Bulgaria, in fact, was not socialist and not a revolution, but just a common political coup d'état. In a national liberation revolution or in a bourgeois/democratic revolution, the privileges could be justified to some extent, but they never are in a socialist revolution, they are simply inadmissible! The socialist revolution comes just to eliminate any and all privileges!

Goods and services for the "responsible comrades," at half-price or for free, at lower prices and from special shops, goods and services of higher quality and various kinds, imported goods and services—all of they were practically inaccessible for the common mortal, "evaluated through his head"[31] worker.

The area of privileges application was too wide. They were not ending with the end of the working time or with the period of working life but were going on until the end of life—lasting into the funeral agency, too. They were not ending with the civil part of society, but spreading wide and were especially strong with the military part of society, too. The uniform officers, the same way as the civil ones, were extending their prerogatives over the workers as a Divine Law.

The privileges—inherited and acquired—do not allow the true possibilities of the person to be revealed. They gloss over them without giving any full and reliable image of them—not to the privilege bearer, nor to this one, who is injured by them.

Privileges of all kinds—value and natural, available and unavailable, legal and illegal, known and unknown, evident and secret—employee's genius had invented various fantastic and incredible forms to suck golden powder through them.

But otherwise, formally, no privileges were admitted, because according to the former and the present Constitution, "all citizens are equal before the law!"

In every rotten state, money always goes just where it is not needed. Then the extravagance of the public money is manifested in the form of noisy boom and useless state entertainment.

---

[31]. Marx, *Capital*, 1:812.

Even the richest state does not permit in itself what happened in our country to prove the possibilities of socialism: triumphant ostentation and maniacal pomposity, showiness and pose—everywhere and in everything. Presenting as real what is unreasonable and non-existing, but as unreal what is reasonable and existing. We had a society of "passions without truth and truths without passion"[32]; a society of dithyrambs, fireworks, and manifestations. There were created many associations and foundations á la Pickwick Club, whose sole purpose was to organize "excursions and glorious travels"[33] not only in England; organizations and societies such as the Blue Socks Clubs.[34] The scope of activity of those "orders of holy sluggards"[35] were expensive receptions and "business trips" for themselves, banquets, and symposia as a sign of hospitality; all that being at the same time a circus, a clown show, at which the world didn't stop to laugh. Everywhere hypocrisy and insincerity, represented as "comradeship and mutual assistance." Of course, "there's no longer any shame in it: hypocrisy is a fashionable vice, and all fashionable vices pass for virtues,"[36] it "is a privileged vice," which "plays its game in peace with a sovereign impunity."[37] People and dances for show; formal stupidities and stupid formalities; an unseen flourishing of private villas as state residences and appropriation of state residences as private villas! That was a window of a social Eden as a cover of misery without end; fair of vanity and tenderizing idleness for ones, heavy yoke, and arduous labor for others. What was this? Splendor? No, squandermania! Bounty? No, wastefulness!

If the above-mentioned five principles refer to socialism, communism as a social system without commodity relations, when the three economic principles died out, will be realized through both legal principles—eligibility and removability everywhere and in everything. The presence of these two legal principles of social self-regulation in communism does not mean, however, the presence of law at all! So, it is necessary that these two principles are real in the social life in socialism first and become established habits, i.e., social relations in force.

---

[32]. Karl Marx, *The Eighteenth Brumaire of Louis Bonaparte*, 3:184.

[33]. Vazov, *Place-hunters*, 4:488.

[34]. Literary clubs in England in the 80s of the eighteenth century united the London aristocratic elite.

[35]. Voltaire, *The Man with Forty Pieces of Silver*, 294.

[36]. Molière, *Don Juan*, 279.

[37]. Ibid.

In the best case, the capitalist state allows a change of one governmental team with another at several—four or five—years, but the average citizen's situation does not change significantly and the exploitation remains. This resembles horseracing, a derby, in which only horses (governments) are changed, but the jockey (the state) is the same and the race goes on. That is why the socialist state is both more progressive and more democratic than the capitalist one as a legal system, because it allows the officials to be recalled **at any time**. Of course, the principle eligibility includes a mandate by competition with a fixed time for the eligible position, but the new and the essential token of higher democracy is the next socialist principle—removability at any time, the recall of the officials by their electors at any time if this is needed, i.e., these two principles in the aggregate mean an *imperative* mandate *everywhere in the social life*. Eligibility and removability are not intended for the representative state bodies only—Parliament, the Court, ministries—but for the local **daily control** mainly as town/city and municipal councils and mayoralties, all local branches of the state agencies, some health and education positions, as well as in all economic enterprises, too. Namely, through this nation-wide daily control from the lowest to the highest level in the state the socialist democracy as a political system is practically done. The modern representative democracy of the capitalist system concerns only the legislative power and nowhere else, while the mentioned here socialist democracy is a direct democracy in all aspects of the social life. Working **direct democracy** everywhere and in everything against the decorative **representative democracy** which is deceptive in its essence! During our past "socialism," there was "eligibility"—for any case, removability—in no case! That is why at a pitiful and bungled attempt in 1985 to introduce a similar eligibility within the totalitarian "democracy" in the enterprises, called "self-management," it turned out that an enormous part of the works managers of the enterprises remained outboard because of workers' lack of desire to elect them surveyors. And what it would be if it was a real democracy of the working class! In various ways, the illusion was created that both the works manager and the workers served the **society**, but not the **state**, served their own, but not another's interests, i.e., they have common interests, the same causes. The works manager, whose role was to carry on the direct surveillance of the workers was, in fact, a sergeant major from the officials' army of the Capital.

The contest, an old form of the capitalist selection of staff, noisily implemented as a new form in our country by the crisis of 1985, was transformed into a new form of the ties, of the behind-the-coulisses machinations, becoming only a new insignia of the old store—the classification was depending on the strongest shoulder again. The contest was noisily announced as a token of democracy, a token of eligibility. The contest form of eligibility is not new, is not essential, and is not a token of socialist democracy only. For centuries, the Capital selected its staff through it. It seemed to be new for us because there was absolutely no eligibility. In our conditions, the contest, as a form of eligibility, remained again a formal eligibility.

Under the pressure of the objective reality, the power in Bulgaria was forced to acknowledge both in oral and in written, i.e., with and without Special report, the existence of storming corruption as mass practice but not as an isolated, single case, as it was justified before. Along with the crisis, it was started to talk loudly about "the new time," the need for changes, etc. Actually, the instinct of this upstart class felt the pulse of the new time, but it remained an instinct of self-preservation only, which provoked the *putsch* or plotted revolt on November 10, 1989.

A long-concealed truth was finally announced—the truth about corruption, worthy to be described by Chandler, Chase, or Hammett, about the decay of the entire social life. Corruption is **impossible** in a **free** society in which there are real eligibility and removability of the officials turned upwards at any time. Just the contrary—the existence of corruption is the best evidence against democracy, a full negation of democracy, an absence of responsibility, lack of freedom in this society. The absence of responsibility was most strongly manifested since the crisis of 1983 to 1985 when it became the season hit, a catch word in the newspapers, the same way as the firms and *glasnost* later. Responsibility under the capitalist mode of production, a responsibility of the rich in front of the poor—this is a take-off, a caricature of good will!

Being infinitely far from Lenin's punishment for the corruption and, alas, proudly waving it as a flag (of peace!) outside the world, our "communist" and yet "Leninist" party looked like boasting of this fact, strongly supporting the principle of Watergate—governmental corruption always refers to past times only!

Corruptissima respublica plurimae lege![38]

---

[38]. *The most corrupt state has the greatest number of laws!* (Lat.).

This maxim was as if a logo of that bureaucratic socialism, which fertilized the entire society with lots of papers, that raised up an endless jungle of laws, decrees, regulations, ordinances, orders, in general— overproduction of normative documents instead of means of subsistence.

Such laws were created that, as Marx notes, it is most profitable to infringe them than to observe them. "Many decrees were released by several people who, because of having much spare time, govern the state, sitting by their fireplaces."[39] There were released "laws that are both of such a bulk, and so dark as not to be read and understood by every one of the subjects."[40]

For these gentlemen-pelicans, that could be some type of socialism, but this was not Marxism! That could be one of the numerous systems of socialism, but this did not mean Marxian socialism. That was an employee's socialism, which Marx and Engels wanted to prevent us from. That was equalitarian and for this reason—utopian socialism. That was the leveling socialism of Louis Auguste Blanqui, who leveled as quite equal both the stars in the universe and the people in the society. In fact, that was an ordinary capitalism. That was a comrade capitalism in which the plain comrade was proletarian, but the party of great comrades was an oligarchy.

The power of one class proves to be a democracy for this class. Any state carries out its own democracy, in its own interest, i.e., it uses in such way its state possibilities in order to satisfy its democratic necessities. The socialist democracy is higher than the capitalist one, therefore, also, because it satisfies the necessities of the greater part of the society—the working class and the people of the free labor.

All civil officials in the socialist state must be elected and, if necessary, removed at any time. With the five principles of the socialism of direct democracy and absolute equality of rights in the society is created "a new and really democratic state"[41], a State of the Spirit. All the positions—management, educational, health, juristic—must be subject to daily control. Control not only by the upside, by the chiefs, but a control that is carried out mostly by the downside, by the working team. Only in this way, the employees will lose their pharaoh inaccessibility. This applies mostly to the forensic system—the day and

---

[39]. Voltaire, *The Man with Forty Pieces of Silver*, 255.

[40]. Thomas More, *Utopia*, 110.

[41]. Marx, *The Civil War in France*, 3:281.

night rapacious birds, the vampires of the society. After William Petty, the law thrives in those parts where the lawyers are famished! Just the contrary—both before and now, because of the anecdotic jurisdiction in our state, the small robbers are in jail while the big robbers are submerging into gold and silk, as Martin Luther says. Really, the science of object alienation is called law, which, ironically today, is a science and even an art for alienating people.

The strict accounting of **every** employee—this is the highest manifestation of the human **rights**, the highest democracy in general, which is possible under socialist power only, that "thoroughly expansive political form,"[42] which the Commune gave. This is the clearest manifestation of the democracy of the working class really as a democracy of a **whole class** and of the **freedom** of this class, in contrast to the play of democracy—the dictatorship of the Capital. Contrariwise, when in a democracy, as Rousseau says, few people possess much more than the average citizen, then the state either perishes or ceases being a democracy!

Democracy is a pretty word. Democracy is a captivating magic. The oppressed classes always wanted and the oppressing ones always promised a democracy. But this was precisely for democracy that the both parts had always fought. The great French Revolution proclaimed the great appeal, "Liberty, Equality, Fraternity." History showed that from the class viewpoint, they could indicate different things, distinct contents; these concepts could be filled with different senses. In the class society, in the society locked in a state, liberty is always at the top of somebody's spear! Equality is the Achilles' heel, into which this spear is plunged. Humanity is the pledge for plunging it by all force.

"There is no word that admits of more various significations, and has made more varied impressions on the human mind, than that of liberty."[43] In order to exist, liberty and justice in a society, there should be equality in this society before them and together with them. Only then can we speak of humanism. Only socially equal personalities are free. And only free and equal in rights personalities could "love each other like brothers."[44] This is why humanism is humanism, but not philanthropy, just because it is **mutual**, between **equal in rights** and

[42]. Marx, *The Civil War in France*, 3:312.
[43]. Montesquieu, *The Spirit of the Laws*, 224.
[44]. Nikola Vaptsarov, *Writings*, 73.

free members of the society. Liberty is a realized indispensability and as such, it is the highest necessity.

However, in order to establish social equality in the *political superstructure*, in the state, it turns out that it is possible only through social injustice. This is not a paradox. As far as the state exists, there will be always both injustice and violence. Social inequality, ultimately, always leads to social injustice, although social injustice does not always lead to social inequality. On the contrary, in the state under socialism, this is just the social injustice, which leads to social equality. Under capitalism, any injustice is a violence as well as any violence is an injustice. Conversely, under socialism, not any injustice is a violence as well as not any violence is an injustice. The working class is placed in a different way in these two systems. The state under capitalism exerts on it a violent injustice, while under socialism the working class through its democracy exerts a just non-violence in the state.

Instead of the clear representation of the essence of the socialist democracy, the cuneiform writing of the opportunism represented to us some illusory universal socialist democracy, the work people were inundated and misled by sweetish and unclear phrases about equality, rights, social justice, and universal love. It was a time when it started to speak of social justice even in the Soviet bloc! But nobody knew what it was. There were even funny pronouncements of the kind "to *increase* the social justice!" By kilogram or by meter, probably! This quintessence was a stupidity and ignorance about fundamental philosophical conceptions as quantity and quality at that by erudite heads with heavy titles going before them. The justice could not have degrees of quality even, and even less be weighed with balances in quantity. We had to listen to paradox brain teasers, cretinism as "insufficiency of social justice" (probably after Gorbachev's appeal for "more socialism!"), as well as "optimizing the social inequality," which are not only far from any science, but make the hearing dirty.

The first condition for the liberty, as Engels says, is the responsibility. The responsibility is the first and the complete condition for the liberty of the personality, of the human rights. The responsibility is the contents of the social relations under socialism and communism. On this very basis—the equal responsibility of all people—the liberty of the individual becomes real under his concomitant subordination to the society. Solely through the responsibility, the liberty of each is compatible with the liberty of all!

Every state carries out social injustice and violence in its own interest. The socialist state carries them out in a way that any injustice and any violence gradually dwindle to nothing in the course of time. Only then—under communism—a universal equality and justice will be possible. Liberty and equality—but yet, without social injustice! Liberty and equality—without democracy! While now we have a democracy, but without liberty and equality!

The man is evil by nature. This is not true. The man is good by nature. This is neither true. The man is neutral by nature. The man is such as the society molds him. The social environment, the surrounding world creates the moral values of the individual, which is only adapted to this environment. In human society, everything depends on whether the natural inequality will be developed into social inequality. When the society kills instead of develops the natural in the man, then most various theories begin to multiply about injured human genetics, about human as a social animal, that he has an innate aggressiveness, etc., all of them intended to defend and to justify the existing social injustice. Some possibilities, natural endowments, or gifts are really inherited, but they are nothing more than an embryo, a germ, some probability. They become a certainty only then if they develop in a suitable social environment (that only the rich may permit themselves!); they may germinate in a suitable social soil only. The social conditions may either develop or choke the natural capabilities. That's why, representing the social inequality as a natural inequality, as something that is rooted in the gene, and vice versa, is an insult to the human dignity and of the good reason, a brute triteness that is worthy for the highest classes only.

Any science has its own laws. Any science has its iron principles, with the violence of which it ceases being a science. Our patriarchs of socialism with the unruffled appearance and priest's infallibility transformed Marxism from science into religion. Even officially, a long time ago, they started to speak about the need for a new faith, i.e., for a new "opium of the people" and that Marxism was a "social religion!" This is a mockery, a sacrilege not of the religion, but of the Marxism!

Chapter Three

The So-Called "People's State"

Kant, the great philosopher, noticed that every great doctrine has undergone three phases. First, it is faced by a murderous silence, then— by a furious criticism, and finally—adapted to the "new conditions" by benevolent disciples, who distort it so much that its creator even cannot recognize it, being guided by the unchanged principle that any principle can be changed! "Truth's fountains may be clear—her streams are muddy."[45]

Marxism, as the top of all social doctrines for all times, was not an exception. The principal distortion of Marxism is always focused on its fundamental point, the essence of scientific socialism—the real recognition of the power of the working class. Just like the myth of the *people's* or *popular capitalism*, which was propagated since the mid-1950s in the countries to the west of Berlin Wall, to the east and the north of it, since the same time it was introduced the myth of the *people's* or *popular socialism*. But the suggestion is always the same. Under any "people's" power—from *people's capitalism* to *people's socialism*—the greatest illusion suggested to the oppressed classes is that the people are sovereign, i.e., that all the people dominate over themselves. In this respect, even John Kenneth Galbraith makes Marxist conclusions, which even in the Internet epoch have the same power:

"Young people are suggested that in a democracy the entire power belongs to the people!"[46]

Yet, old people know that this is not true!

The dream of each opportunist from Lassalle and Proudhon to our days is to represent in a mawkish manner the socialist state not as a power of the working class, but as a kind of *people's state*. The classics of socialism elucidated this matter a long time ago. This is an old

---

[45]. Lord Byron, *Don Juan,* 500.
[46]. John Kenneth Galbraith, *The Anatomy of Power*, 18.

debate—since the rise of Marxism. And yet, in spite of that, in the "overpowered socialism," the faithful "Marxists," in the same old way that Lassalle did it, "developed further" the doctrine of Marx in a manner that reached again this impossible, non-existent, and utopian state, this platonic ideal state. However, history has a dump, too, and it sweeps away any waste when its time comes, "for time discloses the truth."[47]

In his book, *Anti-Dühring*, Engels explains extremely clearly whether, when, and why the *people's state* could exist. He notes that it is justified **only in the sense of propaganda,** at that temporarily, i.e., only when the working class is in opposition, but not when it holds power! It is justified to some extent for the purposes of propaganda only during certain periods of the class struggle of the working class, but is completely untenable from a scientific point of view. Actually, it becomes necessary for the working class, in certain periods of its class struggle, to enter some union with other classes against some common enemy, for example, fascism or a national oppressor, under the slogan of a *people's* or *popular state*. But after the elimination of this common enemy *people's* or *popular state* is immediately disintegrated into its component classes. "In a popular state the inhabitants are divided into certain classes,"[48] Montesquieu affirmed in a Marxian manner a century before Marx! So, the *popular state* is a fiction; it is transient, fleeting, and for this reason— imaginable only. In its rigorous scientific sense of a class instrument, it is practically an empty matter sophism, a complete commonplaceness, an offspring of mental weakness. There is no such state! If it is a state, it is not popular! If it is popular, it is not a state yet! **The State is a violent institution for social injustice** generated by two main classes, which are main ones because they are at enmity. For this reason, by speaking of a state, the main classes which form it cannot be on friendly terms, (like it was the accepted ideology during the ex-socialism), simply because they cannot combine their class interests that are radically opposed, as interests of the whole people. Any people closed in a state, are divided into classes. "For indeed any city, however small, is in fact divided into two, one the city of the poor, the other of the rich."[49] Not Marx, still Plato said the truth!

It is true that by the *Decree on Land*, as by a number of other documents written by Lenin, as well, his party established a "property of

---

[47]. Seneca, *On Anger*, 2:141.
[48]. Montesquieu, *The Spirit of the Laws*, 63.
[49]. Plato, *The Republic*, 142-143.

the whole people," where he speaks about "whole people's cooperation," etc. Really, in an odd and puzzling manner, sound the words said by Lenin immediately after the revolution about the property (and the power) as . . . people's one! These words had written by the same Lenin who before the revolution untiringly fought against the *people's state* and he was its irreconcilable enemy. The same Lenin, who, in his work of genius, *The State and Revolution*, just two months earlier had razed to the ground the *people's state*, at the very first day of the revolution proclaimed . . . a whole people's property on land!

This is very odd and puzzling if we do not take into consideration his complete works as well as the concrete historical conditions, if we lose sight on the whole socialist theory. As odd and puzzling as Lenin himself reminds us (in *The State and Revolution* again), the idea of this *people's state* had the same oddly reads in Marx's work in some detached phrases. Of course, at a conscious abuse of all the doctrine of Marxism, it is very convenient to use these odd sentences, to make them turn like a worn refrain. This is the first.

And the second, during the October Revolution in 1917, the proletariat in Russia represented a not large part of the entire class structure of the society, while the enormous part was the peasantry. That is why it was established as a power of the workers and the peasants, but not a power of the working class only. The workers and the peasants made almost the whole people in practice. For this reason, their worker-peasant power was called a *whole people's power*.

However, something occurred thirty years later in all new "socialist" countries under the Soviet sphere of influence. On September 15, 1946, Bulgaria was proclaimed a people's state. Other peoples also received such social acquisition, a "state of people's democracy"—Poland, Hungary, North Korea, etc., and even a part of Germany!

This "state of people's democracy" represents tautology both from an etymological and philosophical point of view, just like "potential potentialities" or "real reality." The official interpretation was that given circumstances—internal and external—forced communist leaders to make such a compromise, a retreat from Marxism, and this was anew for the purposes of propaganda only. This state, the so-called "state of people's democracy," was proclaimed in the "socialist" camp with the idea that later, once the working class had strengthened its positions, would be developed into a dictatorship of the working class—both in theory and in practice, because propaganda and enthusiasm cannot be eternal. But it was not yet any socialist state. Unfortunately, the "state of people's democracy" was accused later of being a form of dictatorship of the proletariat, to be able to be theoretically "legally" transformed in later years into a still more *people's state*—into a "whole people's state"!

In the same time in the West worked and still works another product of *people's state* concept—the so-called "social state" and "welfare state." *Social state* and its later Nordic modification *welfare state* are invented as a capitalist alternative in reply to the Marxist concept of socialist state. Bismarck's *social state* against Marx's *socialist state* is a capitalist project to conciliation of the keen and irreconcilable class contradictions, which continues already 165 years. *Social* and especially *welfare state* is a Keynes's concept and practice of the organized capitalist class to buy its class peace and class tranquility. *Social* and *welfare state* is a capitalist state based on enormous personal taxes that ensure and strongly develop the parasitism and idleness in the society leading inevitably to its certain rot. Something more, it impends a deepening of the parasitism and idleness through breeding of loafers when every *welfare state* will accept soon the so-called *unconditional basic income*. The modern capitalist state is so rich that it can afford that. The *welfare state* is a compromise between trade unions and large corporations and, in fact, it enervates the struggle of the former against the latter; thus workers' strikes and rebellions are nipped in the bud! Modern *welfare state* is barmy democracy, unreal welfare, and real capitalism!

During all the twentieth century, the middle-class democrat has always considered the power of the working class like a commissar with a black jacket and a Nagant revolver. This image of a Bolshevik revolutionist applying the dictatorship of the proletariat is not the real image of the scientific understanding of working class's political power as it was described above in chapter two. For this power is not political only; it is mainly an economic system. However, even from this point of view, being considered as a political system, the power of the working class, being a class instrument, is the most democratic system ever possible and it must cover the whole period of socialism. Because at any time, until the state exists, there will always be state employees paid to carry out its power and for this reason, it is necessary that these employees are subordinated to the working class as the essential part of the civil society. In other words, the state employees (especially the highest) must be **ceaselessly** subordinated to the working class and the citizens in general, no matter how much "of the people" they are. While the state exists, the subject of class oppression inside it will never disappear because the subject is the state itself!

In this connection, I have to notice here the following thing, namely—how the character and essence of the state under socialism is changed when the society is not divided into rich and poor anymore, i.e., what is this state, which is no longer compound by these two main classes? Just here, however, begin the speculations—that such a state means a classless state, a "whole people's" state. Such knowledgeable cretins, who do not distinguish between 1 and 0, as Karl Popper, for example, bamboozle the general public that the one-class society is . . . a classless one! Popper the faker, who falsified the science, raised the falsification (by his absurd theses) even as a scientific principle! In his blind anti-Marxist "criticism," this guy made the discovery that the socialism is "a society consisting of one class only, and, therefore, a classless society!"[50] The fact that the socialism is a semi-state does not make it a classless society and no state! Popper's completely mistaken notion of this matter looks for a mockery with Marxism, distorting it deliberately, with a concocted-by-himself thesis that the workers, "by eliminating the bourgeoisie, they must establish a classless society, since only one class remains!"[51] One could be astonished at his flat brain that cannot differentiate something from anything, 1 from 0! This is a sign of primitive or manipulative thinking, and falsification of this "authority" is the charging Marx with the frank untruth about his "prediction of the emergence of a classless, i.e., socialist, society."[52] The classless society is not the socialist one, but this subject-matter for Karl Popper is terra incognita! Popper could not understand that the one-class society of socialism contains inside itself dozy potential of the second main class and this is just the state! This one-class society means that only "when, at last, the state becomes the real representative of the whole of society, it renders itself unnecessary,"[53] i.e., the one-class society dies gradually out to a classless society, socialism passes into communism, but the one-class socialism is quite not classless communism!

The new characteristic of the socialist state is that it represents a power of the working class on its state. Because all the same, it is a state!

---

[50]. Karl Popper, *The Open Society and Its Enemies*, 2:150.

[51]. Ibid.

[52]. Ibid.,149.

[53]. Engels, *Socialism: Utopian and Scientific*, 1:146.

But it is a semi-state, as Engels says, because, firstly, it does not have power over another real class, but on its own employees and, secondly, because now it gives the beginning of the end of the state in general, i.e., it is a withering away state.

In spite of its non-euphonic name, the state of the working class is, however, the most democratic of all possible states, being more of the people, i.e., closer to the whole people than the most *people's state* does! The withering away state under socialism will more and more resemble on external sight a state of the whole people, but just because it is a power of the working class. And such it will remain until its end. And when the classes dwindle to nothing and all the people becomes a whole and all peoples merge in one people only, then the working class, that ceased being a class yet, will not need a state anymore. But the withering away state is not a *people's* one, just like the *people's state* cannot be a withering away one.

The force of the withering away state at its high stage will not be expressed in armed collisions and in police cordons, but in a continuous, daily negation of itself in its quality of a state; first, the force will lose its form and then its contents, too, having already created a standard of behavior, a mode of life, which will be transformed into a habit, into tradition, into an ordinary social practice. Just because of that there exists the historical inevitability of state of the working class during the whole period of socialism, during the whole period of transformation of the capitalism into communism in order to be it really a "period of the revolutionary transformation of the one into the other."[54]

---

[54]. Karl Marx, *Critique of the Gotha Program*, 1:184

Chapter Four

State-Monopoly Capitalism

Under the Mask of Socialism

Still, in 1877, Engels wanted to protect us from false socialism. Still then, in *Anti-Dühring*, he wrote that not any nationalization is socialist, because in the contrary case both Bismarck and Napoleon would have to be arranged among the founders of socialism. Still earlier—in 1848, in their Communist Manifesto, Marx and Engels wrote about different types of socialism—feudal, bourgeois, petite bourgeois, "real" . . .

The abolition of private property does not mean that in this way the property is transformed automatically into a social one. Because after private property in the society remains the state! Nationalization, or the full socialization of the means of production with the old production relations still reserved, means a system of monopoly of the production. But that is not socialism at all, as it was represented to us. The full socialization (in Bulgaria and the USSR—100 %) of the means of production transformed them from private property into state property, but not into social property. [The cooperative property was a pitiful appendage only subordinated to the state property, which disappeared de facto with the imposing of the new economic organizations in the rural economy, since 1970, Agricultural and Industrial Complexes (AIC)]. From here it is all theoretic nonsense, where the complete impasse and welter in the theory of socialism originated—in the equalization, in the sign of equality between socialism and state property. Because the state property does not mean that it is a social one, although the social property could be generated by the state one. The state property is as much a social, as it was under Louis XIV and the Ottoman sultans. As Engels writes, "the transformation, either into joint-stock companies or into state ownership, does not do away with the capitalistic nature of the productive forces."[55] On the contrary, the "state ownership of the

---

[55]. Engels, *Anti-Dühring*, 8:312.

productive forces is not the solution to the conflict, but concealed within it are the technical conditions that form the elements of that solution."[56]

With the complete seizure of the means of production of the private property and its setting in the hands of the state, competition is completely negated and dominating in the production becomes the monopoly of the state. Lenin is wrong by writing that socialism is a state monopoly in working class's favor. The economic nature of the monopoly is such that it just cannot act in the interests of the working class. It exists for the extraction of monopoly profit only. And such a profit can be extracted only when the labor power is a commodity and worker's wage represents a monopoly price of the commodity labor power. So, the monopoly is always directed against the working class and never in its favor. The monopoly is a negation of socialism. Marx saw that and explained to us that it, the monopoly, at a given stage stops the development of the productive forces. "The monopoly of capital becomes a **fetter** upon the mode of production, which has sprung up and flourished along with, and under it."[57]

Socialism is not a competition; it is not a monopoly, either. Socialism is not a private property; it is not a state one, either. Socialism is a completely different thing. What is socialism in such case?

To answer this question, we need to approach it without dogmatism, scholastically and without prejudices, but without free essays and general words, as well. Because socialism is an exact science, it uses exact concepts and categories only. One of them is the social property of the means of production. Marx's socialism does not recognize any other property! The so-called "pluralism of the property," a slogan raised in 1989-90 in our side as a manifestation of the so-called "democratic socialism" came to reconcile Marxism with the contemporary theoretic impotence, to salve somebody's erudite conscience, to legalize the private property on behalf of Marx! But Marx was its irreconcilable adversary. His volcano genius gave the best scientific interpretation of capital and of private property. This pluralism of the property does mean only one thing—pluralism of the private property, i.e., an establishment of a variety of its forms without changing its contents.

On the other hand, the primitive comprehension that the state property represents a social, their identification, and their equalization

---

[56]. Engels, *Anti-Dühring*, 8:312.
[57]. Marx, *Capital*, 1:831 (bolded is mine—T.B.)

could not resist the criticism of the time. The state property is not socialism. The state-monopoly property, as it was on the both sides of the Berlin Wall and which continues to be such one even after it dropped down, is not social property. So, state-monopoly capitalism dominated for forty-two years in Bulgaria and for seventy-four years in USSR in its complete, its absolute form and because of that—the uttermost degree of socialization, a top degree of monopolization of the means of production by a sole owner—the state, but not any socialism, as we were adroitly misled by cohorts of demagogic theoreticians. *There was never and nowhere any socialism!* In the twentieth century, we passed through a system of utopian socialism as proof that this was not socialism that was not possible, but the utopia of the writers before Marx and after Marx. We were visited by a utopian socialism, which at the contemporary stage is simply capitalism—state, monopolistic.

State-monopoly capitalism is an inevitable, natural stage in the development of the productive forces, once the capitalist private property already appeared; it is an evolution of the capitalist property, due to the concentration and centralization of the capital. Being obviously a product of this evolution, having normally led to the highest, uttermost degree of monopolization of the property, this proved to be possibly the most parasitic and non-progressive form of capitalism, that was spuriously proclaimed like a "world socialist system," where Bulgaria was one of the members, as well.

The complete socialization of the means of production by the state with reservation of the old capitalistic production relations transforms the economic system into a state-monopolistic capitalism in the highest stage. This is the utter, final degree of monopolization of the means of production, remaining in the hands solely of one and only owner—the state. Engels foresightedly wanted to prevent just this type of sham socialism. Still, he spotted the danger that the state-capitalist is hidden, is huddled up under the garment of socialism. "The modern state, no matter what its form, is essentially a capitalist machine, the state of the capitalists, the ideal personification of the total national capital. The more it proceeds to the taking over of productive forces, the more does it actually become the national capitalist, the more citizens does it exploit. The workers remain wage-workers—proletarians. The capitalist relation is not done away with. It is rather brought to a head."[58] Really, when the

---

[58]. Engels, *Anti-Dühring*, 8:312-313.

particular capitalists are eliminated from the play, all the economy passes completely under the power of the state joint capitalist and the state remains like "a single capitalist company."[59] This was what happened after the Second World War in Bulgaria and in the entire so-called "socialist system"—the invasion of étatism (state management).

Now it's been asked—in the end of the twentieth century what this unprecedented economic crisis is due to, which overthrew not any distinct government, but a whole social system; a crisis which razed to the ground a gigantic political building and in this manner changed all over the world order. Is the theory, in fact, guilty for the failure of communism as a worldwide ideology or is this the existing practice? Is Marxism the culprit or his interpreters? There is just the answer to the question—is Marxism a utopia or a science? In other words, does the theory admit the possibility of such economic crisis like that—a crisis not of the overproduction, but of the deficit? Is it able to explain this crisis?

It turns out that, yes, it can.

The reason is rooted in the nature of the mode of production itself of the absolute state monopoly of capital, which existed in this form like a copy in Bulgaria and as an original in the USSR. This crisis contains in itself all possible disproportions being then just their result. And they can be united into three large groups:

1. Disproportions between accumulation and consumption.
2. Disproportions in the accumulation itself.
3. Disproportions in the consumption itself.

These three groups of disproportions exist always and unceasingly as genetically immanent to any capitalistic mode of production, because they are a consequence of the main contradiction of the capitalist reproduction created by the infringement of the Law of proportionality. And its requirements, with full realization of the product in the conditions of extended reproduction, excluding in this way the advent of crises, are:

1. Initial (necessary) condition:

$$\mathrm{I}\left(v + \frac{s}{x}\right) < \mathrm{II}(c + s)$$

---

[59]. Marx, *Capital*, 1:692.

2. Main (sufficient) condition:

$$I\left(v + \frac{s}{x}\right) = IIc$$

where I s/x is that part of Is which is spent like an income (i.e., the part given for consumption), the other part of Is is the part given for accumulation; I is the first department of the social production and II is the second one; c – constant capital, v – variable capital, s – surplus value.[60]

Under capitalistic production relations, this law is always infringed and just because of that, and just from here, all crises of capitalism have originated—because the equation in the main condition cannot be supported. That wants to say that there is no full realization of the product, but it is stopped at a certain point of the circulation as commodity or money. The equality in the main condition is modified into inequality. And if the inequality belongs to the type $I(v+s/x) < IIc$ that means a **crisis of overproduction** (of articles of consumption), but if it is of the type $I(v+s/x) > IIc$, that means a **crisis of deficit**. The inequality in both cases expresses a transgressed exchange between departments I and II of the social production, disordered "metabolism" of the social organism. Marx was extremely clear while explaining in the second volume of *Capital* how that is done. He treats the crisis of the first type—the crisis of overproduction which is characteristic of the capitalism of the free competition at his time, i.e., before the epoch of the monopoly and the étatism. In the "socialist" system in the apogee of the symbiotic monopolistic-state capitalism, there was the opposite crisis, but its interpretation is similar.

If X of the II department sells to Y of I some articles of consumption, but a purchase does not occur immediately, i.e., a **unilateral sale** is carried out, X (II) will have taken money out of circulation and Y (I) will have piled up commodities (means of production). At his side, X will have a "virtual money-capital" on hand, and at the opposite side, Y will be piled up in the form of commodity-capital equal by its value part of its newly created value. Then the expression $I(v+s/x)$ becomes larger than IIc and the constant capital in II department cannot be restored since the necessary money for it is taken out of circulation, used with an another aim, but not for purchase of the necessary means of production, which remain in this case out of

---

[60]. Marx, *Capital*, 2:585.

the circuit of capital without being marketed—fixed, buried. The fact that the constant capital in **II** is not restored as a productive capital leads to that, the production of articles of consumption decreases because of the deficit of means of production into **II** while at the same time in **I** there is a relative overproduction of them. Thus, on the one hand (in **I**) it is received as a relative overproduction of means of production, piled up commodity-supplies (and even oversupplies), and on the other hand (in **II**)—a deficit of articles of consumption, a deficiency of means of subsistence. This deficit gets as far intensified as the inequality $I(v+s/x)$ > **IIc** is larger, i.e., as the disparity between them increases and it is more difficult to restore **IIc**, and thereby embarrasses, respectively— decreases, the production of articles of consumption, too. Thus, the deficit intensifies and under a complete monopoly on the property becomes **chronic**. In short, while carrying out unilateral sales of articles of consumption from **II** department without respective subsequent purchases of means of production by **I** department, money is taken out of circulation and in it again leave piled up commodities. In this manner, needlessly increasing accumulation of superfluous means of production (in supply) is received with intensely decreasing consumption of means of subsistence at the same time, by forming the disproportion between them. But despite all strains done, the formal "Marxist" science has never been able to give a precise interpretation of this contradiction, but, on the contrary, always being astonished at the "paradox" how, on one hand, there is a keen deficit of commodities for "popular consumption" and, on the other, an enormous part at the same time of piled up supplies by overproduction of means of production!

So, in the conditions of deficit crisis, too, we have the same three interdependent phenomena in the same moment of the reproduction, like those ones, mentioned by Marx about the crisis of overproduction, but in the opposite direction—in his words, we have nothing to do, but to substitute **I** for **II** and vice versa; thus, we have all the picture of these simultaneous phenomena observing a "formation of virtual additional money-capital in class **II** (hence under-consumption from the viewpoint of **I**); piling up of commodity-supplies in class **I** which cannot be reconverted into productive capital (hence relative overproduction in **I**); surplus of money-capital in **II** and reproduction deficit in **I**."[61]

So, to generalize, we can say that the crisis of overproduction of

---

[61]. Marx, *Capital*, 2:565

articles of consumption is at the same time a crisis of deficit of means of production and vice versa, in our case, the crisis of deficit of articles of consumption is actually a crisis of overproduction of means of production.

In this situation, the difficult restoration of the constant capital in **II** department even from the viewpoint of the simple reproduction makes deeper still more its inequality with **I(v+s/x)**. Thus, however, the disproportions get intensified also in the accumulation itself and in both departments it is very ineffective: in **I** needlessly accumulation of superfluous means of production in supply because of an absence of money-capital, while in **II** the accumulation is lagged behind—because of using the money-capital for other purposes (mostly state ones). This fact by itself delays the development of the extended reproduction and holds it back at the level of simple reproduction, disturbing the normal functioning of the capital.

If to all that is added the strangling noose of the state with its unbearably heavy, a deadly tax system that ruins the productive forces, reaching, for example, even to 80 % tax on profits(!), which is, in the full sense of the word, a crime; a system, by which the entire potential of the productive forces is sapped, fully squeezed, the "socially weak" capitals and labor power cannot sustain the pressure, become more and more weak, and begin needing injections of charity: the capitals need subsidies, the labor power—reliefs.

Thus, at the final line, we inherited "industrialization" that was random and for itself, which was not subordinated to any preliminary and after economic analysis, with enormous and extremely inefficient, technologically backward in its design still capital investments in all productions and branches, remained like dead and most expensive monuments of the irrational thought. (In Bulgaria, more than 120 billion levs, which was equal to about 50 billion US dollars at the end of 1989, were frozen in the shabby and worn fixed capital, were irretrievably buried by the strongly disturbed social reproduction.)

The third group includes disproportions in the consumption itself, a consequence of the distribution and redistribution of the national income. In this case, we are interested in the most significant one—the exploitation in the capitalist society, which is the eternal, inevitable, and the main disproportion, always accompanying this society. Low wage (and in Bulgaria, it was a disgraceful low, reaching a molecular level!) always means a high degree of exploitation of the labor power, which exists in our country since that time. To illustrate that, I present a diagram, giving a precise image of the real situation of the working class in "socialist" Bulgaria, which shows its relative impoverishment, a result of the social plague—the capitalist exploitation—which raged with unremitting force for more than forty years. (Data about wages and national income is taken from the statistical guide of 1989)

Diagram 1

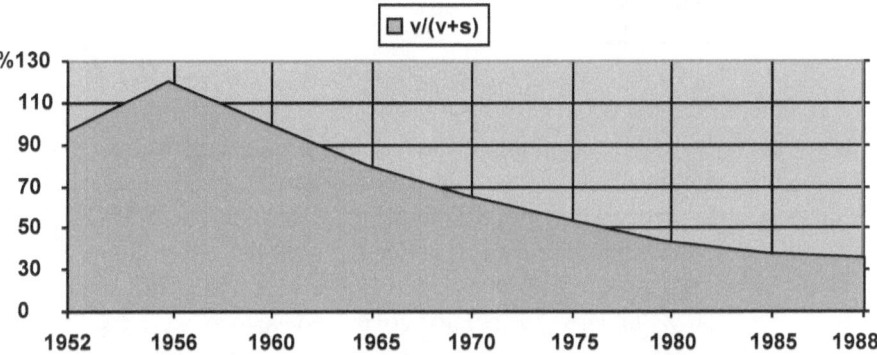

The diagram shows that the impoverishment of the working class and the average citizen in general in Bulgaria was such that it was reduced to the edge of the penury, reduced to beggary, by a cruel, inhuman exploitation, which squeezed all forces of this class. This was an economic state terrorism over a disenfranchised proletariat. The diagram shows in a clear way what the real situation of the workers was in our country, despite all the Pharisee declarations at that time. The tureen (the national income), indeed, was continuously increased in size, but worker's spoon (his relative wage) was continuously decreased. This exploitation was done with the insatiable avidity of the niggardly usurer, with Gobseck's mad thirst for money. The interests of the working class were injured at this final point. Infringement of its interests meant the simultaneous infringement both of its possibilities and necessities. It was a brutal and wild exploitation of the working class according to the principle "from each—above his possibilities, to each—below his necessities!"

"The quantity of labor," Marx says, "by which the *value* of workman's laboring power is limited forms by no means a limit to the quantity of labor which his laboring power is apt to perform."[62] In other words, the possibilities for exploitation on the limited in his necessities worker could be unlimited! And it was so!

---

[62]. Karl Marx, *Value, Price and Profit*, 7:88.

57

That was so until the end of 1989. The same was true in the end of 1999 and in the "sacral" 2000. However, quarter of a century later, after the so-called "socialism," in the end of 2015, the poor man's situation during the neoliberal "democracy" is more tragic than ever! Crying sorrow, desperation, and pain, there is much grief, only grief, and a lack of hope! In the end of 2015, the agony continues with Satan's strength! Like real red Khmers, our "communists" of that time and their clones of today exterminated their own people!

Still, since the coming of the state-monopoly capitalism, two forms of exploitation of the wage labor appear, that have always coexisted since then—the man-by-man exploitation and man-by-state exploitation, one of them is dominant in different times and at different places. For example, in France where in 1985 the state sector took about 35 % of the economy, the exploitation even under the socialist government did not differ by its contents from that one in Bulgaria and in USSR, where it occupied 100 %, under such socialist governments, too!

The absolute monopoly of the state, negating the competition, forces the Law of anarchy and competition of capitalist production to function one-sidedly and in a half-way, i.e., only as Law of anarchy of production no matter of proclaimed its central planning. In this was expressed the tragedy of this mode of production: it was missing the engine, the motor of the social progress—the competition; that is why it was sinking faster and faster. Because what the anarchy does in the production, i.e., the squandering of social labor, is compensated to some extent by the competition. This was the reason to begin speaking of "socialist competition," making several times attempts, in words at least, to break the state monopoly, but unsuccessfully every time. The monopoly is a supreme delight, more supreme than orgasm, as the "oracle" Warren Buffett confesses to the general public. That is why, during the "post-communist" robbery in Bulgaria, called privatization, the monopoly of the big capital was not destroyed. The years of this robbery and unceasing, multiple monopoly orgasms at the end of 2015 will already number twenty-six, after the initial forty-five, and its end is not yet seen! Today the monopolies provoke again the protests and the anger of the powerless people against their powerful rulers!

The exploitation of wage labor, however, has nothing in common with the "defect" of socialism, indicated so by Marx and repeated by Lenin. It is not even a defect. We speak of the fact that at the tract of socialism, the distribution of material goods will not be carried out after the higher principle—as per the necessities, as communism envisages it, but as per the possibilities, i.e., through the wage only, and because of the natural inequality of the possibilities, there will not be the same, i.e., a leveling, satisfaction of the necessities. This "defect" will be forgotten into the upper stage—communism. But that is not a defect at all, and it is necessary during the time of socialism. Otherwise, as it was in the former "socialism," there were forty years of leveling instead of equality of consumption, which is, finally, a social injustice regarding people with better expressed possibilities. So, under socialism the wage remains the best valuation of the real possibilities by which people cover their necessities.

However, this "defect" was a demagogic way suitable to hide the exploitation, to mask social injustice by representing it as a natural inequality, and when it was necessary our preachers of Marxism shook the dust from it by using it. Marx and Lenin kept in mind just the natural inequality in the possibilities, but not the social injustice toward the necessities, while speaking about "richer" and "poorer" people in socialism. This is a fortune, but which is based on put in one's own labor only, but not on the appropriation of another's labor. Quite the contrary, the universal Law of capitalist accumulation was in its element at our "real socialism"—fortune at either pole, in spite of any extravagance, poverty at the other one—in spite of any thrift. This sweat-sucking system of the state monopoly at our side was possible because it kept workers in subordination through shamelessly low wages—a half-century of "communist" practice that continues to exist the same until now, still a quarter of a century after the crash of "communism!" Retaining wages at a low level is an old and tested medieval approach—it existed under King Jacob the First in England. Through low wages, the worker is consciously encouraged to search for "side earnings," i.e., speculations. And "the misfortune of a republic is . . . when the people are gained by bribery and corruption; in this case they grow indifferent to public affairs, and avarice becomes their predominant passion. Unconcerned about the government and everything belonging to it, they quietly wait for their hire."[63]

This picture was evident in Bulgaria as a copy and in the USSR as an original!

Why was the wage so shamelessly low? Because it was a result of rude exploitation with the sole goal—shamelessly high rate of profit!

---

[63]. Montesquieu, *The Spirit of Laws,* 65.

We have an accurate evaluation of our own economic situation in that "socialist" time made in a few lines by yet again, Marx! This is a short, but expert, surgically precise evaluation of Soviet "Marxian" socialism made by Marx himself 120 years before!

> So far as it is *based on a high rate of surplus value, a high rate of profit is possible when the working day is very long, although labor is not highly productive*. It is possible, because *the wants of the laborers are very small*, hence *average wages very low*, although the labor itself is unproductive. The low wages will correspond to the *laborers' lack of energy. Capital then accumulates slowly*, in spite of the high rate of profit. *Population is stagnant* and the working time which the product costs, is great, while the wages paid to the laborer is small.[64]

That is why there was a lack of energy in the workers, which our Pharisees wondered so much about. Because a low wage was corresponding to it! It's a banal truth known by the illiterate persons. That is why the population does not still grow, but melts like the snows of yesteryear, i.e., the nation grows old. That is why the working day was very long and the labor was hard. That is why the product was expensive—because the working time was great and unproductive. And such was for all the "socialist" system!

At the same time, this inhuman system raised the ideological slogan, "care for the man" as an extreme hypocrisy of the *E*. (Establishment)! The "care for the man" manifested itself in succession again, when in 1985 our precious National Assembly (the Parliament) decided that the workers receiving *monthly* (!) wages of 120 levs ($50 US) should be exempted from tax on wages. What an attention, what altruism! Exceptional generosity and humanity! In this manner, these workers were completely arranged in the category of **proletarians**—paupers, who do not pay taxes, because of any property except their children, who must obligatorily make their military service! That was the reality in this "real socialism!" What a dictatorship of the proletariat—the proletarians didn't know that! Yes—dictatorship against the proletariat! A dictatorship of a handful of persons, as Rosa Luxemburg wrote, a dictatorship of a party, a dictatorship of a clique!

***

---

[64]. Marx, *Capital*, 3:286. (bolded by me—T.B.)

In Global Scale

People's state is the ideological platform of the state capitalism, usually representing in its transformed form of a *people's socialism*. (Here I mean the *people's socialism* in so-called "communist" countries by the Soviet bloc as a real political regime, but not the socialist current from the Nordic countries as an ideological tendency. Although there are no any theoretic differences.) The *people's state* is so suitable, the most suitable in fact, to implement capitalistic exploitation. This state capitalism in the modern times of corporative economy under the mask of some "socialism" is actually called fascism!

This word is shocking. But it is the real name of the policy of "iron curtains," of the full depersonalization of personality. This word is still provoking a storm of indignation amongst the worthy gentlemen of the modern "people's" socialism. How is it possible—our society, they say, had nothing in common with fascism, it was no fascist Reich.

Was it not?

And what is the so-called "Stalinism?"

In the epoch of "glasnost (publicity) and democracy," we were poured with facts about Stalin's despotism and his unlimited monocracy. And this is the top of the iceberg only.

How otherwise may we call the physical extermination of *millions* of people who were unsuited to that regime? Were the concentration camps in Siberia of lower quality than those ones in Buchenwald and Dachau? Why allegedly having been enemies, Stalin and Hitler became military friends and allies and in 1939 divided Poland between themselves? Their military units took part in joint parades! And as we already know, since Stalin had no readiness in 1939, he did not raid Hitler, although it occurred in the reverse two years later. Stalin—he was the "Great Chieftain," the Leader that Hitler was in Germany—the Führer!

Until recently, however, some people wanted to convince us that all these outrages and repressions were specific to that time only and they were due to the will of one person only, Hitler or Stalin, but not to the whole political system with its economical and ideological content. Hitler and Stalin are products of the system, but not the opposite—the system was to be their product. Both of them would not be possible if there were no conditions available—the state, coalescent to the big monopolistic capital, to get behind them, to raise them, and to support them until they are suited.

The fear of acknowledging the **entire** truth, the fear of calling the past with its exact name—this is a fear inherited from these years. It was even scientifically acknowledged that the long political season that had faded out was totalitarianism. However, this is the half-truth. Nobody has acknowledged or proved yet that this was fascism, but not socialism! How did Stalinism appear and develop if there were no conditions available for it? And it was only by alluding to the similar "deviations" of Brezhnev for people not to avoid that there was never socialism in fact. That's why his time was diplomatically called the "time of the standstill." So, after every sip of fresh air of a new "socialist democracy" from some "reconstruction" followed submergence and a long period of a standstill. Life in an (old) submarine—dangerous, hard, and short! In a confined space, time, and air! After Lenin, the periscope was taken by Stalin, after Khrushchev—Brezhnev. And if Stalin was the Kremlin Caligula, and Khrushchev—a feeble-minded jester like Claudius, is it not true that Brezhnev was Tiberius?

After Stalin, every next Caesar blamed his predecessor in a cult of him, for becoming the same one. A cult only replaced another one. However, the cult is possible in religion only. Communism was transformed into an occult science with a conjuring character, into religion, into another type of confession. In addition to Buddhism, Christianity, and Islam, it was a new kind of world religion. Religion, from which, as usual, one may win much! The priest's vocation is to distribute (and to observe) the moral of the faith. Reducing communism to occultism, upon transforming socialism into faith, the role of the party secretary was not much different from that of the priest—he had to concern himself not with scientific principles, but with moral ones of the faith that he could not observe! The religious cult—this is the misfortune of humankind. Because of their **ignorance**, people have always perceived their leader not as first among equals, but as a God among a flock!

Because of ignorance, both Hitler and Stalin were perceived by millions of crowds in the same way. The impression is that most authoritarian regimes were led by mentally restricted individuals, but who had a pathological craving for power, individuals with poor and even empty mental luggage, but with unscrupulous ambitions. And if Hitler's fascism is frank cynicism, Stalin's fascism is cynic furtiveness!

What is fascism actually, in short? (In short, because it is not the main topic of this research)

Its **economic** basis is the fusion of the state with the big monopolistic capital, i.e., the state monopoly of the capital. It is a state-monopoly capitalism, which in our time proved to be in its final, completed stage—the stage of absolute monopoly. It is imperialism with all its features, and nowadays—even over-imperialism, mega-imperialism. This is the utmost, highest extent of fusion of the bank capital with the industrial and trade capital in a monolithic financial and state oligarchy, having reached the extreme top, a final degree of centralization of the capital in one and only center.

The **political** basis of fascism is the fusion of legislative, executive, and judicial powers in one center—the biggest evil for any state, according to Montesquieu. "When the legislative and executive powers are united in the same person, or in the same body of magistrates, there can be no liberty . . . Again, there is no liberty, if the judiciary power is not separated from the legislative and executive. Were it joined with the legislative, the life and liberty of the subject would be exposed to arbitrary control."[65]

In this way, the political superstructure represents a kind of sealing with thickly concreted plates, an armored bunker resulting from the compacted coalescence of Parliament, government, Supreme Court and party, which could not be dissociated as per functions and subjects, any form of criticism and freedom being in this way cruelly choked and eliminated—of the personality, of the thought, of the speech.

In this way, on this favorable soil of power only grows the mistreated forms of the one-party political system, which, in its latent form, i.e., in the absence of an organized resistance of the working class, represents a totalitarian police regime. And only at an apparent form of organized class struggle, fascism throws off its mask and manifests itself already as an open terrorist dictatorship of the most reactionary financial capital, after G. Dimitrov's definition. In the above view, we must mention that the democracy of the working class does not negate the multiple-party political system in the state. On the contrary, it even needs it to some extent in order to remain faithful to its principles. Since "the corruption of this government generally begins with that of the principles."[66] The

---

[65]. Montesquieu, *The Spirit of the Laws*, 227.
[66]. Ibid., 177.

party of the workers needs other parties like outside mirrors—to get its principles saved.

The **ideological** support for fascism is the petty bourgeois ideology in the theory of the *people's state*, through which socialism is transformed from class socialism into a people's (national) socialism. The *people's state* is always a police state—the violence in it is often expressed in arbitrariness.

In other words, everywhere, fascism strives for a class "unity," for absolutism, monopoly, for a uniform unification of all differences—in the economy, in politics, in ideology. Fascism is not each one of those things separately, but all of them put together. Fascism is an offspring of the state-monopolistic capitalism and imperialism. It is a decadent state super-capitalism, as a concept in Italian fascism according to Mussolini, but as essence, not as an opposition to the fascism. Fascism in the society is a result from fetishism of the State. Fascism is a product of the apotheosis of the idea of State in the conditions of the developed monopolistic capitalism; it is an idealization of the State in the modern corporative capitalism.

This is the essence of fascism. While as phenomenon it may be showed as extreme nationalism, as anti-democratism, as anti-communism, as racism, as anti-Semitism, separately or together, in general—as state terrorism, even as national nihilism, provided that the oligarchic Establishment is satisfied, i.e., fascism may take various forms and images: "pre-fascism" (authoritarian regime), "initial fascism," "normal fascism" (Italian), "extreme fascism" (German Nazism , Zionism), and even "communism" (Soviet and Asian).

The totalitarian regime finds its expression in the politic "prophylaxis," in the preliminary police investigation and "advises" people who think otherwise and particular persons like a witch-hunt—always in the name of democracy and the peace of citizens. The police surveillance also goes for in "anticipatory work for preventing crimes and law infringements," according to the Programme of the ex-Bulgarian Communist Party. In this way, every idea of freedom and democracy may be easily stigmatized for being terrorism or extremism! "Everything ought to depend here on two or three ideas; hence there is no necessity that any new notions should be added."[67] Thus, in a methodical and certain way, the conscience of the society is lulled to

---

[67]. Montesquieu, *The Spirit of the Laws*, 118.

sleep and Swift's gourd only would help awake from the deep sleep, from the lethargy that had grabbed this society. "As fear is the principle of despotic government, its end is tranquillity; but this tranquillity cannot be called a peace: no, it is only the silence . . ."[68]

Actually, the underlying principle of despotism is fear—fear paralyzing the souls. Totalitarianism is "a government where fear ought to be the only prevailing sentiment,"[69] so, the publicity is a sly monastery whisper; it is a regime "where absolute power is in some measure naturalized"[70] and where the particular person's "security depends entirely on his being reduced to a kind of annihilation."[71] A regime that imposed, in addition to the heavy tax burden, a tax on wit, songs, and laughter, that transformed the almost entire society into a "mass of broken wretches past salvation."[72] We were transformed into a state "where every mouse is under police surveillance."[73] Thus, it created a society of fear, the same like that society on the Moon, in which half of the citizens squealed to the power about the other half.[74] A society in which there are no talents, but only admirers! A society based on fear and ease! A society that is crammed in jails, asylums, and bars! A society in which thought is crucified! A socialitarian, not a socialist society, in which "each particular officer is the vizir."[75]

The cynicism of this system consisted of the fact that this tyranny was represented as freedom, something more—as socialism! And "the people, amazed at so many revolutions, in vain attempted to erect a commonwealth."[76] For forty-five "free" years of "people's" power, "desperate from the liberty, people wanted some smaller slavery."[77] However, the new liberty turned out again to be not a smaller slavery than the preceding one; the replacement of the totalitarian system with a "democratic" one was only a theater in front of the general public! The screenplay of this theater was written by Reagan and Gorbachev in Malta in 1985. That is why there were shifts of the scenery, the actors,

---

[68]. Montesquieu, *The Spirit of the Laws*,120.

[69]. Ibid., 137.

[70]. Ibid., 123.

[71]. Ibid., 137.

[72]. Marx, *Value, Price and Profit,* 7:110.

[73]. Marx, *Capital*, 1:728.

[74]. Janusz Zajdel, *Van Troff's Cylinder.*

[75]. Montesquieu, *The Spirit of the Laws,* 126.

[76]. Ibid., 75.

[77]. Sallust, *Bellum Iugurthinum*, 147.

and the act, but the E producers left the same. For this purpose, these unscrupulous party brigands were reproducing themselves into thousands of copies and they were successfully cloning themselves in all of their heirs, staying at the head of the state since the first day of their democracy. And the unscrupulous clones excelled their originals—the blackest days, days of disintegration, humiliation, and agony took place in Bulgaria. The clones created by the Matrix of the pseudo-socialism, mutants yet were intended to serve something like democracy, something like freedom, something like nothing in the world!

Like a gloomy and sinister paradox since its apparition until now, socialism suffered terrible and terrifying metamorphoses. With the name of the most human doctrine—socialism—the most ominous and naughty crimes against humanity were done. The National Socialism of Hitler created Auschwitz and Majdanek and the people's socialism of Stalin—Gulag and Kolima! And both of them buried more than fifty million people! That's monstrous! But the misfortunes were not over with this, the tragedy did not stop with this. On the contrary! The totalitarianism, the content of fascism, increased. The so-called "cult of personality," the worship for "The Great Chieftain" was solely immanent to the "socialist" system. A cult replaced another and so on—until the end of the century! Anti-democratic regimes of Asian despotism and inhuman tyranny—for all that socialism was guilty!

While in Cambodia, Pol Pot's cutthroats exterminated their own people, in China, the great mandarin, Mao Zedong, undertook jumps of "cultural revolution" that the Chinese were not until the 1990s starting to recover from. He established a social equality—all people were donned in the very same duck uniforms just like the state super-capitalism wants! His associate in North Korea was Kim Il-sung, who was a good associate of him. Until now this regime remains unapproachable like its leader Kim the Third and his dynastic line do. It is amazing that this barrack system still exists there solely all over the world when even Fidel Castro's Cuba gradually began to pull down the fence of it.

In the USSR, Stalin's repressions were confirmed and extended under Brezhnev. With him appeared the theory of the "little man" with his "little truth." One could shed tears from tenderness while seeing with what a paternal care the "big man" discussed the problems of the "little man." Long before him, Chaplin and Brecht created the image and the place of the little man in a world deprived of rights. But that was the little man as criticism, but not as demagogy, like Brezhnev did. To which extent were the serfdom and the feudal absence of rights of the "little man" proved by Gorbachev's reconstruction (perestroika)— laying a normal middle-class democracy provoked a true furor and applauses. This was an abolition of the serfdom in Russia for a second time—at the end of the twentieth century!

> Observe how industriously the Russian government endeavors to temper its arbitrary power, which it finds more burdensome than the people themselves. They have broken their numerous guards, mitigated criminal punishments, erected tribunals, entered into a knowledge of the laws, and instructed the people. But there are particular causes that will probably once more involve them in the very misery which they now endeavor to avoid. [78]

The picture of 1760 was amazingly the same as in 1990. Nothing new under the sun in Russia!

The turbulent twentieth century was a century of fascist dictatorships. Besides the world "socialist" system in Europe and Asia, it teemed with such systems in Latin America, although it was not under the slogan of socialism. That is why the struggle in all these countries was reduced to a struggle for liberalization, for a restoration of a normal bourgeois democracy or for social democracy. However, the struggle further, i.e., the struggle for socialism, was not initiated yet. Because, until nowadays, nobody had answered the question: howsoever, what is socialism?

What happened at the end of the twentieth century in the "socialist" countries was they were overthrowing totalitarian regimes, i.e., fascism in Europe was nominally overthrown not in 1945, but in 1989! Although the fact is that at present, it really smolders all over the world. What happened in Central and Eastern Europe since 1989 is simply a restoration of the common normal bourgeois rights and freedoms. What happened in the Soviet Union, Bulgaria, Hungary, Poland, the German Democratic Republic, and Czechoslovakia was not a return from socialism to capitalism, as lots of people think, but a transition from a form of capitalism to another one—economic more progressive, from a form of a middle-class ruling to another one—seemingly more democratic. However, both until and after the "reconstruction," i.e., during all the tract of "socialism," the labor power went on to be a commodity and the working class—done and exploited. Socialism may

---

[78]. Montesquieu, *The Spirit of the Laws*, 120.

be reality only under the power of the working class and in no other case! Because, in any other case, the eternal for capitalism problems—unemployment, inflation, external debts—have never their solution, but only provoke the substitution of a government with another one, which is also as powerless to cope with them as the previous.

The dream of all peoples—a world without weapons, a world without wars—despite any initiatives, no matter whether they are strategic or not, is only a utopia within the contemporary content of the State. Nowadays, the State is the biggest, the most powerful criminal organization of continuous robbery of social labor. The State is a mafia today, in which the basic principle is the "law" omertá—"who's not mum, is dead!" Now the State is the final phase of the organized criminality. It is "a conspiracy of the rich,"[79] where because of the judicial astrology, "in every situation, powerful rogues know how to save themselves at the expense of the feeble."[80] Until now, the class society represents a power of one family that divided for itself the state as private property!

The contemporary epoch—the epoch of mega-imperialism—is specific with the fact that imperialism has reached only its higher degree, a militant globalism. Why?

First, because the concentration of capital reached unprecedented dimensions and its monopolization (the centralization) enabled an insignificant in number national financial oligarchy to possess the entire own national state, and from Washington's capitol—the entire world! While there was still any competition between the corporations and the banks in the western capitalist community, in the Eurasian "communist" community, the entire state was one corporation and one bank! It is something that had never been in the capitalist world—even during the imperialism described by Lenin in 1916. This allowed being realized an enormous export of capital—to the poor, developing states, conquered themselves economically as colonies. The increasing export of capital imposed its movement to be released from any national barriers. For the purposes of the free movement of capital between the particular countries, various economic unions were created—in Europe, for example, the Common Market in the west, the Council of Mutual Economic Assistance in the east, and later, the European Union as a third world centre when the latter was absorbed by the former, although not in full scale.

---

[79]. More, *Utopia*, 136.
[80]. Jean-Jacque Rousseau, *Confessions of Jean-Jacque Rousseau,* 37.

This unprecedented export of capital transmuted the national corporate capital of the world economic powers into multinational. This was an evolution of the state-monopoly capitalism. If Soviet and Asian "communist" state-monopoly capitalism reached the last stage of fusion of the state with the national capital, the more developed American and west-European state-monopoly capitalism passed into a new, higher stage under which the national corporate capital being liberated from any national borders transmuted into multinational capital. Just the multinational corporate capital demanded to conquer new markets and lands. With that end in view was created the European Union. In the end of the twentieth and the beginning of the twenty-first centuries commenced a new process of evolution of the multinational corporate capital and the transmutation of the corporations into states! These new capitalistic social formations—the corporative vertical states—entered keen conflict with the traditional (the horizontal), i.e., the national states, which for that purpose had to be erased in Europe by the artificial amorphous structure European Union. Just for that reason the next step is the subjugation of the national states in Europe and their complete liquidation by the US and Canada based now multinational corporate capital, by the new vertical states through establishing new statutory regulations—the treaties TTIP, CETA (and TTP for the Pacific region). These secret treaties include out-of-court and over-national mechanism of arbitration tribunals (ISDS) through which the corporations, these new states, could judge and cope offhandedly with the traditional, historically created national states.

Second, the coalescence of the monopolies with the state led to unseen dimensions of the parasitism and the decay of this mode of production—the state-monopoly capitalism in its final degree. In the Soviet bloc, just like the clergy in every medieval Christian state, there was built a parallel parasite structure in the state by the half of population for control of the other half—this was the enormous ranks of the ruling party which along with the padded state administration unleashed unseen earlier parasitism in the society; that led in the last reckoning the need of an unrealized Gorbachev's "reconstruction." But the parasitism in "new Europe" with the additional new, highly paid administration of the European Union and with the class peace's policy of the so-called *social (welfare) state* will prove the decay of this system, as well, which will inevitably topple down under its own weight as it happened to that very Soviet bloc. It is very funny that the totalitarian Soviet Union existed seventy-five years, while the alleged democratic European Union will not last more than thirty! But the crucial contribution to unleashing of the parasitism has the fictitious capital; the speculative games of the fictitious capital trade in Wall Street and the like create parasitism unseen in the earlier imperialism a hundred years ago.

Third, the partition of the world between the Great Powers, the division of spheres of influence, and the fight for markets, in this century since the October Revolution was already carried on not by several states as in 1914-1918, but only by two world powers, two ultra-states—the USA and the USSR. For this purpose, astronomical amounts were allotted for armament, unknown under the earlier imperialism and all of this after the end of the most sinister war in human history—the Second World War, as an offspring of this very mega-imperialism. At the end of the twentieth century, the USA remained the single super force. Both contemporary scepters of imperial power—The World Bank and the International Monetary Fund—were and still are in the hands of US imperialism. Thus, in this unipolar world, the capitalism reached the apogee of the imperialism and its market distribution. The USA remained the only world gendarme and custodian of the "New World Order." It was until 2014/15 when the Eurasian militarism (Russian and Chinese) challenged the US supremacy and this new unipolar order. The war in Syria is such a test.

In the conditions of this "New World Order," a crucial part of the contemporary world economy is a criminal economy, in which the excess profits are accumulated not by the production of material comforts, but by drug-traffic, arms trafficking, and human trafficking, including prostitution. The contemporary world economy is an economy of the global organized criminality whose eminently form is the modern capitalist state. The contemporary world economy is an economy not of the real commodity production, but an economy of the jobbery; this is expressed directly in supply and demand of the capital of the speculation, i.e., in the fictitious capital trade, in the antagonistic games with share capital in the stock exchange. Just Wall Street's stock exchange, i.e., the world speculative capital market, is the contemporary tremendous pump for inflation of the balloons of the world economic crises, the last one of which began in 2007. The aggregate amount of the bonds on the world market, as many economists know, is over one hundred trillion US dollars! Without taking in mind the derivatives! If including those, the aggregate amount is **several *times* more**! This is an enormous balloon as inflated as a red giant star! And when added to this amount the world market of the shares, the passing each other between real and fictitious capital grows to cosmic dimensions! This cosmic balloon will burst very soon! That means the most destructive capitalist crisis in human history lies just round the corner, the global economic apocalypse is just forthcoming! This ruin will be due to the stock exchange antagonistic games, the stock exchange that is, as a matter of fact, a gambling house! Because the securities and shares' trading is sheer gambling! This becomes clear by the direct proportionality between risk and profitability, the more risk—the more profitability, and vice versa! However, this is gambling in which the stakes are not simply money, but millions and billions of human fates. So, this is a destroying-the-civilization-world crime economy!

Fourth, militarism, as a form of manifestation of imperialism, was intensely developed, in spite of all chatter, negotiations, and some reductions of armies and arsenals. The US Empire touched off any number of wars all over the world on behalf of "democracy"—from Vietnam via the Gulf to Grenada. The Soviet Empire (and its then province Cuba) tried to disseminate "communism" with the power of its weapons until 1985, until Gorbachev's appearance—as an "export of revolution." However, this military doctrine was exhausted to its final point in its feeble economy. It was not occasionally that the USSR was called a military giant of an economic dwarf. At the same time, we had to be convinced that in 1988, the USSR spent for military expenses only . . . 33 billion rubles against $300 billion dollars spent by the USA. Black humor! The entire military empire was supported only by a doubtful in its authenticity amount. Simply fun, as a Russian journalist said.[81] This was fun because this was not true. Because, if the USA has a military industry, then the USSR's industry was military! If US imperialism is due to its military-industry complex, the Soviet one was an expression of its industry-military complex. We won't say that US imperialism is a good thing, but simply that Soviet imperialism until 1990 was not the lesser evil! A cabinet reshuffle, the "reconstruction"—in general, this was similar to the *New Deal* of Roosevelt who substituted and replaced in 1933 the "dry regime" of Harding. Gorbachev changed the "dry regime" in the economy and introduced a "new deal"—so-called *new thinking* in politics. *New political thinking* for the USSR in 1985 was the *New Deal*; the same as in the USA in 1933. But they have nothing to do with

---

[81]. Alexander Bovin, *Izvestia* newspaper, March 1989, on Bulgarian TV.

socialism. This was simply a replacement of one governmental team with another within the same capitalist system. This was reformism, but not a "quiet, bloodless revolution," as it was emphasized at that time. There is no such revolution—bloodless, quiet, or tender! The *New Deal* of Roosevelt was an intervention of the state in the functioning of big business, which was welcomed in Germany by Goebbels! But the big business in the United States struck back through the skills of the PR father, Edward Bernays, another mighty manipulator of the public opinion just like Goebbels! In other words, this throwing between wild and controlled capitalism, between "market" and state capitalism, between "democratic" capitalism and totalitarian "socialism" ("communism") exist during all the tract of the state-monopoly capitalism, i.e., since the rise of the monopolies and their fusion with the state until now—all of the twentieth and the first two decades of twenty-first centuries. What was the "New Deal" of Gorbachev? This was a cleaner and reasonable policy, a more realistic policy, restricting and in some places eliminating the rudest forms of Russian imperialism. Gorbachev, however, came out not only as the last utopian of the socialism, but also as an unable statesman if he had allowed his state to disintegrate with the same easiness that he put an end of the "socialism," too.

Roman peace (*Pax Romana*) was a fruit of violence. Contemporary peace (*Pax Americana*) is also a fruit of violence—where and when it is present. Peace is the highest good for all peoples, but how will we live in such a peace in the future—of class violence of the Capital? Like helots standardized in a single world Empire? We saw that after the end of the "cold war" these were the ambitions of the United States—the other Evil Empire! *Quo vadis, homuncule?*[82]

The last paragraph I had written twenty-six years ago. It turned out that I prognosticated quite right the contemporary advance of the State in the global scale. It turned out that just this is the utmost aim of world's masters—passing all people under a single world Empire! Approximately fifteen years ago (since 2000), there began a process of destroying and effacement of the national states through their unification in different geographical over-national "unions"—European, American, African, Asian, Eurasian—as the last stage before their unification in a single global State, in a single world Empire! The aim is a world Empire with effaced territorial borders, with effaced national states being replaced by

---

[82]. Where do you go, manikin? (Lat.)

the vertical states, the corporations; an Empire mixing races and cultures, where the constitutional law is nothing, but the corporate wrong is all! The achievement of this ultimate phase passes through a transition stage in which the national states are tributary formations quite helpless towards the corporations by means of TTIP, CETA and TTP—treaties legalizing lawlessness! The secret negotiations for conclusion of the secret treaties are the height of the underhand age-old domination of the secret number secret societies being guided by a secret center. The sovereign as a concept and legal regulation disappears in full, the court is a survival, and the right is only one—the right of the strong, of the corpo-oligarch! Thus, the enslavement of the mankind is finishing and forever!

Duties' abolition between the European Union and the United States is only the consecutive step to a fusion of two "unions" in one mega "union" and of all such "unions" in a world corporative mega-imperialism without borders. For this purpose, the *Final Solution* of the European peoples Question is already put into effect! In pursuance of the plan of destruction of the European national states with the final purpose a substitution of the native nations and the reduction them to the status of impersonal mass of degenerates without stock it is carrying out an organized migration of countless hordes Arabian and African settlers conquering Europe. The mass invasion of immigrants called euphemistically "refugees" in a common plan with the creation of Islamic State (ISIS, ISIL, Daesh) is the serial bungled and misconducted operation of CIA and its masters just like the "terroristic attacks" on 9/11/2001; it's the serial fiendish plan against the humanity, in this case against the peoples of Europe and their full effacement! It is so transparent, all too clear operation repeating the unique in its madness operation of a wide scope by 9/11! In both cases, it is using the Islamic card. In both cases, it is speaking of closely interwoven foul business and political interests; destroying World Trade Center's towers there were furtive business interests to 3 (three) billion USD but the towers were used politically in front of the general public with the idea of new future foul business plans. Such foul plan is to do for the European civilization with the disappearance of which the revolutions must cease to occur. That is the modern mega-imperialism—the State everywhere creates terrorism and conditions of terrorism!

If humanity will be saved from the nuclear nightmare, how will it have to live further in the clipper of the State? Weapons become more

73

and more powerful, more dangerous, inspiring more and more horror. The controlled nuclear synthesis and the full genetic code revelation along with the information technologies will unleash the imagination enormously in this direction. There are always wars because there is a State and there will always be wars until the change and the dying out of the State. That is why humans have never learned not to kill—either after the First or after the Second World War, being always ready for the Third World War. War is an extreme, brutal, and the most savage expression of State's violence.

Still, Plato discovered the rule that the searching for the truth was in opposite dependence on finding the pleasures. The running high of the pleasures, by transforming them into brutal consumption, narrows the way to the truth. In our days, the Capital, by using the development of the scientific and technical revolution wants to create a society of the "consumption paradise," a society of mass indifference, a militarized techno-tronic society without a working class, for depersonalizing humans and for transforming them into the screws of a military machine called the **State**! The Capital wants to erase the polarity between the working class and state and to create a unified, monolithic, "classless" society. As at the time of Marx and Engels, nowadays also, various "theorists" breed who want to convince us that capitalism is the eternal economic system or at least that it is the best and even has no alternative, by comparing it to the disability of the bygone "socialism." Socialism came out of a Gordian knot that was intricately tied economically, politically, and ideologically. Up to now, it remains a scientific poser for all formal professors, in spite of their strains, who, as the medieval theologians did, undertook defending the faith, but not the God, and they were doing this in a way that until recently socialism served flawlessly as opium for the poor, as religion did formerly. Religion, however, wants to change the consciousness without changing the being. Science changes the being and thereby, the consciousness. If Christianity is a doctrine of relief of poverty, Marxism is a doctrine of abolishment of poverty. Socialism was transformed from science into utopia, and because of that, it was an enigma, an Egyptian hieroglyph. Our blown-over "real socialism," like a Trojan horse, defeated so hard the socialist doctrine inside that it has never been made in its history, even by the most malignant and furious invective on the outside. Now the ugliest social rags are stitched up to socialism. God grants a lot of designers—nothing reverse is strange to them! Socialism was transformed into a scarecrow to frighten the adult children—it was branded as the greatest evil! And of two evils, people always choose the lesser one! In the twentieth century, we passed through a form of utopian socialism, which at the contemporary stage of society's development was simply capitalism. In front of this "socialism," the western capitalism was really preferable—it was the lesser evil than its eastern variant. However, this social lie of the largest size gave "reason" to the ignoramuses to consider themselves more intelligent than the geniuses. Now every layman with the self-confidence of expert "rejects" Marx and Engels at any occasion! Even without it, he has breathed in a bit of library dust. Without ever having reached the coattails of those titans! *Shoemaker, not above the sandal!*[83]

---

[83]. Pliny the Elder, *Naturalis Historia* [XXXV, 85[2] (Loeb IX, 323-325)] where he records that a shoemaker (*sutor*) had approached the painter Apelles of Kos to point out a defect in the artist's rendition of a sandal (*crepida* from Greek *krepis*), which Apelles duly corrected. Encouraged by this, the shoemaker then began to enlarge on other defects he considered present in the painting, at which point Apelles advised him that *ne supra crepidam sutor iudicaret* (a shoemaker should not judge above the sandal), which advice, Pliny observed, had become a proverbial saying.

Chapter Five

The Transition Period

Marxism is a doctrine of the State and Revolution, of society's release from the State via the Revolution.

To differ from the innumerable socialist systems, Marx writes that this socialism represents a permanent revolution. In other words, for no restoration to take place, as it occurs always after every other revolution, socialism, under the conditions already of the state, as well, must be an unceasing revolution, i.e., without "reconstructions." This permanent revolution is expressed in no other thing, not in any eternal Jacobin terror, but in the withering away of the state. Engels interpreted that in a brilliant philosophical manner. The blow, i.e., the revolution—this is a concentrated friction, and the friction, i.e., the state—this is a long-lasting blow. What the blow (the revolution) cannot do, can be done by the friction (the state). The revolution of the working class is actually an explosion of the old state, a concentrated friction against the middle-class, while the state of the working class is an unceasing blow against it, i.e., just the state of the working class represents that permanent revolution, of which Marx writes. For this reason, socialism is a unity of revolution of the working class and of state of the working class.

The revolution is an explosion between productive forces and production relations, between old and fossil, production relations, and new and progressive, productive forces.

There is an impression that among all other social revolutions the Great Revolutions are distinguished, which go by two for the same mode of production. The First Great Revolution only proclaims the necessity for the new production relations, but the productive forces remain within the framework of the old production relations, i.e., the old mode of production remains **dominant**. The Second Great Revolution affirms the new production relations, it comes to establish them utterly and finally as already triumphing production relations, i.e., it gives the beginning of a new mode of production, imposed as dominant, i.e., not like an isolated case only in one or more particular states.

Because the transition to the slave-holding mode of production gradually became through evolution, we cannot speak there about any revolutions. The decomposition of the primitive communism and the transition to a class society, just like the opposite process, as well—the transition from class society to communism, is a gradual process, an evolutionary way.

We can consider as the First Great Feudal Revolution, the acceptance of Christianity for the established church of the Roman Empire at the ecumenical council of Nicaea in 325 CE. As the Second Great Revolution, i.e., a revolution having affirmed the feudal production relations on a world-wide scale, we can admit the coming into force Iustinianus the Great's law of conversion to Christianity of all pagans all over the Roman Empire in year 529 CE. This law played a revolutionary role giving the beginning of the process of the final victory of Christianity as the established church in the Empire, i.e., the beginning of the end of the process of affirming the new production relations having started in 325 CE at Constantine the Great in Nicaea's council. Later, conversion to Christianity as an established church by the different, early-medieval states at different times came to legalize the extant already feudal exploitation, to establish the new mode of production, because the new productive forces required breaking off the link with the old production relations and imposed a border, which must have been passed or, otherwise, the state must have gone to wrack and ruin.

The English Bourgeois Revolution of 1642, with Cromwell at the head, is only a great precursor of the new time, which, however, does not impose any typical capitalistic production relations. That is done by the Great French Revolution of 1789 and the American Revolution at the same time, which answered already the historical inevitability for new production relations, for a radical change in the mode of production in worldwide scale. The same applies in respect to socialism. The Great Socialist October Revolution of the Bolsheviks in 1917 only proclaimed the historical inevitability for new production relations, which already lagged long behind the level of development of the productive forces, while the mode of production remained capitalistic during all the time of "socialism" from 1917 until our days. At the first quarter of the twenty-first century, there will be a new, still one Great Socialist Revolution, which will utterly and finally establish, will irretrievably affirm the new production relations, i.e., the socialist mode of production. It will be the

Last Great Revolution of earth's humanity, which will throw open the doors to spaces that people have never dreamt until those times![84]

Each new mode of production creates a higher level of labor organization, a higher organization of the working time than the preceding one, creating in this way such "conditions, which are **more advantageous** to the development of the productive forces, social relations and the creation of the elements for a new and higher form than under the preceding forms . . ."[85]

It's namely more advantageous for the society, but not more wished for by the individual.

Each mode of production from its nascence to its dying out has periods of transition, when its first germs appear out of the womb of the old period and has periods of maturity, during which it already exists independently, in a pure state, without admixtures of another mode of production.

This transition period is called so because it gives the beginning of new production relations (along with the dying out of the old ones) until their complete victory, i.e., this is precisely the period when the Great Revolutions burst. As we will notice below, if the periods of the distinct class societies shorten according to an exponential law, the transition period is always constant, is always three centuries! This is a remarkable fact!

The Neolithic era, having begun in the eighth to sixth millennium BCE and the Copper Age, having lasted from 5500 BCE to 3500 BCE, represent the period of maturity of the tribe society. At the end of the Copper Age, and at the beginning of the Bronze Age, decomposition starts of the tribe society that would continue until 3200 BCE, when the first city-states in Sumer and the first *nomes* in Egypt emerge, which represents a transition period from primitive communism to class society, from the primitive communal system to the state system. The slave-holding mode of production continues approximately 3700 ± 100 years, from 3200 BCE to 600 CE, as its widest borders. Of course, this

---

[84]. By the way, it is very interesting that Anatole France in 1904 did a similar forecast in his utopian book, *The White Stone.* We see there some amazingly exact prognoses about the socialism and the European Union, but he makes a mistake, I think, concerning this main event, supposing it a quarter century earlier.

[85]. Marx, *Capital*, 3:925 (bolded by me—T.B.)

is a conditional periodization, because the economic processes do not go from a specified date to another specified date. The period of maturity of the slave-owing system lasts from the fifth century BCE—the time of the classical Hellenic democracy, to the end of the third century CE—the decline of the Roman Empire.

The transition period from a slave-holding mode of production to a feudal one goes from the fourth to the sixth century inclusively, when the first feudal states of the early Middle Ages arise in Europe—the East Roman Empire, the Huns Empire with its direct successor the Bulgarian Empire, and Franks Empire. The conditional borders of this transition period are from 306 CE—the year of ascension of Constantine the Great, the first Christian Roman emperor, until the end of 602 CE, the death of Emperor Mauricius Tiberius, up to which is finally affirmed the started by Iustinianus the Great the real transformation of the Roman Empire from a late-antique state to an early feudal one. The duration of the feudalism was approximately 1350 ± 50 years. The period of maturity of this social system, the flourishing state of feudalism, was from the tenth to the fifteenth century.

The transition period from the feudal mode of production to capitalistic was between the sixteenth and the eighteenth century inclusive. The conditional borders of this transition period are from 1492—the year of Columbus' discovery of America for the Old world and the beginning of the great geographical discoveries, until 1789, the year of the Great French Revolution and the American Revolution. The feudal production relations dominated in the world until the end of the eighteenth century. It is difficult to speak about capitalism before this date. In 1758, a miracle happened, an epochal event—the first bourgeois in England "was seen with an equipage of his own"[86]! Not until 1800, the most advanced states like England, United States, France, had already developed capitalist relations in their contemporary meaning. Capitalism in its mature, developed form, as an affirmed mode of production, can be accepted only since the appearance of the machinery and the heavy industry but not since the period of the manufacture which is only an overture, a transition period to capitalism. That is the so-called *primitive accumulation of capital*. This is precisely the transition period to capitalism, the period that continues from the beginning of the sixteenth to the end of the eighteenth century.

---

[86]. Marx, *Capital*, 1:656

"Although we come across the first beginnings of capitalist production as early as the fourteenth or fifteenth century, sporadically, in certain towns of the Mediterranean, the capitalistic era dates from the sixteenth century."[87]

Indeed, it dates from the sixteenth century, but only as a beginning of the transition period, mixing different types of production relations. Because the transition period represents a period with the old withering away, but still remaining **dominant** production relations, which in fact makes it belong to the old social system. That's why the manufacturing period, taken as a transition period, is chronologically assigned to feudalism. Under the manufacturing period, which is not yet real capitalism, the capital, at its childish age, "failed to become the master of the whole disposable working time of the manufacturing laborers."[88] The manufacture has not been able "to revolutionize (the social) production to its very core"[89], "it towered up as an economic work of art"[90] of the feudal mode of production. The mature capitalism expressed itself politically for the first time scarcely during the revolution of 1830 in France, when the working class appeared for the first time on the historical stage as a detached class, as a separate, detached social force. So, the contemporary capitalism has a relatively short history, a relatively short biography—only two hundred years!

For this reason, just like the manufacturing period represents a transition period to capitalism and is arranged within the feudal mode of production and the transition period to feudalism is arranged within the slave-holding mode of production, socialism, being a transition period to communism, must be put chronologically to capitalism, because it is also a class society on commodity-based relations.

Today there is talk already about cosmic civilizations seeking their regularities. The basic mistake of all scientists is that they jump over whole stages of the historical development of the society; they mix completely different states of the society, completely different levels of its organization. That's why they only guess the planet Earth's cosmic civilization. And human society will become a cosmic civilization in the literal meaning of these words, i.e., mastered its solar system, only when

---

[87]. Marx, *Capital*, 1:783.
[88]. Ibid., 411.
[89]. Ibid.
[90]. Ibid.

it survives its class antagonisms, i.e., after the withering away of the State.

That is why, while examining the development of the class society only, i.e., from the rise of the State to its withering away, we can establish the following fact, discovered also by Enrico Fermi—human society's development runs according to an exponential law. But which law more precisely? Still, Engels had noticed that the productive forces grow in the course of time in geometric progression.[91] Actually, the productive forces develop in geometric progression with the quotient $q = e$. So, if the slave-ownership had lasted an average of about 3700 years, there would be 1360 years for feudalism, as much as it had actually lasted! For this reason, while calculating according to the same law, there would be 500 years of duration of the developed value-based production relations—capitalist and socialist, which is the end of the commodity relations, of the exchange in general, and along with this the end of the State, as well! All the period of existence of the State includes a period of more than 5550 years, being an incubation period only. The epoch of the State is a pregnancy of the Earth, a uterine period of the development of the embryo—*Homo Cosmicus*!

Humankind determined the historical ages of the class society in a strangely accurate way. Actually, if the State was eternal, capitalism in the distant future would look like hoary antiquity. All the division of history in antiquity, middle ages and modern times is true only because the State will die out in the not much distant future. From that time on, Man will write annals of quite another history and quite another chronology.

So, it turns out that the State is left about three centuries of life, its last transition period—until the end of the twenty-third century. The new era, Communism, will come with the beginning of the twenty-fourth century!

Formal science complained that "the new objective laws governing the historical development of the social form of matter's movement are still far away from being revealed."[92] Actually, no dogmatic school could ever understand, or less could reveal any objective laws—neither historical nor dialectical—in the development of the society. Each

[91]. Marx, *Capital*, 1:41.
[92]. Deyan Pavlov, *Knowledge and Aim*, Narodno Delo newspaper, 26.09.1986.

dogmatic school does not see further than its nose because it stands on paid agents of the system, nourished men of the power, like Karl Popper, for example, engaged to prove "in a scientific way" how the society can become open after its history was already over! The task of such opened wise guys is to open our eyes to the society scientifically, but they always forget that even in the most opened class society, the sum of the cages, slums, and hovels make by their inhabitants a quite closed society. Such ersatz thinkers are always defenders of their own class peace and because of that, for them, "history has no meaning"[93]! That is good that the history does not depend on them, and thus, their meaning has no history!

---

[93]. Popper, *The Open Society*, 2:300

Chapter Six

Withering away of the State

This was the clearest issue threshed out by all "socialists of the Chair and of the State and by their hangers-on"[94] of the former "socialist" system! They all knew that the state would wither away one day. Just one day—in a distant and vague future. This withering away was perceived like a dim concept in an unspecified time, which, however, in all the cases was not concerned to the current moment and concretely to us. It was always early and that is why it was always "postponed" for the distant future—upon the complete victory of the socialist production relations when the toilets even would be made of gold, when the social productivity of labor of socialism would dominate that one of capitalism.

One cannot wait for the economic victory over the capitalistic mode of production and scarcely then, the state starts to wither away. This quintessence of the highest instance is a folly, not praiseworthy, an empty jugglery of words. The withering away of the state and the growth of the social productivity of labor under socialism—this is an integrated process. This is just by the withering away of the state that the productivity of labor can grow stormily, at revolutionary rates within short times. It is not necessarily that the productivity of labor grows and then the state withers away, but the state must withers away in order to grow the productivity of labor with a higher than usual of the capitalism rates. Thus, it will be proved in practice the "advantages of socialism" as a more progressive and economically stronger system. Contrariwise, with the increase of the state apparatus, the productivity of labor lags incessantly behind—in an absolute and relative way. Officialdom and barracks are fetters, which trammel the development of any society, but they are especially heavy chains to its free motion under socialism.

Social injustice within the state is a result of the dictate of any class in the society. That is why, the social injustice under socialism along with all other principles of the power of the working class, are established

---

94. Marx, *Capital*, 2:11

in accordance with its interest for the withering away of employees' bureaucracy. The measures of the Paris Commune are the real way to the real withering away of the state.

The class violence of the withering away state is directed to itself, to its institutions—officials, army, police (and this is not in the form of violence, but as an economic policy!)—which, in spite of their new contents, represent in themselves hidden poisons with slow, but sure effect. Therefore, it's with a consequent effect. They can reproduce the bureaucracy with its dangerous "virus" influence. This invisible quasi violence of the socialist state over itself is necessary to open the path of progress, to become a mode of life, a practice of "introducing the new," as it was said in our country before. The withering away of the state means the scientific and technical progress is to be used and to be directed in a way that more and more labor power is employed to productive work, but not towards bureaucratic obligations. Then the government of the society will gradually and lightly yield to its self-government, "which is a charming form of government, full of variety. . ."[95]

Of course, at the very beginning of the socialism—immediately after the victory of the socialist revolution—this withering away of the state will be very slow, extremely difficult, and for that reason, hardly perceptible at an international encirclement of the Capital, not only in the case when the revolution overcomes in one undeveloped state, but even in several advanced countries, too. **But it must be started!** Because the society "needs only a state which is withering away, i.e., a state so constituted that it begins to wither away **immediately**, and **cannot but wither away**"[96]

The society needs really this state precisely—which is ready immediately to start to wither away and cannot but wither away! Only then and for this reason the socialist state is a "semi-state," a state not "in the true sense of the term,"[97] as Engels calls it—because it is withering away.

However, today again, just as it was 160 years ago, just as it was 95 years ago, the withering away of the state is perceived in a stupid and ironic way by certain, uncultivated circles as an abolition of the state in one day only, the withering away is understood as a liquidation of the

---

[95]. Plato, *The Republic*, 336.

[96]. Lenin, *The State and Revolution*, 33:23 (bolded is mine—T.B.).

[97]. Marx, *Critique of the Gotha Programme*, Engels to Bebel, 1:161.

state and that's why the demand for such socialism is malignantly represented as anarchism and nihilism. Such an "understanding" only proves its infinite distance from Marxism. "The state is not 'abolished.' *It dies out*," says Engels. "This gives the measure of the value of the phrase 'a free people's state,' both as to its justifiable use at times by agitators, and as to its ultimate scientific insufficiency; and also of the demands of the so-called anarchists for the abolition of the state out of hand."[98]

The state is necessary to the low development of the productive forces and to the low social consciousness of the tribe society just to develop the productive forces and to raise the social consciousness. However, at a stage of their development, it ceases being necessary and must "die down of itself," after Engels's exquisite expression. The social inequality in the face of the private property has led to the social injustice and violence in the face of the state. In order to turn back the society, ensnared in a state, to the initial position, but in a higher degree yet, it is necessary to follow the opposite direction—by social injustice to social equality. In this way, in the new classless society—communism— the spiral of evolution is closed but at the next higher degree. Nowadays, the state is the greatest evil for the society, inherited from the centuries.

The withering away of the state concerns all political organizations inside it, including the party itself, which has carried out the socialist revolution. This is withering away of the politics entirely and of the law in general. That means that the final goal of this party is the raising of the consciousness of the **whole society** at the level of the communist prime teachers and sages, but not a continuous breeding of the "communists" by their documents, of the party men "who have made for themselves a shield from the coat of religion, and who, under this respectable garment, are still permitted to be the worst of men."[99] That means to raise the social consciousness to a degree where it will drop out the need of a special political organization—the party; where it will be "rooted out of the minds of . . . the people all the seeds, both of ambition and faction."[100] And that means that the communist society is a society . . . without communists! But precisely this is the real civil society, i.e., a society that is fully (100 %) released from any state. Any other "civil society" is simply a bad imitation; it is just not a **civil** society.

---

[98]. Engels, *Anti-Dühring*, 8:315.
[99]. Molière, *Don Juan*, 280.
[100]. More, *Utopia,* 138.

In order to raise the social consciousness within the socialist state, in his book, *A Great Beginning*, Lenin recommends a successful ratio between party and class—at a four-million working class in Russia and Ukraine at that time, the party must include from 100,000 to 200,000 members, i.e., in the worst case 5% party's members. In Bulgaria in 1989, the Bulgarian Communist Party had 984,000 members against a working class of less than two million, = 50%! An incredible dilution, having led to the image of the party man at that time—lazy and omnivorous like a Benedictine friar! Communism is expressed not in the increase of party's apparatus, as it was in Bulgaria at that time, nor in its dilution, but in its reduction in the course of time; not by the number of the official communists, but of those that were outside them—by the level of the social consciousness. The withering away of the state means the society to be transformed by a society of hierarchical structure into a society of synodical structure.

The most characteristic feature that the state is socialist is that this state is withering away. The dying out of the state is expressed in the continuous increase in the number of the workers, at that of the highly skilled, while the dying, i.e., the putrefaction, of the state is expressed in the continuous increase in the number of the employees, at that of petty clerks. The state is negated in both cases, but whereas in the first case, it is a negation of the negation, because the society is released from the state, in the second case, it is only a naked negation, because it is an inevitable self-destruction. If the Capital will not be stopped, it will be fatal in the immediate, but not in the distant future. The enslaved part of the society will not differ from the common torrent of the things— objects and men will be a common, workable mass for the Capital, even in the physical sense. The society, divided into godlike Eloi and common-mortal Morlocks,[101] will be a dying corpse. Computer robots and bio-robots; satanic cloning and artificial insemination, as well as the "improvement" of the gene, all that for the purpose of the production of good citizens and brave soldiers; injecting of death batch production; ablution of brains, erasure of memory, i.e., alteration of the consciousness, of one's own "ego"—all that terrifying vividness of manipulation in a futuristic techno-tronic society, in which the State nips in the bud any resistance; a society at 481°F—a society without books and without values. The human life of the poor will be worth nothing and such moral qualities like duty, honor, conscience, and dignity will simply lose their

---

[101]. H. G. Wells, *The Time Machine*.

meaning and will be erased and forgotten by the social consciousness. If will not be stopped, the modern capitalism will build up in the near ten or twenty years a world exceptionally by smart machines—everywhere and in everything, from the phone to the home, from the car to the robot domestic servant! But this world will be by thinking machines and without thinking people, a world in which any man's initiative of thought will be erased! Actually, not quite—thinking's development through acceleration of the synapse impulses in the brain will be only for specially selected men, only for the subordinated to the general intention for world domination, only for scientists who will confirm the class status quo; thinking men will be only picked elite, a confraternity, subservient to the omnipresent Order! Even the thinking will be a special function of select society! This privilege, however, will be given only for precisely appointed and canalized thinking. Thus, the thinking will be an option accessible only for an insignificant percentage of "God's" elect men, while the enormous mass of bio-population will be lacking in a thought cretins enslaved amongst clever robots. The brute, barbarian violence will yield to the quiet, refined, and totalitarian regulation of human behavior in the society. For this purpose, a personal chip with full peculiar data will soon be implanted in every man and woman. In this world, the nuclear arsenals and the truncheons will become just funny and useless, outdated and uncouth toys for frightening. The science in the hands of the State and the Capital will inevitably lead to a suicide of the human civilization—no matter that it will be suddenly, by a global military conflict, or after a long agony of moral degradation and disintegration. In this Orwell's society, fascism, led to its extreme stage and changed past recognition, will cause a mutual destruction of the society as an autoimmune disease. For this reason, the withering away of the State is a necessary and sufficient condition for the movement of the society ahead and upward, for the free development of humanity as a cosmic civilization of the second and third type.

The dialectical unity of possibilities and necessities means that there could have interests in a classless society, too, but not only within the state. Nowadays, the interest perceives as a pecuniary measurement only, from its vulgar and material side only, as a commercial, philistine flair after the maxim "the interest, more or less, otherwise stoops the fez!"[102] The interests within the classless society have a very different basis and that's why they have a very different content.

The mature slave-holding system gave the first ideas of the ideal social constitution—Plato (*The Republic*). The mature feudalism gave the utopian socialism—More, Campanella. The mature capitalism already gave the scientific socialism—Marx, Engels. Today, it is high time to lay the beginning of the realization of these ideals.

Communism is a society with a crystal, but not with an amorphous structure. This is the time when the society will no longer be individualistic, but the individual will be a social personality. Communism is a perfect society, but not an ideal State! Communism is a high society and the working class's democracy is a path, at that the single path, to the high society. This is the time when the only organization of human society all over the world will be the United Nations Organization; the time when "that blessed thing called money"[103] will wither away; when even the toilets, as per Lenin, and the chamber-pots, just like with the utopians, will be made of gold; when the Earth will be the City of the Sun, when the human society will represent a mighty planetary reason—this is the Age of the Noosphere! And if the man is the last known degree of highly organized matter, having the cell as its main constructive unit in the evolution of nature, then this classless society is a qualitatively new degree, the next higher degree of organization of the matter with the constructive unit being the man. But for that purpose, it does not meet the case that the world is interpreted; because "the philosophers have only *interpreted* the world, in various ways; the point, however, is to *change* it."[104]

---

[102]. Bulgarian proverb

[103]. More, *Utopia,* 137.

[104]. Karl Marx, *Theses on Feuerbach,* 2:66.

Supplement

Upon a more attentive sight on history and astronomy, we observe a striking connection between their most luminous peaks—the revolutions in the first one and the solar activity in the second one. However, while the dependency between the process of forming solar spots and all cataclysms on earth such as epidemics, earthquakes, floods, volcanic activity, record temperature values, etc., has been long ago proved, it is more than surprising that the fact goes ignored related to the same connection between human history and the activity of our luminary, without which, actually, there cannot be any human history. From fear, maybe, because it is a heresy, it looks like being "non-Marxist" to suppose that the social-economic conflicts, i.e., the **events** in earth's society depend in any way on the sun's caprices. In fact, maybe, they are not determined, but to a very great extent, depend really on the fiery Apollo's cycles, on the energy, mass, and light of the good old sun, whose children we are. It turns out that all great historical events, i.e., those events that remain in humankind's memory, are related to the fury of Amun-Ra. It turns out, seen by the side of the Creator of the Universe that we, human society, are a sophisticated (bio-) chemical reaction that has not finished yet!

The fact is surprising that Chizhevsky, who had established the dependency between solar activity and all considerable catastrophes on earth, did not go a little ahead and did not establish the connection with such social "epidemics" and "pandemics" like wars and revolutions. Yet, Kondratiev, having established the cyclic recurrence of the long waves of the economic crises and wars, did not relate them to the shorter cycles of the solar activity. In fact, this connection could be more probably seen by Marx and Engels, who noted the ten-year cycles of the economic crises of capitalism than Kondratiev, who studied only the long waves of forty-seven to sixty years, which might be more hardly connected to the solar cycle. But Marx and Engels lived too early . . .

Really, it is impossible to ignore the fact that **all** important revolutions coincide **in an absolutely exact way** with maximums of the eleven-year solar cycle of activity!

Starting from the English Bourgeois Revolution of 1642, with maximum solar activity in 1640, this dependency is available upon the following revolutions, too—in 1789, for example, when the Great French Revolution and American Revolution took place, the maximum of solar activity was in 1788. Follow: the revolution in France in 1830, with the dethronement of Charles X, maximum in 1830; the revolutions of 1848 in France again, German and Italian states as well as the revolutions against the Habsburgs in Austria, Hungary, the revolutions in Denmark, Switzerland, Poland (*Springtime of the Peoples*) and other European countries, maximum in 1848. Then the Commune of Paris comes in 1871 as a consequence of the French-Prussian War of 1870, maximum 1870. In 1905, the bourgeois-democratic revolution in Russia exploded against the tsarist autocracy and the Russian-Japanese War, maximum—1905. In Russia again, the February Revolution and the Great October Socialist Revolution took place in 1917, maximum—1917!

All that could not be occasional, all that could not be a simple coincidence, a play of chance. Because not only the global social conflicts but the local armed actions, the local wars coincide with the solar cycles, too. But in difference with the revolutions, they may appear during a minimum of solar activity. For example, the Balkan Wars of 1912–13 coincide with the minimum of 1913; the September rebellion in Bulgaria in 1923 coincides with the minimum of 1923; however, in 1956-57, the Soviet armed interventions in Hungary and East Germany took place together with the maximum of 1956; in 1967–68, such a local conflict in Czechoslovakia and the maximum of solar activity is in 1967, in which year the aggression of Israel in Palestine begins; in 1979–80, martial law was introduced in Poland, then the Iran-Iraq war commenced, maximum in 1979.

The First World War, as a global conflict, did not begin at the exact time of maximum, but at the lowest point of an ascending cycle—in 1914, because the main event, the global event that had an epochal importance for the whole world was the October Revolution of the Bolsheviks in 1917, which coincides exactly with the maximum in 1917. The most sinister global conflict known until now in overall history—the Second World War—began in 1939, i.e., in the maximum time, 1939. In 1990–91, an unknown solar activity was expected—the highest one since the beginning of the scientific observations, i.e., for 360 years until that time. The facts were confirmed again—we witnessed an unknown political activity in the whole of Eastern Europe as well as in Latin America and worldwide—the Soviet bloc and the Soviet Union fell apart and the Desert Storm War was carried out in the Persian Gulf. An empire toppled down, which had given birth to many local wars.

Now, in 2012–13, during the peak in a row of solar activity, there is such powerful social activity that we are seeing in all of Europe, North Africa, and the Near East—the Arabian Spring in Libya, Tunisia, Egypt; the war in Syria; the civic disturbances in Greece, Bulgaria, and Turkey as well as strikes in France, Italy, and Belgium; all movements *Occupy*—in the United States, England, and Germany, and other civic disturbances, too, like in Brazil and Russia.

Of course, the subject matter of this connection is very complex and large, imposing a special study. I simply expose some facts here.

References to Book One

(All quoted material is from text in the Bulgarian language.)

Byron, George G. *Don Juan*. Sofia: Narodna Kultura, 1986.

France, Anatole. *The White Stone*. Varna: Georgi Bakalov, 1983.

Galbraith, John K. *Anatomy of Power*. Sofia: Hristo Botev, 1993

Korotki, Emile. *Fragments by the Unwritten*, Leningrad: Hudozhnik RSFSR, 1966

Lenin, Vladimir Illyich. *Collected Works* in 55 volumes. 2nd edition, Sofia: Partizdat, 1982.

———— The *State and Revolution*, vol. 33.

———— *The Immediate Tasks of the Soviet Government*, vol. 36.

———— *A Great Beginning*, vol. 39

———— *Letters*, vol. 50

Marx, Karl & Engels, Friedrich. *Selected Works* in 10 volumes, Sofia: Partizdat, 1984-1985.

Engels, Friedrich. *Anti-Dühring*. vol. 8

———— *Socialism: Utopian and Scientific*. vol. 1

———— *The Origin of the Family, Private Property and the State*. vol. 5

———— *The Peasant War in Germany*. vol. 4

———— Preface to *The Civil War in France*. vol. 3

Marx, Karl. *Critique of the Gotha Program*, vol. 1

———— *Theses on Feuerbach*, vol. 2

———— *The Civil War in France*, vol. 3

———— *The Eighteenth Brumaire of Louis Bonaparte*. vol. 3

———— *Value, Price and Profit*, vol. 7

———— *Wage Labor and Capital*, vol. 7

———— *Capital: Critique of Political Economy*, Sofia: Partizdat, vol. 1 (1988) Seventh edition, vol. 2 (1989) Fourth edition, vol. 3 (1990) Fourth edition

Molière. *Don Juan*, Comedies, Sofia: Narodna Kultura, 1977.

Montesquieu. *The Spirit of Laws*. Sofia: Naouka & Izkustvo, 1984.

More, Thomas. *Utopia*. Sofia: Narodna Kultura, 1984.

Pavlov, Deyan. The Institute for Modern Social Theories, Sofia, in 1986

Plato. *The Republic*. 2nd edition Sofia: Naouka & Izkustvo, 1981.

Popper, Karl. *The Open Society and Its Enemies*, in 2 volumes, Volume Two: *The High Tide of Prophesy: Hegel, Marx and the Aftermath*. Sofia: Otvoreno obshtestvo, Zlatorog, 1995

Rousseau, Jean-Jacques. *Confessions*. Sofia: Narodna Kultura, 1982.

Sallust. *Bellum Iugurthinum.* Sofia: Naouka & Izkustvo, 1982.

Seneca, Lucius Annaeus. *Selected Dialogues*: *On Anger*. Sofia: Naouka & Izkustvo, 1987.

Vaptsarov, Nikola. *Writings: Spring Poem.* Sofia: Bulgarski pisatel, 1983.

Vazov, Ivan. *Works: Place-hunters.* vol. 4. Sofia: Bulgarski pisatel, 1982.

Voltaire. *Philosophical Novelettes: The Man with Forty Pieces of Silver*. Sofia: Narodna Kultura, 1983.

Wells, H. G. *The Time Machine*. Varna: Georgi Bakalov, 1984.

Zajdel, Janusz. *Van Troff's Cylinder*. Varna: Georgi Bakalov, 1983.

Zdravomyslov, Andrey G. *Necessities, Interests, Values*. Sofia: Partizdat, 1988.

Narodno Delo newspaper, 1986

Trud newspaper, 1989

BOOK TWO

The Economic Theory of Socialism

Critique of Political Economy

Introduction

For the purposes that socialism is converted from a utopia into reality, first of all, it should be an economic system more effective than capitalism. Historically, socialism must be a social and economic system with a social productivity of labor more developed through which to get its way in the competition with capitalism. Logically, socialism must be a radically different economic system. But neither before, nor after the "reconstruction" (Gorbachev's "perestroika"), it was such thing, but subordinated to the same economic laws, and using the same scientific conceptions, immanent in the capitalist mode of production. The so-called "socialism" exceeded the mangiest recommendations of Keynes! Such a regulated state capitalism, such an intervention of the state in the economy like "socialism" does, Keynes had not even dreamed possible! The exceptional assistance of the state for the monopolies and their coalescence in a constitution—still after the receipt of Keynes! There is no better application of Keynes's doctrine than the "socialism" of the twentieth century! Keynesian doctrine is an ideology of étatism, which strangely, was proclaimed as an essence of socialism! Keynes—the ideologist of the national debt, of the chronic budgetary deficit, and the inflation! His idea is the militarization of the economy, increasing workmen's taxes, regulation of incomes through a "moderate inflation" in favor of the rich and the "solution" of the economic crises by regulation of the money circulation. All that was so well carried and applied in the "socialist" system that Keynes himself would have to wonder and to be proud of his "communist" disciples! Actually, Keynes, by observing the Soviet Union, had understood well the role of the state and the monopoly of the capital and sincerely recognized, by contrast with Stalin and the others after him, that they were used in a wonderful manner for the confirmation and for the perpetuation of the sovereignty of capitalism but not for its abolition. His "planned capitalism" is the same "planned socialism" of the twentieth century!

That the socialization of the means of production through the monopolization of the production is a preparation, a "phase of transition to a new form of production,"[105] having in view the socialism and the social property of the means of production is true as far as this is only a historical, but not an economic stage towards them. This acute, "a self-dissolving contradiction," Marx had very precisely seen and foreseen that "it establishes a monopoly in certain spheres and thereby requires state interference."[106] This contradiction "reproduces a new financial aristocracy"[107] (how much Marx was right!), no matter it will call itself Communist Party of Soviet Union or DuPont Financial Circle. It reproduces "a new variety of parasites . . . , a whole system of swindling and cheating by means of corporation promotion, stock issuance, and stock speculation."[108]

The socialization of the means of production at a large scale is actually a **centralization** of the capital increasing to gigantism and there is not an evidence of social property. On the contrary, the social property of the means of production does not require their exclusive socialization, because it is a social **relation**. The centralization of the capital is not socialism—the misfortune comes from the fact it is capital and it is exceptionally centralized.

Until nowadays, among the Marxist theorists the confusion reigns that the state-monopoly property is "the closest approach to the future socialist society."[109] But this is an absurdity! This absurdity, however, existed and originated from Lenin's mistake that the state-monopoly property is the closest material preparation for socialism—a capital mistake with respect to the capital! The first act of socialism—the complete state property, has not, howsoever, something to see with the monopoly. It is a property of a state but not of a monopoly, after which it becomes social, according to a strictly given way, according to strictly given economic laws. There may be a material preparation for socialism without state property and without monopoly property before that is available. Passing to socialism is possible as from the private property, as from the non-monopoly property, provided that strictly given production relations are established. Socialism is neither private property, nor a state, nor a monopoly one.

There are command economies all over the world and especially in

---

[105]. Marx, *Capital*, 3:507.
[106]. Ibid.
[107]. Ibid.
[108]. Ibid.
[109]. Toncho Trendafilov, et al., *Political Economy (Short course)*, 144.

East Asia with a completed oligopoly and monopoly structure, without being proclaimed as socialism. There is not only in the so-called "communist" China, but until 2012, also in the most powerful there capitalist Japan, in Korea, Taiwan, and Singapore (particularly in Singapore!), etc. At the same time, together with Europe and the United States, they are singled out as market economies! Although the bankruptcy of the market economy was proclaimed by Engels 120 years ago!

The étatism hitherto, the nationalization of the economy, represented as socialism obviously succumbed to the time. That's why "reconstruction" was needed, which, however, was turned to face the "free initiative" of the private property, although it inevitably stumbled over its old production relations of the state monopoly. But then, that led to the ignorant statements that socialism is an unrealizable utopia, even a religion (!) leading to "the absurd idea of social property in the commodity production!"

Is this, however, really true?

Chapter One: $p' = \text{const.}$

The Law of the Same and Constant General Rate of Profit

The Rate of Profit and the Law of Value

The truth about society is given in *Capital* by Marx: about capitalism—in a direct text, and about socialism—in a coded way. A work like *Capital* has a hypnotizing effect on any reader and it is very difficult for him to be released from this hypnosis and to begin an analysis. Howsoever, one, after having a good knowledge of *Capital*, should understand that all the internal contradiction, the entire antagonism of the capital is contained in only one formula:

$$p' = S' \frac{v}{c+v}$$

In the common case, the infinite difference among the rates of profit in the various branches of social production is a necessary and sufficient condition for the existence of capitalist private property. The rates of profit are different, "since capitals in different spheres of production viewed in percentages—or as capitals of equal magnitude—are divided differently into a variable and constant capital, setting in motion unequal quantities of living labor and producing different surplus values, and therefore profits. . ."[110]

But "there is yet another source of inequality in rates of profit. This is the different period of turnover of capital in different spheres of the production,"[111] because even with equal capitals and all other equal conditions, a greater mass of surplus value is obtained where the velocity of turnover is higher.

---

[110]. Marx, *Capital*, 3:175
[111]. Ibid.,177.

The third cause of difference of the rates of profit is the different degree of exploitation of the labor power, i.e., the different rate of surplus value. So, different rates of profit are gotten mostly from the effect of these three factors, and in this manner, the leading branches and companies, thanks to their higher technical level, having an individual rate of profit higher than the average (general) rate of profit, gained in the war of competition by extracting surplus profit. For this reason, the existence of the capitalist private property, i.e., its approval and its functioning, is due to the different rates of profit, which are reached by an appropriation of surplus value unevenly with respect to the invested capitals: once as increased rate of surplus value, second time—as surplus profit. In other words, the more the organic composition of a capital is higher, the velocity of turnover and the exploitation of labor are larger, the more this capital increases its inequality with another capital, which has a lower organic composition, less exploitation of labor and slower turnover. In this way, the ratio of the appropriated mass of surplus value of an invested capital is different, unequal with the same ratio of all other capitals. Just in this fact, the private appropriation of surplus value is expressed under the social character of the production at the same time. On the one hand, the different rates of profit in the different branches create such relations of production, which suppose a private appropriation of the social product, i.e., **private property**. On the other hand, the different rates of profit create the production relation of **capital**. So, the uneven rates of profit are the source of the **capitalist private property** and hence—of social inequality, too.

What would happen, however, in case we take a converse look at the things, i.e., in case we admit **the same** rate of profit for all spheres of the production? What does that mean?

If the rate of profit is the same for all capitals with a different composition and turnover, a relative equality in the profits is obtained, i.e., at a relative extent, any producer appropriates the same mass of surplus value, independently of the infinite difference of the invested capitals, having different technical equipment with a corresponding labor power and accomplishing different turnovers. The profit, expressed in percentages, is everywhere the same, when "in different spheres of production capitals of equal magnitude would have equal rates of profit, in spite of their different organic composition."[112] The

---

[112]. Marx, *Capital*, 3:175.

same rate of profit means that the different productivity of labor, the different rates of surplus value, just like the different turnovers of capitals are brought into service for the purpose to appropriate such a mass of surplus value, which is proportional to the invested capital with the same ratio with all other capitals. In this manner, the effect of the Law of extraction of maximum surplus value, respectively—maximum profit is stopped. The different producers are already placed under equal conditions of production, i.e., with equal production relations.

The first question, which now immediately appears is this: is the same rate of profit possible?—Yes, it is possible, despite all speculations and seeming contradictions—in precisely given conditions.

Of course, someone would reproach us that a process of production, taking place at a same rate of profit, is a complete absurdity. An absurdity entering contradiction with the Law of value, but with good reason, too! It is not possible, according to good reason, either in an economic way or with high-handed methods, that the production enterprises can be forced to obtain a same rate of profit. Moreover, the immense provocation imposed by the Law of value at the time of solving problems which, thanks to the law, "have not a solution" if the problem is contradictory to the law! But how can we solve these problems without violating the Law of value for the capitalist mode of production—Marx showed us. The same had to be done for the socialist mode of production, too. And the solution already exists—"not only without a violation of the law of value but on the very basis of it!"[113]

Why doesn't the Law of value allow the same rate of profit? Here we plunge into the most serious depth of the problem. Marx's explanation is: because the different capitals have different organic compositions, which, because of the different quantity of living labor contained in them, create a different quantity of surplus value, which, related to the different invested capitals, gives different rates of profit. And this is so. It is about the capitalistic mode of production. If the rate of profit depended only on the organic composition of capital, then the same rate of profit would be impossible because of the interdiction, which the Law of value raises. But you see, the rate of surplus value also exists and then the interdiction drops down! In other words, the same rate of profit is not possible if it depends on the organic composition only. But there exists in the capitalist commodity production the rate of surplus value,

---

[113]. Marx, *Capital*, 2:25.

too—and then, things are changed. This is just the magnitude of the rate of surplus value, which assigns the rate of profit to be the same. The rate of surplus value, according to the organic composition, is regulated so that after the advancement of the capital to be gotten the same rate of profit. If s' would be 100 %, 250 %, 500 %, etc., at a given rate of profit, depending on the organic composition so that the entire newly created value after the realization of the commodity is divided into such a proportion, that the surplus value s, remaining after this division, to be in such proportion to the total invested capital, so as to give the same rate of profit with every other capital. The rate of profit can be the same, in spite of the different quantity of necessary labor put in the production, as the Law of value requires, thanks to s', thanks to the regulating role of s'. Even though at the same rate of profit, the quantity of necessary labor put in the production of the commodity, is different again. It is one at $s' = 62$ %, quite another at $s' = 250$ %, but p' is the same in both cases, = 50 %! In other words, this interdiction, which the Law of value imposes, would be absolute, if it was not s', the effect of s'. The necessary labor at the same rate of profit is different and thanks to the rate of surplus value, it is just as much as objectively necessary, but not so much as the capitalist would like. Namely, the rate of surplus value determines the necessary labor to different levels, itself being determined by the level of the organic composition of capital.

The Law of value does not admit the same rate of profit, Marx says (and Engels also), since, because of the different organic composition, there is a different quantity of living labor, which produces a different quantity of surplus value and hence—a profit. That is true *only at the same rate of surplus value!* Marx expressly notes many times in *Capital* that the difference among the rates of profit is due to the assumption of the same rate of surplus value; he assumes the same rate of surplus value for different rates of profit! In chapter 8 of volume III, he writes:

"In the present chapter we assume that the intensity of labor exploitation, and therefore **the rate of surplus value** and the length of the working day, are **the same** in all the spheres of production. . ."[114]

Approximately forty pages further, Marx emphasizes again:

"The fact that capitals employing unequal amounts of living labor produce unequal amounts of surplus value, presupposes at least to a

---

[114]. Marx, *Capital*, 3:166 (bolded by me—T.B.)

certain extent that the degree of exploitation or **the rate of surplus value** are **the same . . .**"[115]

Marx assumes the same rate of surplus value to obtain different rates of profit. I do the inverse.

It is true that under the capitalist mode of production, the same rate of profit is completely impossible; it would be an exceptional fortuitous event. Under capitalist mode of production, the same rate of profit is really impossible because any capitalist, in his striving for maximum profit really reduces the rate of surplus value to a magnitude to be approximately equal to the rates of surplus value of all other capitalists. That's why, the theoretic assumption of Marx upon studying the average rate of profit is not theoretical only, but is really existing fact under the capitalist system. And that's why under this prerequisite—the same rate of surplus value—the different organic composition of the capitals gives different rates of profit. But in the opposite case—when the rates of surplus value are different—the rate of profit can be the same, regardless of the different organic composition; in this way and only in this way, it—the same rate of profit—stops the social relation of **capital**, thereby only the capital ceases being capital.

At first sight, the same rate of profit seems impossible not only because of the inertness of the simplest domestic thought but also because of the Law of value, according to which a different quantity of labor creates a different value and hence—a profit. The question is how a different quantity of labor, creating a different value, can give the same rate of profit?

In order to get this, such a rate of surplus value is necessary, that it corresponds to any different organic composition in a way that the mass of surplus value to be at any moment in such a ratio with the capital that, despite its different organic composition, gives the same rate of profit, i.e., the relation of s to v is such that regardless of the quantity of living labor which sets in motion a different quantity of substantial labor, the mass of surplus value that is obtained from the total new value created by it enters into the same relation to its capital, as any other mass of surplus value that is related to its capital; such a rate of surplus value that decreases or increases as much the different masses of surplus value at the expense of the simultaneously increasing or decreasing of the variable capital, as they are equal each other by their relations to their

---

[115]. Marx, *Capital*, 3:205(bolded by me—T.B.)

capitals. In this way, the living labor in the organic composition is different again, but the surplus value that it has created, because of the adopted exactly determined rate of surplus value, would no longer be expressed in a different rate of profit. Even at the same rate of profit, despite the same rate of profit, because of the different organic composition, the living labor, which is put in the production of the commodity, is quantitatively different again in the same way that it is different at the different rates of profit. It is due to the regulating s', to the different s'. This means that the same rate of profit is due not to the same quantity of living labor put in the commodity, which is impossible, but to the different rate of surplus value, which is completely possible!

The different organic composition is not a barrier for the same rate of profit. On the contrary, just according to the organic composition of capital, such a rate of surplus value is established, which secures such mass of surplus value that the same rate of profit is obtained. "To say that the profits of unequal capitals are proportional to their magnitudes would only mean that capitals of equal magnitude yield equal profits, or that the rate of profit is the same for all capitals, whatever their magnitude and organic composition."[116]

The same rate of profit is impossible in the developed commodity production not because of the Law of value, but because of the capitalist mode of production itself! Because the Law of value has two meanings:

1. The value of commodity is determined by the socially necessary labor time, but not by the individual labor time; and

2. The exchange of the commodities is made at their values.

Both meanings are completely kept, but not infringed under the same rate of profit as much as they do under different rates of profit. Something more—as we will see further, in respect of meaning two, namely by the same rate of profit, but not by the average one, the Law of value is proven satisfied. The rate of surplus value through its respective organic composition determines the quantity of living labor, which has to be just as much as necessary to enable the commodities to be really purchased and sold precisely **at** their values, as the Law of value requires. The rate of surplus value through the organic composition determines how much the necessary labor is to be employed in the production of the commodity—neither more nor less, so the commodity

---

[116]. Marx, *Capital*, 3:176.

is sold **at** its value, in full agreement with the Law of value, i.e., it not only doesn't contradict the Law of value, fulfilling the same rate of profit, but on the contrary—it is in a complete correspondence to it! Even at the same rate of profit, the Law of value is strictly and best kept just through the different organic composition, but not despite it. Something more—the Law of value no longer acts as an elemental regulator of the distribution of the labor power all over the branches, but it does act on its proportional development into all production branches. Through the Law of the same rate of profit, in contrast to the Law of the maximum profit, the migration processes of capital and labor power from given branches to other ones are stopped, because the motivation of maximum benefit in a given branch and a given production falls away, i.e., the elemental transfusion of capital and of socially necessary labor between the branches is stopped. Besides, the same rate of profit stops and eliminates the **centralization** of capital as well as the elemental pricing caused by the competition.

The Law of value does not allow the same rate of profit solely at the same rate of surplus value!

The same rate of profit as such appears as a **general** rate of profit. It's a general, which is no longer an average rate of profit. In order to be the same in the course of time, however, the rate of profit should be supportive as a constant quantity, i.e., it should be invariable, too. That's why, we should accept as a constant the same general rate of profit, to place **p′ = const.** We get the reason of being able to do this, i.e., to accept the same general rate of profit (through the law of **p′ = const.**) from the following fact, presented by Marx:

> Thus, although in selling their commodities the capitalists of the various spheres of production recover the value of the capital consumed in their production, they do not secure the surplus value, and consequently the profit, created in their own sphere by the production of these commodities. What they secure is only as much surplus value, and hence profit, as falls, when uniformly distributed, to the share of every aliquot part of the total social capital from the total social surplus value, or profit, produced in a given time by the social capital in all spheres of production.[117]

And a little further:

[117]. Marx, *Capital*, 3:185-186

So far as profits are concerned, the various capitalists are just so many stockholders in a stock company in which the shares of profit are uniformly divided per 100 . . . [118]

We may accept the general rate of profit as the same—our reason is the above quotations of Marx, i.e., it does this in order to have a uniformly distribution of the total social surplus value on every respective share of the total social capital, in order to get this share of the capital pro rata its aliquot part of surplus value's production. This, which is in fact only an impracticable claim under capitalistic production relations—the equal participation in the total social mass of surplus value of the capitals proportionally to their magnitudes, is a starting point and a really feasible *condicio sine qua non* under socialist production relations. This uniform distribution of the total social mass of surplus value pro rata to the share of every capital is the first step to the real social appropriation of this total surplus value, i.e., the first step to **social property** of the means of production, expressed as a value in the constant part of these capitals, just because of the uniformity of distribution of the total social surplus value. With the law of **p' = const.**, the property becomes social because:

1. Regarding the **capital**: The total social surplus value, the total social surplus product, produced in the society are through this law prepared for social consumption, for social, but not for private appropriation through their even distribution in the society according to the magnitude of individual capital invested therein, according to the extent of the particular capital invested. Provided that all producers appropriate the same mass of surplus value compared to their capital invested, the separate favor, the private appropriation of more surplus value becomes impossible because of the terminated effect of the Law of maximum profit. This means that nobody may appropriate for himself more surplus value than all other producers in the society do. And that means that the relations of appropriation, i.e., **the relations of property** become **social**! In this way, new production relations are established, **a social property of the means of production** is established! The property is social because all the producers of commodities use their means of production in relations that

---

[118]. Marx, *Capital*, 3:186

are economically equal between them, despite their different capacities; they are in alike and equal in rights economic relations to the product of their means of production, independently of the difference in their power. And for establishing this as a *relation*, but not only as a *sense* of property to the social means of production (as this was proclaimed in Bulgaria until 1989), this is achieved with an economic law only. This equal relation to the means of production is based on the same rate of profit obtained from these otherwise differently productive capitals. So, this is the first time after the decomposition of the tribe society that equality in the society is achieved, i.e., a social equality is established. The same way that private property meant social inequality, social property means social equality.

2. Regarding the **income**: Another manifestation of the new production relations, i.e., of the relations of appropriation, this is the income of the immediate producers. Since nobody in the society appropriates a surplus value more than anyone else, the profit—its converted expression—ceases being a personal income which it is by the private property. The profit ceases being a personal income and there is no other income but the wage! This law—p' = **const.**, the Law of the same rate of profit is applied in order that the workers employed in any branch of the social production get their possible maximum (according to the organic composition) of wages, but not the possible minimum as it is under private capitalistic property. That is the idea—after the realization of the commodity produce on the market, the created new value is to be divided by the rate of surplus value into **s** and **v** so that **s** should *always* give the accepted same rate of profit necessary for the further extended reproduction, and all the rest from **(v+s)** should be used for an income like wages of the immediate producers—the workers. Or, if at other, i.e., capitalistic, conditions the more surplus value **s** of the created new value **(v+s)** appropriated by the capitalist would give a rate of profit that is completely different from all other rates of profit, with these conditions, the surplus value should remain such that to provide the same rate of profit at the cost of increased wages; the purpose is to remain as much surplus

value from the newly-produced value as to provide the normal extended reproduction of the enterprise under the same rate of profit, but not an atom more. All the rest—for wages! It is obvious that thus the means of production are really used as social property—once **s**, regarding the capital, and then **v**, regarding the income; **s**—for production consumption and accumulation only, **v**—as a maximum wage. So, the same rate of profit is not at all a spoke in economy's wheel. On the contrary, this is a powerful motivation and purpose for its impetuous development ahead, because those that move it ahead, the workers, have the prerequisite for it—the desire to increase continuously their incomes through a maximum growth of their wages.

As concerns determination of the magnitude of the general rate of profit, this is made on the ground of the scheme of extended reproduction. "But this additional amount of 20% is itself determined by the surplus value created by the total social capital and its relation to the value of this capital, and for this reason, it is 20% and not 10 or 100."[119] Naturally, upon establishing the magnitude of the general rate of profit, we should take into consideration the relative weight of the rate of profit in the leading branch. In this case, upon any dislocation of the layers, i.e., of the leading branch, there would be a new relative weight, and along with this, a new calculation of the general rate of profit. So, the magnitude of the general rate of profit may be the same and invariable, but still is determined by the general economic development of a given country for a given period of time; "because beyond certain limits a large capital with a small rate of profit accumulates faster than a small capital with a large rate of profit."[120]

So, the same general rate of profit cannot be eternal. According to the Law of the tendency of the rate of profit to fall it has to downwards and that's why this must be terraced down at certain periods of time, to fall at certain stages in the course of time. The growth of the organic composition of the total social capital should show by itself when this should be done—on a ten to fifteen-year basis, or more or less quickly.

In order to advance a given capital, it is already based on a strictly determined general rate of profit, but not on such one that is vague to

---

[119]. Marx, *Capital*, 3:972.
[120]. Ibid., 292.

anybody (under capitalistic mode of production). The advance of wages, as well, is already strictly predetermined both by a completely clear and concrete rate of profit and by a completely clear and concrete rate of surplus value. Clear, concrete, and known p' and s'—things that nobody is interested in under capitalistic mode of production: neither the capitalist nor the workers. But which are alphabetic truths under the social mode of production, in which the collective of every enterprise is both owner and host. However, in order to be the property not only in a group, but social, as well, each collective must be placed into the same production relations to any other in the entire society. And this is made through the Law of the same rate of profit. In this way, the property is social and concrete at the same time, but not common and therefore—nobody's one.

Only now, under the social property of the means of production, the labor power is not alienated from the means of production, it is not detached from them because only now it already **possesses** these means of production as its own property. That's why it is no longer a hired labor power. Once the labor power is already an owner of the means of production, thus it ceases being a **commodity**! Because the sufficient condition for the labor power to be a commodity—the worker could not sell commodities because of an absence of his own means of production and therefore he is coerced to sell the only commodity he always has with itself, his labor power, is excluded yet. The labor power ceases being a commodity and thereby, the social relation of expansion of the value—a capital!

It turns out, as Engels truthfully noticed, that the same rate of profit is a starting point in the development of the capitalistic mode of production. It is a starting and endmost, final point of the contemporary economic production relations which have begun as capitalist but ending as socialist ones. The same rate of profit is the start and the finish of the highly developed commodity production. Since the very beginning of the transition period to capitalism, i.e., the period of primitive accumulation of the capital,

> for the first time, we meet with a profit and a rate of profit. The merchant's efforts are deliberately and consciously aimed at making this rate of profit equal for all participants. The Venetians in the Levant, and the Hanseatics in the North, each paid the same prices for his commodities as his neighbor; his transport charges were the same, he got the same prices as

every other merchant of his "nation". Thus, the rate of profit was equal for all. In the big trading companies, the allocation of profit *pro rata* of the paid-in capital share is as much a matter of course as . . . the mining profit *pro rata* of the mining share. The equal rate of profit, which in its fully developed form is one of the final results of capitalist production, thus manifests itself here in its simplest form as one of the points from which capital started historically. . .[121]

While in its completed form the equal rate of profit today, in high-tech era, is turned out the point of which capital may finish historically.

***

Price and Value

Under capitalistic mode of production of classic capitalism, the leading branches and companies impose their superiority in the cruel conditions of the competition, by extracting a surplus profit as a difference between their individual rate of profit and the general, which is an average rate of profit, because "the equalization process of capitals, which divorces the relative average prices of the commodities from their values"[122] leads to the situation where except for their produced value, they realize and appropriate also a part of another's produced value. This is the reason that the values of the commodities differ from their prices—through the price the stronger capital takes away another's produced value, adding it to its own. Upon such a passing each other between price and value, the capital having a higher organic composition than the average, through its production price, which is higher than its own produced value, is in a position to attract, to rob, and to appropriate more value from the total produced value as a surplus profit. While the capital with a lower organic composition than the average, in the rural economy, for example, whose price is lower than the value produced by it, is in this way injured and loses its share in the total value produced with its participation, too.

A completely different result is produced at the same rate of profit. It appears to be general, being not a basis for injury to some producers of commodities while the others get richer. Under the same general rate of profit, the value of commodity is always expressed in the same

---

[121]. Marx, *Capital*, 3:1019-1020.
[122]. Ibid., 935.

magnitude as a price, i.e., the price always corresponds to the value of the commodity, the price **reflects** truly and precisely the real value of the commodity. The price, as a transformed expression, becomes a mirror image of the value, too. Exchange value and value coincide. Now, no longer accidentally, "the surplus value, and thus the profit, actually produced in any particular sphere of production, coincides with the profit contained in the selling price of a commodity."[123] When value and exchange value coincide, then the price—this is the value of a commodity, and the value—this is just the price of the commodity.

The same general rate of profit already enables the entire surplus value to be realized, respectively the entire profit, which is produced in a given industrial branch, but not left it to the accidental distribution between the particular capitals as this is done under the average general rate of profit. The cost prices, Marx says, are specific for every sphere of social production. But the profit that is added to them does not depend at all on the conditions of a given sphere of production.

Table 1

Capitals c	Rate of surplus value s'	Mass of surplus value s	Rate of profit p'	Constant capital c		Cost-Prices	Value of commo-dities	Price of commo-dities
				Circulating capital	Wear of fixed capital			
10c + 90v	55.6 %	50	50 %	5	3	98	148	148
20c + 80v	62.5 %	50	50 %	10	7	97	147	147
30c + 70v	71.4 %	50	50 %	15	10	95	145	145
40c + 60v	83.3 %	50	50 %	20	13	93	143	143
50c + 50v	100 %	50	50 %	25	17	92	142	142
60c + 40v	125 %	50	50 %	30	20	90	140	140
70c + 30v	166.7 %	50	50 %	35	23	88	138	138
80c + 20v	250 %	50	50 %	40	27	87	137	137
90c + 10v	500 %	50	50 %	45	30	85	135	135

---

[123]. Marx, *Capital*, 3:196.

When the value of a given commodity is not higher than its production price, in this case, the capital would not set in motion more living labor, ergo, it would not realize and appropriate more surplus labor than any other capital would do. And this may be already done not only at an average but also at any other composition of the capital.

The process of equalization of capitals under the same rate of profit is absent, and thereby, the detachment of the prices from the values of the commodities ceases, as well. The average rate of profit creates an average production price while the same rate of profit creates an utmost production price as an upper limit of any price. Then the price of commodities, as we said, coincides with their value, thus with the labor realized in them, while "the average price of commodities differs from their value, thus from the labor realized in them."[124] Besides that, "the average profit of a particular capital differs from the surplus value which this capital has extracted from the laborers employed by it,"[125] whilst, at the same rate of profit, the profit obtained coincides exactly with this surplus value that a particular capital had produced with the laborers employed by it.

The depreciation methods must influence neither the value formation, nor price establishing, nor their coincidence under the same rate of profit. For this purpose, it is of great importance how the depreciation allowances are calculated—through a constant (established) percentage rate or with a digressive method of accelerated depreciation or through an anticipated percentage rate. The transfer of the value in parts of the fixed constant capital on the value of the commodity should remain with its contents as a principle, although being different in its forms. The system of accelerated depreciation is not necessary because it is only a way of decreasing the profit and the tax on it through increasing the cost price, i.e., it supposes the so-called "hidden budget financing" of the enterprise. This is the first. And the second—the accelerated depreciation increases the prices of the commodities. As a final result of both factors, it pans out a passing each other between value and price, which is inadmissible in the economic system with a social property of the means of production. At first sight, regarding the high technology products with fast moral wearing, it looks like accelerated depreciation is necessary. But the hidden budget financing is a state regulation still, which is an antagonism for any market economy.

---

[124]. Marx, *Capital*, 3:935.
[125]. Ibid.

So, the method of the accelerated depreciation should drop out, because it is really contradicting the Law of value and the depreciation allowances should be formed according to the classic method of the constant (established) percentage rate.

After all aforementioned, one can see that the exchange of the commodities is made **at** their values practically yet, but not in theory only.

It is possible, however, that some letter-eating critics who look for some contradistinction to Marx quote the following text:

> The exchange of commodities at their values, or approximately at their values, thus requires a much lower stage than their exchange at their prices of production, which requires a definite level of capitalist development.[126]

The purpose of such an argument is to make us fall into disagreement with Marx and to attribute to me some sins that I do not have. In other words, that exchange of the commodities is impossible just **at** their values, this is the first, or, the second, that, in the best case, this concerns a passed, an archaic stage of social development and that it in no case applies to today's level, or worse, to a future, still higher level of economic development of society. I will respond that the exchange of the commodities is accomplished, of course, at their production prices, as the higher level of contemporary social development and in the future, a still higher level of this development is required, but in contrast to the capitalist system where the production prices are passing each other and vibrate around the values of commodities, in the socialist system, thanks to the same rate of profit, the production prices coincide with the values of commodities and in this sense, and only in this sense, and in full accordance with the Law of value, we may say that they are exchanged **at** their values *too* at the contemporary high level, and whatever higher level of economic development is, i.e., not in the way of a craft industry organization but in the way of a high technology organization of the production.

Warren Buffett, "the Oracle of Omaha," who has spilled aphorisms all over the Internet in order to pour some sense into the young generations' heads, dumbfounds the world by his piece of wisdom— "price is what you pay; value is what you get." Great! "The Greatest Investor" makes a difference between price and value! The mountain

---

[126]. Marx, *Capital*, 3:208.

labored, and gave birth to a mouse! If Buffett would read only two lines by Marx, he would know that 150 years ago the great scientist had put this differentiation as an underlying principle in his political economy. Maybe Buffett understands that he cannot lump together these two scientific concepts, since exchange value and use value are "intrinsically incommensurable magnitudes,"[127] as Marx could teach him. In this connection, I have to note that the non-studying of Marx's theory has led to the full degradation of all economic sciences in the present days. Together with the satanic economic ideology of Milton Friedman's neo-liberalism, an ideology of savage and brutal violence over the person, peoples, and the states of the so-called "shock politics" ("shock therapy," as well) and "monetarism," on the opposite polar of the contemporary economic science as a counterpoint is praised to the skies in the ideology of the "just" capitalism of John M. Keynes. This bipolar ideological model creates in the society a deadlock and it is impossible to break it under capitalist economic laws and because of that, the society is offered as a sacrifice incessantly to these two doctrines and is sadistically thrown from Scylla to Charybdis and vice versa. A desire to become a bridge between these two mortal rocks shows the US economist Professor Paul Krugman, a Nobel Prize winner, who says, "I'm esteeming the free market Keynesian,"[128] i.e., Krugman is a suspension bridge between Friedman's neoliberalism and Keynes's state regulation; he is a close bond for reconciliation and unification of their mutual modern absurdities and because of that for great services rendered to the dominant class he got his Nobel prize!

The same general rate of profit, however, comes not only to establish a social equality through the new production relations. It serves to do away with all disproportions in economy inherited from capitalism. The law of $\mathbf{p'} = \mathbf{const.}$ erases them gradually in the course of time while the Capital continuously extends and intensifies the social inequality, enhances, and resounds all differences in the economic development of persons, branches, and nations. The law of $\mathbf{p'} = \mathbf{const.}$ is a border that does not allow, a barrier that does not admit the rebirth of the private property. It stops any attempt of robbing of another's labor, being the first law not admitting *the transformation of money into capital*. The same rate of profit provides symmetry, equilibrium in society, a

---

[127]. Marx, *Capital*, 1:594
[128]. Television interview by the journalist Boyko Vassilev on *Panorama*, a political program on Bulgarian TV Channel BNT1, November 15, 2013.

harmony of the interests of the person and the society—then the possibilities and the necessities of the person and the society are mutually satisfied.

***

The Wage

When we admit the same general rate of profit and lay down **p′** = **const.**, then we shall establish the magnitudes of the basic wages according to the level of technical equipment of labor, i.e., the wage enters a direct dependency on the level of the productivity of labor:

$$\Delta S^{'} = \Delta \frac{c + v}{v}$$

The above formula shows that the increase in the rate of surplus value corresponds the increase of the productivity of labor. This means that under this law, the rate of surplus value has the content of the income tax—it increases differentially with the increase of the wage, i.e., the labor of lower productivity is taxed with a lower rate of surplus value and vice versa. But, in this situation, as it is clearly shown, the income tax, as well as any other tax on the wage, becomes completely otiose—the rate of surplus value accomplishes this function, too. So, in the conditions of the social property of the means of production, all and any taxes on the wages of the productive workers are abolished.

This is the only case when the wage is bound in an immediate and automatic dependency on the productivity of labor; in all other cases, under capitalism, the wage "never rises proportionally to the productive power of labor"[129]. Only in this case the payment of the labor power gets an objective assessment, by contrast with the subjectivism of the different FLP (factors of labor participation), grades, qualification degrees, and other similar balderdash introduced to beguile and "stimulate" the commodity of labor power and which represent only different ways of internal distribution "of the 'labor fund' determined and vouchsafed to us by God and Nature,"[130] but negated by Marx and Time.

How is the magnitude of the wages established in practice?

If under average composition of the capital in a given country 1:1 and the same general rate of profit **p′** = 50%, we accept an annual rate of surplus value **S′** = 1200% with 12 turnovers of the capital, this means

---

[129]. Marx, *Capital*, 1:667.
[130]. Ibid., 674.

that the simple rate of surplus value is $s' = 100\%$. And if the newly created value for a month is, for example, $(v+s) = \$2000$, the monthly wage amounts to $1000. This wage becomes a further basis for establishing the wages under any organic composition. If we now want to establish the wages at a higher productivity of labor, for example at a composition of 4:1, having the same number of turnovers—12 per year, this means that $s' = 250\%$ and with the same newly created value of $2000, the wage should be $570. But this new value is created for a much shorter working time yet—if it is for 8 hours per day in the first case, this is done for 2 hours per day only in the second one. Or, if the worker gets a wage of $1000 per month for 8 labor hours in the first case, in the second case his wage amounts to $2280 at the same duration of the working day.

Here's the inverse case. If we have to find the wages provided that the productivity of labor is lower, for example at a composition of 1:4, this means that (at the same turnovers) $s' = 62.5\%$ and at the same newly created value of $2000, the wage amounts to $1230, but for 4 times more working time, i.e., for 4 months instead of one month on an 8-hour basis. And in the case of an 8-hour working day, the monthly wage will be $307.5 against $1000 under 1:1 composition and $2280 under 4:1 composition.

Chapter Two: S′ = const.

The Law of the Invariable Average Rate of Surplus Value

The Wage—A Self-Expanding Value

Marx developed his theory of the capital by discovering the surplus value and expressed the capitalist exploitation through the rate of surplus value. It is through the latter only that it becomes clear what capital is. Capital is a self-expanding value because of the unceasing, unrestricted, and uncontrolled expansion of the rate of surplus value. The unquenchable thirst of the capital for human sweat and nerves is shown by the continuous expanding rate of surplus value, sapping more and more living labor, shortening more and more worker's necessary labor time. Or, in other words, the capital represents a function, which expands unceasingly in the course of time. As a consequence of its activity, as a result of its expansion, is the function *relative wage*, expressing the relative impoverishment of the working class namely on the shoulders of which this expansion is done. Three cases are possible upon studying this function:

$$\text{a)} \ \Delta \frac{v}{v+s} < 1; \quad \text{b)} \ \Delta \frac{v}{v+s} = 1; \quad \text{c)} \ \Delta \frac{v}{v+s} > 1;$$

We must immediately note that case **c)** is not characteristic for the capital. This case, when the growth of the average wage exceeds the growth of the national income is a result of a prolonged and vast retaining of the wage first upon the continuous increase of the national income, which can appear as an occasional phenomenon only for short moments in the time of crisis—for example in the early 1960s in Italy, in 1968 in France, etc., as well as in 1987 in Bulgaria.

However, in order to have $\Delta v > \Delta(v+s)$ as a constant practice, that can be done with the costs of the accession of the surplus value. This case is an infringement, a disorder in capital's distribution processes and can appear only by exception. However, there is such an exception in our practice—from 1952 to 1956—as a result of a misunderstood dictatorship of the proletariat. This is a disease, a pathological state of the capital, which was turned back to its normal state after the coup d'état of 1956, i.e., the April Plenum of the Bulgarian Communist Party restored not the Leninist principles in the party, but normal capitalist relations in the distribution. And since this case is not typical under capitalist production relations, we are interested in the development of **v** to (**v+s**) only in the interval from **1** to **0**. Because the functions of the capital, for being a capital, i.e., a self-expanding value, are expressed only if $\Delta v < \Delta(v+s)$. In that case, the relative wage represents an unceasingly descending function in the interval **[1;0]**, a function, limited both upside and downside.

The capital is a social relation, at which the relative wage is always minimum and tending towards zero. That, of course, is true in a mathematical sense only, because the workers are not chameleons to "live on air."[131] Although, at the end of 1996 in Bulgaria, they were turned into just that! "The zero of their cost is, therefore, a limit in a mathematical sense, always beyond reach, although we can always approximate more and more nearly to it."[132] Our socialist (!) financial oligarchy was too near to refute this scientific postulate! The red oligarchy already knew very well by Marx that it was "necessary to reduce the laborer's wages to a minimum 'to keep him industrious.'"[133]

When the growth of the average wage of the working class lag behind the growth of the newly created value, i.e., at $\Delta v < \Delta(v+s)$, that means a progressively descending consumption of this class, expressed in its diminished solvent demand of articles of consumption. The latter, on its part, represents one of the factors that originate the economic crises. The depression of wage below the value of labor power leads to the continuous robbery of the necessary product of the working class, i.e., of that part of the newly created product, which is essential to its normal reproduction. In this manner, the solvent demand of the workers enters a conflict with the production of consumer commodities as an

---

[131]. Marx, *Capital*, 1:662.
[132]. Ibid.
[133]. Ibid., 657.

element of the fundamental capitalist disproportion between $I(v+s)$ and IIc, which leads to acute contradictions, to collisions between them, which develop like social storms, like crises. And if in either form of the contemporary monopolistic capitalism with a prevailing private property, the crises are expressed in overproduction, in excess, representing a "hemorrhage" of commodities leading to a possible "apoplexy" of the system, then in its other form—with a prevailing (or full) state property—they are expressed in deficit, in shortage, the diagnosis is a commodity insufficiency with possible "infarct." That's why, one of the causes of all crises of capitalism is the lagging, the descending consumption of the working class compared to the growth of the newly created value, i.e., the discrepancy between $\Delta(v+s)$ and Δv, between the increase of the newly created value and the increase of that part of it, which is spared out for consumption by the workers, the wages, which mathematically represents the inequality $\Delta v < \Delta(v+s)$. However, upon transforming this inequality into equality, i.e., upon $\Delta v = \Delta(v+s)$, when the expansion of the average wage of the working class is equal to the expansion of the created new value, that wants to say that the consumption of the working class does not lag behind the expansion of this new value, created by itself, which is distributed within the entire society. The realization of this equality, however, is possible only under an invariable average rate of surplus value. Translated into a popular economic language, the equality $\Delta v = \Delta(v+s)$ means that the growth of the average wage of the working class in a given country must correspond to the same degree of growth of the national income. Or, because of the unceasing expansion of the wage in the course of time as a function of the expansion of the newly created value, the wage in a social scale, as a social relation, represents a **self-expanding value**. Capital is a self-expanding value, because, depending on the advanced value $(c+v)$, its expansion is added to it—the surplus value s. Wage is a self-expanding value, because, depending on the newly created value $(v+s)$, its expansion is added to it—Δv. In this manner, the wage in a social scale can be not only expanding but also a self-expanding value. That, however, does not mean that the individual wage is always a self-expanding value. On the contrary, it depends on the realization of the commodity produced by the worker, i.e., it contains the possibility to be reduced according to the result, as we shall see further.

So, the capital is always a self-expanding value, but the self-expanding value is not always a capital!

Because of its constant private strive for extracting maximum surplus value, it is impossible for the capital to maintain its rate invariable but always increases it (promiscuously or in a regulated way). It was a constant practice of the red capitalism the ceaseless enhancement "by upside" of the production quotas during an invariable productivity of labor, i.e., through enhancement of the rate of surplus value, through enhancement of the exploitation, the state-capitalist was thrusting its brutal and abrupt hand in the worker's pocket. Such invariable average rate of surplus value means that a conscious, controlled by the society production process is realized, i.e., a production process, which runs under the conditions of a social property of the means of production. When the process of expansion of value is not under supervision, then the expansion of value appears in front of us in the form of capital. **The property** at the contemporary stage of development of the productive forces is a manifestation of the value. Whether the property will be social or private that depends only on the process of expansion of value—is it controlled or not. Just like the fundamental task of the physics nowadays is to carry out a controlled process of thermonuclear fusion, the fundamental task of the political economy is to carry out a controlled process of expansion of value. And that can be reached only when it is mastered and regulated the rate of surplus value by the society. Just like earth's energy would fantastically be increased as a consequence of a mastered thermonuclear process, in the same way, society's energy would fantastically be increased under a mastered value process. If Capital's march will not be stopped, it will work irrevocable havoc with the human civilization, including thermonuclear energy, as well! By itself, the Capital is the most powerful means of mass extermination!

The self-expanding wage means that the labor power is not processed during the production process as a commodity and does not go out of it like a commodity, i.e., the production process is deprived of exploitation of the labor power. And that, by itself, means **social justice**. Social justice is expressed in the absence of exploitation in the society, in rejection of the organized robbery of human labor. The exploitation, i.e., the social injustice, is actually an organized criminality, promoted to the rank of fundamental law—a constituted crime!

Social justice is expressed in the relations of distribution. The distribution of material goods in the conditions of the capitalistic mode of production is always done to the detriment of the working class. With the existence of the inequality, $\Delta v < \Delta(v+s)$, the distribution relations are always infringed, just like with the inequality, $\Delta v > \Delta(v+s)$. The mathematical inequality in both cases expresses social injustice, in the first case—for the working class, in the second—for all other classes and social groups. There can be equitable distribution processes for the entire society depending on the distribution of the newly created value for consumption only if the equation $\Delta v = \Delta(v+s)$ is present. Or, if by the law of $\mathbf{p'} = \mathbf{const.}$, production relations of equal rights are established first, by the law of $\mathbf{S'} = \mathbf{const.}$ equitable distribution relations are established then. "The specific distribution relations are thus merely the expression of the specific historical production relations."[134]

The invariable rate of surplus value does not mean that it is also universal, i.e., the same one for all producers. As we already saw, at $\mathbf{p'} = \mathbf{const.}$, it is different and is determined by the technical level of the production—$\Delta S' = \Delta(c+v)/v$. Or, in other words, the rate of surplus value is increased not only during the capitalistic production but during the socialist production, too. But this increase is not arbitrary and does not testify at all to an exploitation of the labor power. Social justice, i.e., the absence of exploitation, under socialism is expressed not in obtaining the "full product" of labor, according to the pre-Marxian utopian notions and yesterday's worldly ones, but of the inadmissibility to take from this product more than a given limit—the limit of the necessary labor time. The mite that the society and the state take from the worker is such part of the labor that cannot generate classes and class contradictions. The unpaid part of the worker's labor is used for accumulation, for extended reproduction of its own enterprise, and for covering the necessities of the unproductive part of the society. This is the cause to have a rate of surplus value under socialism also and not to pay the "full labor" of the worker and not to get Lassalle's "undiminished proceeds of labor." And the more the worker is highly skilled, the more the relative unpaid part of his labor becomes larger, although his wage gets colossal dimensions in absolute value. That is why, there will be some difference in the property status under socialism, too, but this is not a class difference anymore. This difference in the property status is precisely a result of the social equality and the social justice but not in spite of them. Since any equality in the monetary society, after Marx, as well, is based on some inequality. This is not a paradox. Why? Why is this difference in the property status not a class

---

[134]. Marx, *Capital*, 3:996.

difference, why does it not engender classes? Because it is based on one's own labor only, this property status is obtained by each one according to his or her own labor, according to his or her own possibilities. And what does it mean? What is the sense of "according to one's own labor?" And why is this expression not valid for the capitalist, too?

"According to one's own labor" means precisely that limit, which is quite different, strictly individual to each worker—the limit of the necessary labor time! This is precisely the labor within the necessary labor time, which means a work achieved "according to one's own labor," i.e., according to the necessary labor, put in by any worker, which is strictly different and individual. This limit of the necessary labor does not allow any worker to take less than the labor put in by him, i.e., to get injured (and even exploited), nor to take more than that (thus to be favored). Namely, this strictly individual limit of the necessary labor corresponds to the different levels of workers' possibilities and is objectively determined only by the different levels of the productivity of labor, which allows different levels of satisfaction of the necessities, i.e., a different property status, without, however, allowing the class stratification of rich and poor men. Because everybody gets the monetary equivalent of *his or her own* **necessary** labor—the *wage*, but not to appropriate of *anybody else's* **surplus** labor as a *profit*, which transforms him or her into a capitalist. No one capitalist accumulates his fortune "according to his own labor," because his labor is not a necessary labor but a surplus labor, his fortune does not come from putting in his own necessary labor, but from grabbing the surplus labor of anybody else. The profit is a surplus value, appropriated without payment by the capitalist, but not his wage, for which he put in labor. More precisely, capitalist's work does not find any expression in a wage as own **necessary** labor, but in the surplus value, which finds an expression in the profit as an appropriation of **surplus** labor that is a sum of many units of anybody else's unpaid labor. The difference is that in the one case the income represents profit from capital, in the other— wage from labor. And the proportion between wage and capital amounts to the scale of the proportion among objects of the solar system or in the classical model of the atom (from $1:10$ to $1:10^{10}$ and more). While the proportion between wage and wage can be only in the range of several times (from $1:1$ to $1:5$, even $1:10$), i.e., where it finishes the relation between wage and wage, there begins the relation between wage and capital. That is why, there is a difference between the wages in socialism, too, but here this difference is not a capital relation. The difference is obligatory because of the different complexity of the labor put in the society. However, this difference results from the difference coming and imposed by the production process in it. There is a difference, but it is not capital's but labor's one, it is not between capital and labor, but between labor and labor. The difference is not capital's one, and just, therefore, it does not generate any classes. The difference is not capital's one because the only source of income in this society is the labor, in contrast to capitalism where the sources of the incomes are three—capital, land, and labor. This is just then and only then, that may appear and may compare the difference between the different kinds of labor, expressed through the wages at different scales, at different proportions. Something, which is impossible in the other case—that's why the proportion between the incomes is capital's one, while in the case of socialism this is not like that! When the labor power is not a commodity, the difference between wage and wage is not the same as between wage and capital. That's why "richer" in socialism does not mean a capitalist anymore, but only "according to one's own labor!"

***

The Individual Wage

So, one of the causes of the proportionality in an economy is the invariable average rate of surplus value. But, in order to master **S′**, it is necessary that the law of **p′ = const.** is already established. Only then the real production process runs and realizes as such, at **S′ = const.**. The process **p′ = const.** is a necessary prerequisite for maintaining an invariable rate of surplus value. Placing **S′ = const.**, we receive:

$$\Delta p' = \Delta \frac{v}{c + v}$$

From here, we may determine the individual wage as a function of the real production results. In this chapter, we are interested in studying the cases where the productivity of labor is invariable only and because of that, we shall examine only them amongst all that Marx had examined:

1. According to the rate of profit:

a) $\Delta v < \Delta(c+v)$—the rate of profit falls;

b) $\Delta v = \Delta(c+v)$—the rate of profit remains invariable;

c) $\Delta v > \Delta(c+v)$—the rate of profit rises.

The case, 1.a), is interesting as far as it expresses the likelihood for decreasing, preserving the same, or for an insufficient increase of the wages of workers whose results of labor did not receive social acknowledgment, i.e., whose commodities had not been marketed due to various reasons and thus had provoked a fall of their individual rate of profit below the general one. And the case, 1.c), means a decreasing productivity of labor when the increase of the wage outstrips the increase of the capital.

It is clear that the cases 1.a) and 1.c) are not desirable and shouldn't be admitted—they don't act in anybody's interest.

The case, 1.b), is of essential importance to us—this is just that it expresses the wanted dependence of the wage on the dynamics of the capital: at an invariable rate of profit, attended by an invariable rate of surplus value, the growth of the individual wage must follow the growth of the capital!

2. Economy of means of production:

If a capital $C = 85c+15v$ produces a surplus value of $20s$, its rate of profit $p' = 20$ % and the rate of surplus value $s' = 133$ %. If any new organization of labor leads to an economy of constant capital, let us say with $5c$, then, under equal other conditions, it would increase the rate of profit to 21 % and the capital would look like $C = 80c+15v$, the rate of surplus value remaining invariable. But, in order to remain the rate of profit, which has a priority, because it is a motivation and purpose of the production, invariable, i.e., 20 %, the saving of constant capital must find its expression into increasing the wages as the rate of surplus value slumps in a way to let the increase of the wages take off the same increase in the rate of profit. In this case, preserving the same rate of profit leads to slumping of the rate of surplus value from 133 % to 119 % at an invariable newly created value, which increases the wages with 1 unit at the expense of such decrease of the surplus value. The value of the commodity of 120 units $(85c+15v+20s)$ decreases to 115 $(80c+16v+19s)$ as the economy of $5c$ leads to an enhancement of the wages with $1v$. Thus, using rational the means of production, even at an invariable productivity of labor, the commodity gets cheaper, and (along with this) the wage becomes greater! It's not a miracle, just an economy!

The "stimulus" for increasing the wages on these conditions is decreasing the materialized labor through technical innovations, rationalizations, etc. Under all other equal conditions, only better husbandry, more rational use of the existing means of production through innovations, discoveries, inventions, savings, in general—improvement of the production process at a given level of productivity of labor creates such conditions that lead to the immediate enhancement of the wages. That's how a careful attitude to the means of production is created, although they are social property! Because according to the distorted ex-notions, the social property could not educate such an attitude in the worker and thus, the property transformed into "nobody's" one, a basis for wastefulness and spillage. Somebody approves of us that only the private property "stimulates" good husbandry. It will always be so when the state-monopoly property is represented as social!

Should we remind those Messrs.-"communists" who were wondering and puzzled why the workers were indifferent to the "social," i.e., the state property as to "nobody's", what was the reason of their alienation to the means of production. They had forgotten that this is always done at "the transformation of the laborer into a work horse."[135] They had forgotten that always under capitalist production relations only, "in fact, the laborer looks at the social nature of his labor, at its combination with the labor of others for a common purpose, as he would at an alien power; the condition of realizing this combination is an alien property, whose dissipation would be totally indifferent to him if he was not compelled to economize with it."[136]

So, economizing is possible without capitalist's constraint when each saving of means of production influences the immediate increase of worker's wage. This is the only way to create a conscious, careful attitude to the social property—to the existing means of production, to the wastes, to the quality of the commodity, etc.

So, we could summarize the aforementioned in the following conclusions:

If, in case of invariable productivity of labor, the constant capital decreases because of economical use, then the rate of surplus value that has been invariable until this moment slumps to a new level, in order to

---

[135]. Marx, *Capital*, 3:107.
[136]. Ibid.,106

preserve the rate of profit invariable, increasing the wage. Otherwise, every growth of the capital at an invariable rate of surplus value must lead to a growth of the wage to the same extent, as well. Of course, with the presumption of a full product realization!

So, under invariable rate of surplus value, the growth of the wage as a social relation should be $\Delta v = \Delta(v+s)$, while the growth of the individual wage should be $\Delta v = \Delta(c+v)$.

This is only with the self-expansion of the wages that workers will get convinced by themselves in the reality of socialism. The wage costs more, much more than all "documents," "programs," "conceptions," etc., securities took together. With the growth of the wage, the consciousness grows up, too—both personal and social—as determined by being. Well, our theologians of Marxism were otherwise materialists, too. But only on their dinner!

The production process under the social property of the means of production is running at a constant rate of surplus value. And if the process $\mathbf{p' = const.}$ is necessary to establish the new production relations, the process $\mathbf{S' = const.}$ comes to develop freely the productive forces. This is just $\mathbf{p' = const.}$ that enables $\mathbf{S'}$ to get a constant value, too. In the opposite case, when the law, $\mathbf{p' = const.}$, is not satisfied, then $\mathbf{S'}$ could never be $\mathbf{const.}$ The new, socialist, mode of production is set in motion when the production relations win through $\mathbf{p' = const.}$ and on this basis, the productive forces begin to work freely under $\mathbf{S' = const.}$. And if in the first case we speak of social equality, the second expresses a social justice. And really—unthinkable is the social justice, it is a fiction without a social equality established **before**. The justice is a function of the equality, it is born from it.

The laws, $\mathbf{p' = const.}$ and $\mathbf{S' = const.}$, once having established equality and justice in a given society, make simultaneously its further differentiation into classes impossible. They exclude the possibility the society to be divided into poor and rich men, to be eternalized the classes. The law, $\mathbf{p' = const.}$, makes the regeneration of the social inequality impossible, even if it would be occasional and unconscious, and on the basis of it—the social injustice, too, i.e., in the way that this was done in the daybreak of human society with the origin of the private property and the state—quite unconsciously and without force—and thereby the entire human history to be repeated once again.

Chapter Three: $\dfrac{v}{c+v}$ = const

The Law of the Preservation of the Labor Power (under Increasing Productivity of Labor)

{Since the schemes of accumulation and extended reproduction were scrutinized at the last minute before printing the book, it was impossible to me to make an upheaval in the structure of the book and this chapter panned out unusually voluminous and with a certain themes' abruptness. That is why, in an eventual new edition the matter of *accumulation and extended reproduction* as well as *a policy of taxation* will be placed as separate chapters.}

Scientific and Technical Progress and Unemployment

The invariable rate of surplus value is neither universal nor eternal. In the production process for the employed workers, there is a limit beyond which the rate of surplus value could not remain invariable, it undergoes a change obligatorily. There is such a bound when it is no longer possible that s' remains the same; "in variations of v there is a certain limit everywhere beyond which it is economically impossible for s' to remain constant."[137] This occurs at a revolution in the value. It comes at a moment of higher productivity of labor when it is impossible yet for the same labor power to work with the same labor time. The cause of change in the rate of surplus value that has been invariable until this moment is expressed in the fact that the individual labor time enters into contradiction with the socially necessary labor time because of the decrease of the quantity of living labor, which sets in motion the same

---

[137]. Marx, *Capital*, 3:80.

quantity of materialized labor. It's a contradiction, which under the capitalist production relations, degenerates into a conflict and is always settled by force throwing a "reserve army" of unemployed people into the street. It's a force born by the existing social injustice—the exploitation of the capital. For example, if the productivity of labor grows up four times at once, this means that instead of four workers creating a new value, let us say, $2000 under $s' = 100\%$, under equal other conditions, now this is one worker creating this new value, but, for example, under $s' = 300\%$ (!), i.e., under thrice the greater exploitation of his labor power, regardless of the fact that his wage has grown up twice from $250 to $500. His wage has doubled, but his exploitation has tripled! Because in this case, the capitalist will appropriate not $1000 but $1500! And only the capitalist will decide whether he would not appropriate more, thus leaving less to the worker, i.e., to increase arbitrarily more the exploitation degree. In addition, the remaining three workers should be dumped just like garbage. In this way, the relation between the value of the variable capital and the value of the total capital $\dfrac{v}{c + v}$ is suddenly changed in favor of the total capital. But what will happen if we admit this proportion as a constant, as invariable until the moment of settling this contradiction?

It turns out that this contradiction—between individual and socially necessary labor time—may be solved in this way only, only if we admit the above proportion as constant for a given period of time. What is panned out?

Then, with the slump of the rate of profit provoked by the impetuous increase of the productivity of labor, thanks to the new equipment, the rate of surplus value must slump, too, and it does this to the same extent. This means that the same workers may work at the new productivity of labor—four in our case, the same labor power, as the new productivity of labor is reduced to the old one, to the productivity of labor existing to this moment through a **diminution of their labor time**.

The continuous increase in the productivity of labor—this is an objective economic process, which has the effect of a natural law. It always leads to such a moment when the same labor power cannot continue to work anymore at the same labor time, because of the decreased quantity of living labor put in the production of the commodity. Then it is necessary either to reduce the labor power with the labor time remaining the same, where the rate of surplus value enhances, or to reduce the labor time, preserving the labor power, where the rate of surplus value slumps. But "the shortening of the working day is, therefore, by no means what is aimed at, in capitalist production, when labor is economized by increasing its productiveness."[138]

Yet, it was in 1867 that Marx explained in volume I of *Capital* that the machine could marvelously increase workmen's spare time instead of increasing the exploitation. In this way, the workmen could feel no fear or even terror, but only joy and even pleasure of their work. But yet, this is blasphemy! Who is the self-respecting capitalist who could have thought of a similar thing! That would have meant a complete self-management of worker's labor time! That would have meant that the worker could be a master of his leisure and labor time, instead of being a controlled appendage of the machine. That means a freedom of the labor and power of the worker, which make the capitalist completely useless because his mainstay is undermined in this manner. And because of that he, the capitalist, will bring all his elite professors and police apparatus, to prove that the above measure is an absurdity, that this is impossible, because in such way the commodity becomes more expensive or another gammon like that. There is nothing to wonder about! Nowadays, so many pieces of idiocy are offered as scientific truths! Thus, a lout of Turkish origin had recently proved to us that Homer was an Ottoman and Europe owed its culture to the age-old, dull ignorance and out of enlightenment of Ottoman hordes! In fact, these miserable and ridiculous anecdotes are only an insignificant part of all the modern historical falsifications, lies and swindles as quite serious official state policy of Turkey!

That is why I shall add the following to the argument that the commodity becomes more expensive in this case, which is possibly the most serious objection.

First, the value of commodity, Marx says, is determined by the socially necessary labor time but not by the individual one. Thus, in the case when the individual labor time passes each other with the socially necessary labor time, the price of the commodity is determined by the socially necessary labor time again. This means that in spite of the slump of the individual rate of profit below the general, which in this way is not the same for the given production in a certain period of time, the price is always established by the general rate of profit.

Second, in the given case, at increasing leisure time with preserved

---

[138]. Marx, *Capital*, 1:358.

invariable wage and invariable productivity of labor, there is not an atom of increase of the cost prices for wages, which on its side would have raised the price of the commodity.

So, an increase in the price may be originated neither by the rate of profit nor by the cost prices. And, in fact, these are the factors which determine it.

Third, the value of commodity increases only upon the increase of the value of the constant capital but not of the variable capital. The value of commodity:

remains unchanged if the increase or decrease in advanced capital is caused by a change in the magnitude of the value of the variable portion of capital, assuming the labor productivity remains the same. In the case of the constant capital, the increase or decrease in its value is not compensated for by any opposite movement. But in the case of the variable capital, assuming the labor productivity remains the same, an increase or decrease in its value is compensated for by the opposite movement on the part of the surplus value, so that the value of the variable capital plus the surplus value, i.e., the value newly added by labor to the means of production and newly incorporated in the product, remains the same.[139]

Here Marx gives the following eloquent example:

$$400c + 100v + 150s = 650$$
$$400c + 150v + 100s = 650,$$

i.e., at a variation of **v**, the value, and thereby, the price does not vary.

But,

$$400c + 100v + 150s = 650$$
$$450c + 100v + 150s = 700,$$

i.e., at a variation of **c**, the value, and thereby, the price varies, too.

Fourth, the quantity of labor, determining the value of commodity, depends only on the **labor time**, necessary to the production of the commodity but not of the mass of the labor power.

Two workers, working at eight hours per day, at invariable productivity of labor, put in the production of the commodity the same quantity of labor as that one of eight workers, working at two hours per

---

[139]. Marx, *Capital*, 3:968-969.

day, equal to a labor time of sixteen hours. So, the larger mass of labor power under preserved productivity of labor does not raise even a jot in the value of the commodity and hence its price. While the increased leisure time at the same productivity of labor means only a more expensive paid labor power, an increase of the wage through a decrease of the labor time. "Hence, if **v** rises through a rise in wages, it does **not** express a **greater**, but only a **dearer** quantity of labor, in which case **s'** and **p'** do not rise, but fall."[140]

Under all other equal conditions, the rise in the wage lowers the rate of surplus value. And vice versa, as in our case, the lowered rate of surplus value, under all other equal conditions, means a rose wage.

The capital **locks** the labor time, it fixes, it strictly keeps the individual labor time towards the socially necessary labor time. Because of the subservience to the value under capitalism, there is unemployment, which, on its contemporary high level of development, takes colossal dimensions. In this way, the class gap between the rich and the poor widens increasingly, the richness is converted into a perverse luxury and poverty—into clochard pauperism. The modern hi-tech industry allows

> as the substances consumed by the capitalists and their dependents become more plentiful, so too do these orders of society. Their growing wealth and the relatively diminished number of workmen required to produce the necessaries of life beget, simultaneously with the rise of new and luxurious wants, the means of satisfying those wants. A larger portion of the produce of society is changed into surplus produce, and a larger part of the surplus produce is supplied for consumption in a multiplicity of refined shapes. In other words, the production of luxuries increases.[141]

Unemployment—this is one of the forms of social inequality. This is inequality not only between the rich and the poor but among the poor themselves, too—when some among them lose their right to work, which right becomes a privilege. This is inequality at which "this qualitative change in mechanical industry continually discharges hands from the factory, or shuts its doors against the fresh stream of recruits..."[142]

---

[140]. Marx, *Capital*, 3:67 (bolded by me—T.B.)

[141]. Ibid., 1:493.

[142]. Ibid., 503.

At the unemployment available, i.e., the "reserve army" of workers, the main conflict of the capitalistic mode of production emerges again— between labor and capital. Marx describes that in a brilliant way:

> There are not too many necessities of life produced, in proportion to the existing population. Quite the reverse. Too little is produced to decently and humanely satisfy the wants of the great mass.

> There are not too many means of production produced to employ the able-bodied portion of the population. Quite the reverse. In the first place, too large a portion of the produced population is not really capable of working and is through the force of circumstances made dependent on exploiting the labor of others, or on labor which can pass under this name only under a miserable mode of production. In the second place, not enough means of production are produced to permit the employment of the entire able-bodied population under the most productive conditions, so that their absolute working period could be shortened by the mass and effectiveness of the constant capital employed during working hours.

> On the other hand, too many means of labor and necessities of life are produced at times to permit of their serving as means for the exploitation of laborers at a certain rate of profit. Too many commodities are produced to permit of a realization and conversion into new capital of the value and surplus value contained in them under the conditions of distribution and consumption peculiar to capitalist production, i.e., too many to permit of the consummation of this process without constantly recurring explosions. [143]

However, with the law, $\dfrac{v}{c+v}$ = **const.**, the reverse effect is obtained: the development of the productive forces and in particular— the labor force, is of paramount importance. For this reason, the labor time is reduced in order to preserve the labor power as socially necessary, instead of throwing it as "useless," so that a reserve army of unemployed is always ready for action and is constantly maintained. It is the only way of not having unemployment available. Unemployment does not have another decision!

---

[143]. Marx, *Capital*, 3:300-301.

Furthermore, the effectiveness of the production is increased just like the time of buy off, the time of come-back of the means of production becomes much shorter when in similar situations the condensed labor power, otherwise "useless", puts itself to work in shifts. It is a more effective manner to use the means of production. It is a saving of time, money, and nerves on a social scale, as well. In the opposite case—throwing away the unemployed—the saving in variable capital by the private property is compensated by the allocation of a dole by the state in spite of not at the same extent. If we neglect the political color, the acute class collisions lead to social entropy, to a great loss of time and money for the society. The strikes are worth much. In this respect, the process discussed $\dfrac{v}{c+v}=$ **const.** creates saving in labor time on a social scale, i.e., the time of strikes could be used productively.

***

Accumulation and Reproduction on an Extended Scale

At a new, higher productivity of labor, when we replace $\dfrac{v}{c+v}=$ **const.**, in order to preserve the same labor power, the result, as we already said, is the preservation of the same productivity of labor. So, the new equipment, by preserving the old productivity of labor, is used to raise the qualification of the workers employed until this moment, which is necessary to them to operate this new equipment. This "training" process also runs under the conditions of an invariable, but already lowered rate of surplus value until the moment of a restored equilibrium between the means of production and the labor power, which remains condensed while waiting for them, with the new, the higher productivity of labor. This means an increased accumulation in nature, an accumulation, which passes from money to commodity; the means of production are provided from a money form already in a commodity one. The duration of this period depends on the level of development of the productive forces—the more powerful they are, the more it is short and vice versa, i.e., this is a period when the production of means of production must satisfy the necessities of the labor power for them, to satiate its "hunger" of them. And it is hardly upon the respective coincidence, upon the full correspondence of the labor power with the means of production, required by the new equipment that the productivity of labor is increased and the individual labor time is restored, is resumed to its preceding level, i.e., this individual labor time corresponds to the socially accepted labor time. Such a saturation with means of production, corresponding to the necessities of the labor power under the respective productivity of labor, is present during the process $\mathbf{p'} = \mathbf{const.}$ If, at a dying out state, at a high level of development of the productive forces the conditions for a new production may be immediately created, i.e., the means of production to be immediately given up to the labor power which is released from the old production under a new, higher productivity of labor, the duration of the process

$$\frac{v}{c + v} = \mathbf{const.}$$ will be reduced to its minimum, the time of this process

will reduce to zero or become close to zero, thus making the productivity of labor increase much more quickly, with much more accelerated rates. The producers will be interested in shortening this period as much as possible, i.e., to make faster accumulation in order to be able under the higher productivity of labor to increase their wages, although the individual labor time is already increased. So, the fall in the individual rate of profit, in this case, reinforces the accumulation at accelerated rates. "A fall in the rate of profit and accelerated accumulation are different expressions of the same process only in so far as both reflect the development of productiveness."[144]

It is just here that we must stop a little more on this subject-matter of exceptional importance—the accumulation of the social capital in the conditions of the social property. There are two schemes of reproduction and accumulation of social capital in the theory—that one of Marx and that one of Lenin. Both of them do not have a practical application under capitalistic mode of production. Why?

Both theoreticians have scrutinized the accumulation under invariable rate of surplus value, i.e., the case which just interests us—when $\Delta v = \Delta(v+s)$. But while in Marx's theory, "the conclusion cannot be drawn that department **I** predominates over department **II**,"[145] i.e., there is equilibrium between the production of means of production and the production of articles of consumption, the accumulation is even in both departments, because it is carried out under an invariable productivity of labor. In Lenin's theory, the production of means of production prevails on the production of articles of consumption. Such

---

[144]. Marx, *Capital*, 3:281.
[145]. Vladimir Illyich Lenin, *On the so-called Market Question*, 1:73.

equilibrium between the two departments of the social production is necessary if we ignore the impetuous development of the technical and scientific revolution that imposes, as we saw in this chapter, on a given period of the reproduction cycle the acute need of purchase of more in the number and more expensive means of production. The case examined by Lenin corresponds to this need because in this case the relation $\dfrac{v}{c+v}$ is lowered not "as a tendency toward a progressive fall,"[146] but like "an absolute form"[147] for any year spent according to the growth of the productivity of labor.

But the social productivity of labor usually does not have growth every year in this "absolute form," at these rates which he presents. The scheme of Lenin is inapplicable since its construction is not presented and is not supported in a correct way. This is an additional reason that Lenin's scheme does not have a practical application. But his idea is of value.

Lenin made an enormous contribution to the theory and practice of the state and revolution. But his most significant contribution to the economic theory is precisely the scheme of extended reproduction with increasing productivity of labor. It is an extremely valuable elaboration of his young mind. It is an original whim, leaving an ineffaceable and useful trace in the political economy and the economic science in general.

If we consider the accumulation of capital as a process running in the course of time, this one as parts of s, from the surplus value, intended for accumulation, we see a relative decrease of the variable part of the capital during the accumulation in descending order $\frac{1}{2}$, $\frac{1}{3}$, $\frac{1}{4}$ ... $\frac{1}{8}$, etc., i.e., the accumulation of the variable capital v, in accordance with the organic composition, forms the line $\left\{\dfrac{1}{n}\right\} \to \mathbf{0}$, while at the same time the accumulation of the constant capital c follows an ascending order $\frac{1}{2}$, $\frac{2}{3}$, $\frac{3}{4}$, ... $\frac{7}{8}$, etc., i.e., forms the line $\left\{\dfrac{n}{n+1}\right\} \to \mathbf{1}$. It becomes clear that the variable capital as a function of the total capital during the process of accumulation is a natural logarithm by it, i.e., $v = f(C) = \ln C$, and its first derivative gives a moment value from this line precisely:

---

146. Marx, *Capital*, 3:248.
147. Ibid.

$$v' = (\ln C)' = \frac{1}{C}$$

Like any derivative, this one of **v** expresses the **velocity** of a given process, in our case—the velocity of the process of accumulation through the prism of the variable capital. In other words, it is the accumulation, which is carried out under an invariable productivity of labor, i.e., the accumulation according to the scheme of Marx. If we now find the second derivative of **v**, it will give us other dependence—precisely that which we seek:

$$v'' = (\ln C)'' = -\frac{1}{C^2}$$

If the first derivative expresses the velocity, the second derivative expresses the **acceleration** of the process of accumulation, i.e., the extent of accumulation of the variable capital, at which it lags behind the accumulation of the constant capital, considering the development of the scientific and technical progress on the organic composition of the capital. That wants to say, with regard both to the individual and social capital, an accelerated accumulation of constant capital in the form of means of production at increasing productivity of labor at the expense of relative reducing accumulation of variable capital in the form of wages. So, if the accumulation is carried out according to the scheme of Marx, we need the first derivative of the function of variable capital, while if the accumulation is carried out according to the scheme of Lenin—the second derivative of the same function.

Marx has scrutinized two illustrations of extended reproduction. Let us see the first one, the main, when **I(v+s/x) = IIc**. He assumes there different rates of profit but the same rates of surplus value in the two departments; the organic composition in **I** department is comparatively high.

 I. 4000 c + 1000 v + 1000 s = 6000

 II. 1500 c + 750 v + 750 s = 3000

I c/v = 4:1; **I p'** = 20%; **I s'** = 100%; **a'** = 50%
II c/v = 2:1; **II p'** = 33,3%; **II s'** = 100%

After the accumulation the scheme looks like that:

 I. 4400 c + 1100 v + 500 s (consumption fund) = 6000

 II. 1600 c + 800 v + 600 s (consumption fund) = 3000

Here we can see that **after** the accumulation all the product of consumption created in **II** department is equal at its value to all the national income—**(c+v+s)II = (v+s)**, [= 3000]; the same is concerning the product in **I** department, the production of means of production—**(c+v+s)I = Ic+IIc**, [= 6000].

In the end of the next year the accumulation of the social capital and the extended reproduction are:

I.   4400 c + 1100 v + 1100 s = 6600

II.   1600 c + 800 v + 800 s = 3200

So, here we can see that although the different rates of profit in both departments, because of the invariable average rate of surplus value, **Δv = Δ(v+s)**, [= 108.57%]. After the accumulation, the scheme looks like that:

I.   4840 c + 1210 v + 550 s (consumption fund) = 6600

II.   1760 c + 880 v + 560 s (consumption fund) = 3200

Here again, we can see that **after** the accumulation **(c+v+s)II = (v+s)**, [= 3200]; and the product in **I** department—**(c+v+s)I = Ic+IIc**, [= 6600]. In the end of the next year the accumulation of the social capital and the extended reproduction are:

I.   4840 c + 1210 v + 1210 s = 7260

II.   1760 c + 880 v + 880 s = 3520

As it is seen, here again **Δv = Δ(v+s)**, [= 110%]. The same cycle is repeated every next year until the social production is running on an invariable average rate of surplus value. At an invariable productivity of labor, all proportions are kept in the course of time and the accumulation is even in both departments, there is an equilibrium between the production of means of production and the production of articles of consumption; the accumulation of **v** goes with a constant step = 1/C. But what occurs under the scheme of Lenin?

By his scheme, Lenin makes conclusion that the production of the department **I** must predominate over the production of department **II**. He takes technical progress into consideration. However, in order to intensify the effect, Lenin matches unreal ratio between **v** and **c** in the additional capital for accumulation; this ratio is not subordinated under any law but is quite arbitrary. Let us see his scheme.

1st year

    I.   4000 c + 1000 v + 1000 s = 6000

    II. 1500 c + 750 v + 750 s = 3000

I v/(c+v) = 1/5 (20%) ; **II** v/(c+v) = 1/3 (33.3%)

    I(1000 v + 500 s) = **II** 1500 c,

add. cap. **I** 500 s = 450 c + 50 v   v/(c+v) = 1/10
add. cap. **II** 60 s = 50 c + 10 v   v/(c+v) = 1/6

I. 4450 c + 1050 v + 500 s (consumption fund) = 6000
II. 1550 c + 760 v + 690 s (consumption fund) = 3000

As we see, Lenin assumes in both departments the relation of the variable capital towards the total capital in the additional capital for accumulation = 1/2**C**. However, this assumption is not submitted to any law, but at random. After the first year, the accelerated accumulation is still keeping the proportions unchangeable: **(c+v+s)II** = **(v+s)** [=3000], and **(c+v+s)I** = **Ic** + **IIc** [=6000]. As we see, in the end of the second year, after the accumulation, Δ**v** = Δ**(v+s)** [=103.43%].

2nd year

    I.   4450 c + 1050 v + 1050 s = 6550

    II. 1550 c + 760 v + 760 s = 3070

I. v/(c+v) = 19.09% ($\approx$1/5) ; **II.** v/(c+v) = 32.9% ($\approx$1/3)

I(1050 v + 525 s) = **II** 1575 c [=1550 c + 25 s]

add. cap. **II** 28 s = 25 c + 3 v   v/(c+v) $\approx$ 1/9
add. cap. **I** 525 s = 500 c + 25 v   v/(c+v) $\approx$ 1/21
add. cap. **II** 28 s = 25 c + 3 v   v/(c+v) $\approx$ 1/9

I. 4950 c + 1075 v + 525 s (consumption fund) = 6550
II. 1602 c + 766 v + 702 s (consumption fund) = 3070

Here, in the second year, the accumulation of the variable capital suddenly and without cause lags behind the accumulation of the constant capital in **I** department abruptly with a step more than $-1/4C$, while in **II** department the lag step is $\approx -1/3C$. After this second year, the accelerated accumulation changes the proportions: $(c+v+s)II > (v+s)$ [3070 > 3068], and pans out the impossible inequality $(c+v+s)I < Ic + IIc$ [6550 < 6552]. If the first inequality expresses annual production of articles of consumption exceeding the real solvent social consumption, an overproduction of articles of consumption, the second inequality is quite impossible because expresses accumulation of means of production in both departments which is bigger than the real produced means of production, i.e. a part of accumulation is fictitious! As we shall see further, both these disproportions become larger under this basic assumption in the next years. In the end of the third year we see that after the accumulation, because of the invariable rate of surplus value, again $\Delta v = \Delta(v+s)$ [=101.71%].

3rd year

      I. $4950\ c + 1075\ v + 1075\ s = 7100$

      II. $1602\ c + 766\ v + 766\ s = 3134$

I. $v/(c+v) = 17.8\%$ $(\approx 1/6)$; **II.**$v/(c+v) = 32.3\%$ $(\approx 1/3)$
I $(1075\ v + 537.5\ s) =$ **II** $1612.5\ c$ [$= 1602\ c + 10.5\ s$]

add. cap. **II** $11.5\ s = 10.5\ c + 1v$ $v/(c+v) \approx 1/12$
add. cap. **I** $537.5\ s = 517.5\ c + 20\ v$ $v/(c+v) \approx 1/26$
add. cap. **II** $22\ s = 20\ c + 2\ v$ $v/(c+v) = 1/11$

I $5467.5\ c + 1095\ v + 537.5\ s$ (consumption fund) $= 7100$
II $1636.5\ c + 769\ v + 730.5\ s$ (consumption fund) $= 3134$

4th year

      I. $5467.5\ c + 1095\ v + 1095\ s = 7657.5$

      II. $1636.5\ c + 769\ v + 769\ s = 3172.5$

I. $v/(c+v) = 16.7\%$; **II.** $v/(c+v) \approx 32\%$

and so on.

In the third year, the lag step of variable capital's accumulation in **II** department is $\approx -1/4C$ while in **I** department is more than $\approx -1/5C$. That means it is 2 times and more bigger than in the first year. Without reason again. The only ratio that is unchangeable is $\Delta v = \Delta(v+s)$ [=101.25%]. However, the disproportions every next year go deeper. Here we can see that in the third year the rift in the lute of Marx's scheme becomes bigger in comparison with the second year—after the accumulation again $(c+v+s)II > (v+s)$, [3134 > 3132], while $(c+v+s)I < (Ic+IIc)$, [7100 < 7104], which is impossible. A certain negative tendency and a new disproportion we can note here in the ratio between the constant capital in II compared to I department. If IIc/Ic during the first year is 37.5%, during the second one already is 34.8%, during the fourth year it falls to 29.9%. In Marx's scheme, this fall is lighter and constant—from 37.5% to 36.36% for all scrutinized years. That wants to say that the accelerated accumulation of the social capital in this view speedily develops the capitalist imbalances in the extended reproduction.

As it is seen, under these rates and ratios of accumulation, the scheme is unreal. The conclusion that Lenin draws is initially „based on improbable assumptions and is, therefore, wrong," because as a result of them a part of the accumulation is fictitious. Something more, he even ask the question: *Is it conceivable that technical progress, which reduces the proportion of v to c, will find expression only in department I and leave department II in a state of complete stagnation?* In other words, to take another step forward and to go to extremes with the assumption in I department $v = 0$, i.e., that no accumulation at all should take place in department II, but all the accumulation occurs only in department I. That, as Lenin says, is already a misuse of the schemes. As a whole, the conception itself of outstripping accumulation in I over II department as generally valid law of the developed commodity production is right. It could be drawn a logical conclusion that the accumulation in II department must lag behind the accumulation in I by the reason of the objective economic law of increasing social productivity of labor which is expressed in the continuous diminution of v to $(c+v)$. But in this scheme, the slow moving accumulation in II leads to deepening of the capitalist disproportions and contradictions.

This scheme of Lenin, however, was turned into a dogma by the Soviet academic science which was blindly subordinate to it. Something more, it was accepted as mandatory for the socialism, although Lenin especially noted that it concerns the *capitalist* reproduction. The economic thought at that time considered that the accumulation of means of production as an end in itself, the accumulation for the sake of accumulation itself, expressed impetuous industrialization, impetuous economic upsurge. But record-breaking production of cast iron and steel at the expense of failing TV sets and cosmetics, for example, led to dead-end this model of spurious socialism. The slow moving accumulation in **II** department in comparison with **I** at that time meant just that—falling off production and deficit of articles of consumption, of lower quality and morally outdated: cars, household electronics, furnishings, foods range, etc. Lenin's wrong scheme with otherwise right idea of outstripping accumulation of **I** department over **II** was put into practice by the Soviet state-monopoly capitalism without any criticism and that's why we really were witnesses of a permanent crisis of a deficit of articles of consumption in return for overproduction of means of production.

The scheme of Lenin is a scheme of the disproportions; they are pronounced under these rates and ratios of accumulation that he assumes. As I already noted, in order to intensify the effect, Lenin matches unreal ratio between **v** and **c** in the additional capital for accumulation; this ratio is not subordinated under any law but is quite arbitrary. We saw that under organic composition in **I** department 4:1 he assumes a division in the additional capital 9:1; in **II** department the organic composition is 2:1, but Lenin's division in the additional capital is 5:1. A scheme of accelerated accumulation is possible, but with quite another and quite realistic ratios. This could achieve when the division of the additional capital is subordinated to the Law of accelerated accumulation which was examined above, with a step of additional $v = -1/C^2$. Along with it, what would happen if we set the same social capital in other economic conditions, in the conditions of the same rate of profit, i.e., under socialism? So, what scheme we can see then?

1st year

      I.   4000 **c** + 1000 **v** + 1000 **s** = 6000

     II. 1500 **c** + 750 **v** + 450 **s** = 2700

I c/v = 4:1; **I v/C** = 1/5;
II c/v = 2:1; **II v/C** = 1/3

p' = 20%; **Is'** = 100%; **IIs'** = 60% ; **IIc/Ic** = 37.5%
a' = 50% ; product = 8700

I (1000 **v** + 500 **s**) = **II** 1500 **c**

add. $\mathbf{Iv} = -1/\mathbf{C}^2 = -1/25$
add. $\mathbf{IIv} = -1/\mathbf{C}^2 = -1/9$

add. cap. **I** 500 **s** = 404 **c** + 96 **v**

I(4000 **c** + 404 **c**) + (1000 **v** + 96 **v**) = 4404 **c** + 1096 **v**
II(1500 **c** + 96 **c**) + (750 **v** + 43 **v**) = 1596 **c** + 793 **v**

I 4404 **c** + 1096 **v** + 500 **s** (consumption fund) = 6000
II 1596 **c** + 793 **v** + 311 **s** (consumption fund) = 2700

(**c**+**v**+**s**)**I** = **Ic** + **IIc** [= 6000] ; (**c**+**v**+**s**)**II** = (**v**+**s**) [= 2700]
total consumption fund = 811 **s**

2nd year

     I.   4404 **c** + 1096 **v** + 1100 **s** = 6600
     II. 1596 **c** + 793 **v** + 478 **s** = 2867

I c/v = 4.02:1; **I v/C** = 19.93% ≈1/5
II c/v = 2.01:1; **II v/C** = 33.19% ≈1/3

Δ**v** = Δ(**v**+**s**) [= 108%];

p'= 20%; **Is'**= 100.36%; **IIs'** = 60.28%; **a'**= 50%
IIc/Ic = 36.24%; product = 9467

I (1096 **v** + 550 **s**) = **II** 1646 **c**

add. **Iv** ≈ −1/25; add. **IIv** ≈ −1/9

add. cap. **I** 550 **s** = 444 **c** + 106 **v**
add. cap. **II** 225 **s** = (50 **c** + 22 **v**) + (106 **c** + 47 **v**)

I(4404 **c** + 444 **c**) + (1096 **v** + 106 **v**) = 4848 **c** + 1202 **v**
II(1596 **c** + 50 **c** + 106 **c**) + (793 **v** + 22 **v** + 47 **v**) =
1752 **c** +862 **v**

I 4848 **c** + 1202 **v** + 550 **s** (consumption fund) = 6600
II 1752 **c** + 862 **v** + 253 **s** (consumption fund) = 2867

$(c+v+s)I = Ic + IIc\ [= 6600]\ ;\ (c+v+s)II = (v+s)\ [= 2867]$
total consumption fund $= 803$ s

3rd year

    I. $4848\ c + 1202\ v + 1210\ s = 7260$
    II. $1752\ c + 862\ v + 523\ s = 3137$

I c/v $= 4.03{:}1$; v/C $= 19.87\% \approx 1/5$
II c/v $= 2.03{:}1$; v/C $= 32.98\% \approx 1/3$

$\Delta v = \Delta(v+s)\ [= 109\%]$;

p′ $= 20\%$; **Is′** $= 100.67\%$; **IIs′** $= 60.67\%$;
IIc/Ic $= 36.14\%$; product $= 10397$; **a′** $= 50\%$

I $(1202\ v + 605\ s) = $ **II** $1807\ c$

add. **Iv** $\approx -1/25$; add. **IIv** $\approx -1/9$

add. cap. **I** $605\ s = 495\ c + 110\ v$
add. cap. **II** $238\ s = (55\ c + 24\ v) + (110\ c + 49\ v)$

I $(4848\ c + 495\ c) + (1202\ v + 110\ v) = 5343\ c + 1312\ v$
II $(1752\ c + 55\ c + 110\ c) + (862\ v + 24\ v + 49\ v) =$
$1917\ c + 935\ v$

I $5343\ c + 1312\ v + 605\ s$ (consumption fund) $= 7260$
II $1917\ c + 935\ v + 285\ s$ (consumption fund) $= 3137$

  $(c+v+s)I = Ic + IIc\ [= 7260]$; $(c+v+s)II = (v+s)\ [= 3137]$
    total consumption fund $= 890$ s

—————. —————. —————. —————. —————. —————. —————.

4th year

    I. $5343\ c + 1312\ v + 1330\ s = 7985$
    II. $1917\ c + 935\ v + 570\ s = 3422$

I c/v $= 4.07{:}1$; **I** v/C $= 19.7\% \approx 1/5$
II c/v $= 2.05{:}1$; **II** v/C $= 32.78\% \approx 1/3$

$\Delta v = \Delta(v+s)$ [= 109%];

$p' = 20\%$; $Is' = 101.37\%$; $IIs' = 60.96\%$;
$IIc/Ic = 35.88\%$; product = 11407; $a' = 50\%$

In the end of the year:
I 5880 c + 1440 v + 665 s (consumption fund) = 7985
II 2105 c + 1019 v + 298 s (consumption fund) = 3422

$(c+v+s)I = Ic + IIc$ [= 7985]; $(c+v+s)II = (v+s)$ [= 3422]
total consumption fund = 963 s

———. ———. ———. ———. ———. ———.-----

5th year

    I.   5880 c + 1440 v + 1460 s = 8780
    II. 2105 c + 1019 v + 625 s = 3749

I c/v = 4.08:1; I v/C = 19.67% ≈1/5
II c/v = 2.07:1; II v/C = 32.62% ≈1/3

$\Delta v = \Delta(v+s)$ [= 109.5%];

$p' = 20\%$; $Is' = 101.39\%$; $IIs' = 61.3\%$;
$IIc/Ic = 35.8\%$; product = 12529; $a' = 50\%$

In the end of the year:
I 6470 c + 1580 v + 730 s (consumption fund) = 8780
II 2310 c + 1111 v + 328 s (consumption fund) = 3749
$(c+v+s)I = Ic + IIc$ [= 8780]; $(c+v+s)II = (v+s)$ [= 3749]
total consumption fund = 1058 s

———. ———. ———. ———. ———. ———.-----

6th year

    I.   6470 c + 1580 v + 1590 s = 9640
    II. 2310 c + 1111 v + 674 s = 4095

I c/v = 4.095:1; I v/C = 19.63% ≈1/5
II c/v = 2.08:1; II v/C = 32.48% ≈1/3

$\Delta v = \Delta(v+s)$ [= 109%];

$p' = 19.7\%$; $Is' = 100.6\%$; $IIs' = 60.67\%$;
$IIc/Ic = 35.7\%$; product = 13735; $a' = 50\%$

In the end of the year:
I $7112\ c + 1733\ v + 795\ s$ (consumption fund) = 9640
II $2528\ c + 1208\ v + 359\ s$ (consumption fund) = 4095

$(c+v+s)I = Ic + IIc$ [= 9640]; $(c+v+s)II = (v+s)$ [= 4095]
total consumption fund = 1154 s

———. ———. ———. ———. ———. ———.-----

7th year

      I. $7112\ c + 1733\ v + 1730\ s = 10575$
      II. $2528\ c + 1208\ v + 730\ s = 4466$

I $c/v = 4.1{:}1$; I $v/C = 19.59\%$
II $c/v = 2.09{:}1$; II $v/C = 32.33\%$

$\Delta v = \Delta(v+s)$ [= 109%];

$p' = 19.5\%$; $Is' \approx 100\%$; $IIs' = 60.4\%$;
$IIc/Ic = 35.55\%$; product = 15041; $a' = 50\%$

and so on.

As it is seen, the scheme in this view works and yields good results. In contrast to Lenin's scheme, in which the disproportions become increasingly deeper every next year, in this scheme the proportions are kept during all the time—always $(c+v+s)I = Ic+IIc$, and $(c+v+s)II = (v+s)$. For four years the capital from 7250 (5500 c + 1750 v) has increased to 9507 (7260 c + 2247 v), which means more than 131% growth, while in Lenin's scheme the capital has increased from the same basis of 7250 to 8968 (7104 c + 1864 v), which means 123.7% growth. And that represents 6% more accumulated capital in comparison with Lenin's example. The constant capital in this new scheme grows to 132%, i.e., $\Delta c \approx 1/3$, while in Lenin's illustration the constant capital grows a little more than 129%, although his extremely accelerated accumulation scheme leads to a bigger exceeding share of Ic over IIc—in our case, IIc/Ic is 35.88%, while in Lenin's scheme this relation is

29.93%. As concerns the variable capital (and respectively the growth of average wage), the difference is very distinct: Δv = 128.4% in our case, while in Lenin's case Δv is barely 106.5%! This difference between them gives a relation of 120.55% in favor of our case! Similarly, the increase of the national income in our scheme is $\Delta(v+s)$ = 118.5%, while in Lenin's one $\Delta(v+s)$ = 106.5%. Total social product is 11407 and it has a growth of more than 131.1% against 10830 which is 120.3% growth in the scheme of Lenin. This fact shows 5⅓% product more provided that its initial basis is 10% less!

Conclusion: irrespective of its exaggerated relations of accumulation, it is worth most of the scheme of accelerated accumulation that Lenin (for the first time) makes an attempt to stir the static scheme of Marx of even capital's accumulation. This is a step ahead.

In comparison with Marx's scheme: for five years the social capital under conditions of the same rate of profit has increased from 7250 (5500 c + 1750 v) to 11471 (8780 c + 2691 v), which represents 158.22%, while in Marx's scheme the capital accumulated is 11566 (8784 c + 2782 v) and its increase is 159.53%. In other words, the raising of the social capital is almost the same as at Marx's scheme, but the organic composition in I department has increased to 4.1:1, while in Marx's illustration even after five years the ratio remains as before the same 4:1. Besides that, after the accelerated accumulation, in I department there is 0.44% more constant capital than under even accumulation; that would lead at a future time to more produced social product. However, the higher rate of surplus value, along with the higher rate of profit in II department in Marx's model in comparison with these rates in our case, create a bigger social product by reason of bigger product of articles of consumption created. The initial difference of 300 units in the first year reaches over 600 units after five years, i.e., the total social product in Marx's scheme grows absolutely and relatively more than the product in my scheme, and after five years from exceeding of 3.45% is already raised to 4.46%. This effect would be obliterated and the total social product would be bigger if the general rate of profit (and respectively the rates of surplus value in both departments, too) would be increased more than 20% or the rate of accumulation would be increased more than 50%, or would be increased all of them. Really, Marx and Lenin assume in their schemes always constant rate of accumulation. But what would happen if we accept an increasing rate of accumulation such as it really must be under the socialist relations of production? What scheme shall we get then? Let us see it.

1st year

    I. $4000\ c + 1000\ v + 1000\ s = 6000$

    II. $1500\ c + 750\ v + 450\ s = 2700$

I $c/v = 4{:}1$; **I** $v/C = 1/5$;
II $c/v = 2{:}1$; **II** $v/C = 1/3$; **IIc/Ic** $= 37.5\%$
$p' = 20\%$; **I** $s' = 100\%$; **II** $s' = 60\%$; $\underline{a' = 50\%}$;
product $= 8700$; **(c+v)** $= 7250$

I$(1000\ v + 500\ s) = $ **II** $1500\ c$
add. **I** $v = -1/C^2 = -1/25$; add. **II** $v = -1/C^2 = -1/9$

add. cap. **I** $500\ s = 404\ c + 96\ v$

I$(4000\ c + 404\ c) + (1000\ v + 96\ v) = 4404\ c + 1096\ v$
II$(1500\ c + 96\ c) + (750\ v + 43\ v) = 1596\ c + 793\ v$

I $4404\ c + 1096\ v + 500\ s$ (consumption fund) $= 6000$
II $1596\ c + 793\ v + 311\ s$ (consumption fund) $= 2700$

(c+v+s)I = Ic + IIc $[= 6000]$; **(c+v+s)II = (v+s)** $[= 2700]$
             total consumption fund $= 811\ s$

——————. ——————. ——————. ——————. ——————. ——————. ——————.——

2nd year

    I. $4404\ c + 1096\ v + 1100\ s = 6600$

    II. $1596\ c + 793\ v + 478\ s = 2867$

I $c/v = 4.02{:}1$; $v/C = 19.93\% \approx 1/5$
II $c/v = 2.01{:}1$; $v/C = 33.19\% \approx 1/3$

$\Delta v = \Delta(v+s)$ $[= 108\%]$;

$p' = 20\%$; $\mathbf{Is'} = 100.36\%$; $\mathbf{IIs'} = 60.28\%$; $\underline{\mathbf{a'} = 51\%}$

$\mathbf{IIc/Ic} = 36.24\%$; product $= 9467$;

$(\mathbf{c+v}) = 7889$; $\Delta(\mathbf{c+v}) = 109\%$

$\mathbf{I}(1096\ \mathbf{v} + 540\ \mathbf{s}) = \mathbf{II}\ 1636\ \mathbf{c}$

add. $\mathbf{Iv} \approx -1/25$; add. $\mathbf{IIv} \approx -1/9$

add. cap. $\mathbf{I}\ 560\ \mathbf{s} = 452\ \mathbf{c} + 108\ \mathbf{v}$

add. cap. $\mathbf{II}\ 214\ \mathbf{s} = (40\ \mathbf{c} + 18\ \mathbf{v}) + (108\ \mathbf{c} + 48\ \mathbf{v})$

$\mathbf{I}(4404\ \mathbf{c} + 452\ \mathbf{c}) + (1096\ \mathbf{v} + 108\ \mathbf{v}) = 4856\ \mathbf{c} + 1204\ \mathbf{v}$

$\mathbf{II}(1596\ \mathbf{c} + 40\ \mathbf{c} + 108\ \mathbf{c}) + (793\ \mathbf{v} + 18\ \mathbf{v} + 48\ \mathbf{v}) = 1744\ \mathbf{c} + 859\ \mathbf{v}$

$\mathbf{I}\ 4856\ \mathbf{c} + 1204\ \mathbf{v} + 540\ \mathbf{s}$ (consumption fund) $= 6600$

$\mathbf{II}\ 1744\ \mathbf{c} + 859\ \mathbf{v} + 264\ \mathbf{s}$ (consumption fund) $= 2867$

$(\mathbf{c+v+s})\mathbf{I} = \mathbf{Ic} + \mathbf{IIc}\ [= 6600]$; $(\mathbf{c+v+s})\mathbf{II} = (\mathbf{v+s})\ [= 2867]$

total consumption fund $= 804\ \mathbf{s}$

——— . ——— . ——— . ——— . ——— . ——— . ———

3rd year

      I. $4856\ \mathbf{c} + 1204\ \mathbf{v} + 1212\ \mathbf{s} = 7272$

      II. $1744\ \mathbf{c} + 859\ \mathbf{v} + 520\ \mathbf{s} = 3123$

$\mathbf{I}\ \mathbf{c/v} = 4.03{:}1$; $\mathbf{I}\ \mathbf{v/C} = 19.87\% \approx 1/5$

$\mathbf{II}\ \mathbf{c/v} = 2.03{:}1$; $\mathbf{II}\ \mathbf{v/C} = 33\% = 1/3$

$\Delta\mathbf{v} = \Delta(\mathbf{v+s})\ [= 109\%]$;

$p' = 20\%$; $\mathbf{I}\ \mathbf{s'} = 100.66\%$; $\mathbf{II}\ \mathbf{s'} = 60.54\%$; $\underline{\mathbf{a'} = 52\%}$

$\mathbf{IIc/Ic} = 35.9\%$; product $= 10395$;

$(\mathbf{c+v}) = 8663$; $\Delta(\mathbf{c+v}) = 110\%$

$\mathbf{I}\ (1204\ \mathbf{v} + 582\ \mathbf{s}) = \mathbf{II}\ 1786\ \mathbf{c}$

add. $\mathbf{Iv} \approx -1/25$; add. $\mathbf{IIv} = -1/9$

149

add. cap. **I** 630 **s** = 509 **c** + 121 **v**
add. cap. **II** 236 **s** = (42 **c** + 19 **v**) + (121 **c** + 54 **v**)

I (4856 **c** + 509 **c**) + (1204 **v** + 121 **v**) = 5365 **c** + 1325 **v**
II (1744 **c** + 42 **c** + 121 **c**) + (859 **v** + 19 **v** + 54 **v**) = 1907 **c** + 932 **v**

I 5365 **c** + 1325 **v** + 582 **s** (consumption fund) = 7272
II 1907 **c** + 932 **v** + 284 **s** (consumption fund) = 3123

(c+v+s)I = Ic + IIc [= 7272]; (c+v+s)II = (v+s) [= 3123]
         total consumption fund = 866 **s**

——————. ——————. ——————. ——————. ——————. ——————. ——————

4th year
      I.   5365 **c** + 1325 **v** + 1338 **s** = 8028
      II. 1907 **c** + 932 **v** + 568 **s** = 3407

I c/v = 4.05:1; **I v/C** = 19.8% ≈1/5
II c/v = 2.05:1; **II v/C** = 32.83% ≈1/3

Δv = Δ(v+s) [= 109%];

p′ = 20%; **I s′** = 101%; **II s′** = 61%; **a′= 53%**
IIc/Ic = 35.55%; product = 11435;
(c+v) = 9529; **Δ(c+v)** = 110%

In the end of the year:
I 5938 **c** + 1461 **v** + 629 **s** (consumption fund) = 8028
II 2090 **c** + 1013 **v** + 304 **s** (consumption fund) = 3407
(c+v+s)I = Ic + IIc [= 8028]; (c+v+s)II = (v+s) [= 3407]
         total consumption fund = 933 **s**

——————. ——————. ——————. ——————. ——————. ——————.

5th year
      I.   5938 **c** + 1461 **v** + 1470 **s** = 8869
      II. 2090 **c** + 1013 **v** + 620 **s** = 3723

I $c/v = 4.06:1$; **I** $v/C = 19.75\% \approx 1/5$
II $c/v = 2.06:1$; **II** $v/C = 32.65\% \approx 1/3$
$\Delta v = \Delta(v+s)$ [= 109.6%];

$p' \approx 20\%$; **I** $s' = 100.6\%$; **II** $s' = 61.2\%$; **a' = 54%**

IIc/Ic = 35.2%; product = 12592;
$(c+v) = 10502$; $\Delta(c+v) = 110\%$;

In the end of the year:
I 6579 **c** + 1614 **v** + 676 **s** (consumption fund) = 8869
II 2290 **c** + 1102 **v** + 331 **s** (consumption fund) = 3723

$(c+v+s)I = Ic + IIc$ [= 8869]; $(c+v+s)II = (v+s)$ [= 3723]
total consumption fund = **1007 s**

——— . ——— . ——— . ——— . ——— . ——— .———

6th year

    I.   6579 **c** + 1614 **v** + 1610 **s** = 9803
    II. 2290 **c** + 1102 **v** + 666 **s** = 4058

I $c/v = 4.08:1$; **I** $v/C = 19.7\% \approx 1/5$
II $c/v = 2.08:1$; **II** $v/C = 32.5\% \approx 1/3$

$\Delta v = \Delta(v+s)$ [= 109%];
$p' = 19.6\%$; **Is'** $\approx 100\%$; **IIs'** = 60.4%; **a' = 55%**
IIc/Ic = 34.8%; product = 13861;
$(c+v) = 11585$; $\Delta(c+v) = 110\%$;

In the end of the year:
I 7295 **c** + 1784 **v** + 724 **s** (consumption fund) = 9803
II 2508 **c** + 1198 **v** + 352 **s** (consumption fund) = 4058

$(c+v+s)I = Ic + IIc$ [= 9803]; $(c+v+s)II = (v+s)$ [= 4058]
total consumption fund = **1076 s**

——— . ——— . ——— . ——— . ——— . ——— .———

Todor Bombov

7th year

      I.   7295 **c** + 1784 **v** + 1780 **s** = 10859

     II. 2508 **c** + 1198 **v** + 726 **s** = 4432

I c/v = 4.09:1; **I v/C** = 19.65%
II c/v = 2.09:1; **II v/C** = 32.3%

Δ**v** = Δ**(v+s)** [$\approx$ 110%];

p′ = 19.6%; **I s′** $\approx$ 100%; **II s′** = 60.6%; <u>**a′** = 56%</u>
IIc/Ic = 34.4%; product = 15291;
(c+v) = 12785; Δ**(c+v)** = 110%;

and so on.

Now, let us do a comparative analysis between these two illustrations of the scheme under the same rate of profit; the former is with a constant rate of accumulation, the latter is with an increasing one. So, what can we see?

First of all, the common feature is that still in the third year, but especially in the fourth and fifth years, in both illustrations, it senses a tension between the rate of profit and the rates of surplus value in **I** and **II** departments, an increasing tension. As a result of the accumulation of capital and growing of the organic composition of the capital as well as in order to keep the rates of surplus value invariable, the rate of profit must fall and it really falls from 20% in the first year to 19.5%, respectively 19.6%, in the seventh year. Another common fact is that this scheme in both its illustrations gives an economic growth with enviable rates at an average of 10% annually! Henceforth differences begin. After an equal start, in the beginning of the seventh year, we can see the following results under an increasing rate of accumulation **a′** in comparison with the case of a constant one:

total social product: 15291 > 15041, i.e., 250 units or 1.66% more; for all the term a growth $\approx$ 176%;

a) *product of department I*: 10859 > 10575, i.e., 2.69% more and with a tendency of increasing rates; for all the term a substantial growth $\approx$ 181%;

b) *product of department II*: 4432 < 4466, i.e., 0.77% less, but there is a pronounced tendency of quick erasure of the differences and a near at hand outdistance; for all the term a growth > 164%;

social capital: 12785 > 12581, i.e., 204 units or 1.62% more; for all the term a growth > 176%;

a) *growth of the constant capital*: in the department **I**: Δc = 7295 (182.4%) > 7112 (177.8%), i.e., 2.57% more, but as a growth of initial basis is 4.6% more; in department **II**: Δc = 2508 (167.2%) < 2528 (168.5%), i.e., an insignificant difference both as a growth of 0.8% and as a growth of initial basis 1.3%. In other words, here is pronounced the outstripping accumulation of department **I** over department **II**; but in spite of that there is a tendency to erase the differences near at hand;

b) *growth of the organic composition*: in the department **I**: from the initial common basis of 4:1 to 4.09:1 against 4.1:1, i.e., almost the same growth; in department **II**: from 2:1 to 2.09:1 against 2.09:1, i.e., quite the same growth. But the outstripping accumulation of department **I** over **II** is more pronounced in the case of increasing rate of accumulation—for example, if **IIc/Ic** in the first year as a common basis is 37.5%, in the seventh year it is 34.38% against 35.55% (the latter result of 35.55% is reached in the first case still in the fourth year). If we examine the reciprocal relation **Ic/IIc**, we shall see that the outstripping accumulation of constant capital in **I** over **II** department is more strongly expressed in the case of the increasing rate of accumulation than that one of constant rate: 291% against 281% at a common initial basis of 267%.

social consumption fund: 1076 < 1154, i.e., 7.25% less; for all the term a growth of 133% against 142%; this fact expresses the descending share of the state expenditures and dying out of the state

growth of the national income and the average wage—these two indexes are mighty effects by the combined work of the outstripping accumulation of department **I** over **II** and the increasing rate of accumulation.

a) *growth of the national income*: the national income marks higher rates of growth under the scheme with increasing rate of accumulation. This tendency is clearly noticed from the fourth year on. Here is an illustration (in square brackets are put the exceeding absolute differences and their relative expressions in comparison with the scheme with constant rate of accumulation):

    1) 3200 = 3200;

    2) 3467 = 3467;

    3) 3795 < 3797; [−2; −0.05%];

4) 4163 > 4147 [16, 0.39%];

5) 4564 > 4544 [20, 0.44%];

6) 4992 > 4965 [27, 0.54%];

7) 5488 > 5401 [87, 1.61%].

It can clearly notice the abrupt leap in the seventh year even after the accelerated development in previous three years and that means that in the next years the national income production will increase with still higher rates and this difference will become more and more striking.

b) growth of the average wage:

1) 1750 = 1750;

2) 1889 = 1889;

3) 2063 < 2064; [−1; −0.048%];

4) 2257 > 2247 [10, 0.44%];

5) 2474 > 2459 [15, 0.61%];

6) 2716 > 2691 [25, 0.93%];

7) 2982 > 2941 [41, 1.39%].

Here again, the rates of growth of the average wage from the fourth year on are increasingly accelerated.

As it is seen, the case of increasing rate of accumulation is much better and makes the scheme unusually mighty. So, in the finale we have a scheme with not only theoretical but with practical meaning, too; a dynamic scheme instead of the static scheme of Marx; an accelerated scheme but not the extreme scheme of Lenin; a working scheme of socialism.

The rate of accumulation should not remain invariable, as Marx and Lenin accept it. It must increase each year. The mass of accumulation is the part of the surplus value, intended for accumulation only; the other part of it, i.e., the consumption fund, represents the allowances for the budget as a tax on profits. As for the social capital, the mass and the rate of accumulation depend on the condition $I(v+s/x) = IIc$. Since the accumulation has priority, in this equation, as we already saw, it has to determine firstly s—the mass of surplus value for social accumulation, and then x—the mass of surplus value for social consumption. The consumption fund in **I** department expresses the aggregate tax on profits, providing its share in state's budget. We can indicate this fund, this mass of surplus value for social consumption x, with t_p, and the mass of accumulation s with a; since the growth of the tax on profits in the course of time with the withering away of the state tends gradually to zero, i.e., $\Delta t_p \to 0$, the rate of accumulation must be incessantly increased and its limit being equal to **1**:

$$\lim_{\Delta t_p \to 0} a = \frac{\Delta a}{\Delta t_p} = 1$$

Like any other rate, the rate of accumulation is a derivative, too—the same function (surplus value), just like **s'** or **p'**, but with another argument—not **v** or **C**, variable or total capital, but t_p, tax on profits. Each year the relative share of tax on profits' growth intended for the budget within the total produced surplus value must decrease, being expressed in the tendency $\Delta t_p \to 0$. That means that in the course of time, more and more mass of surplus value is intended to accumulation and less for state expenditures until all the mass becomes intended for accumulation only—at the border period when the state dies out completely. It is clear that just like the rate of profit, the rate of accumulation could not be more than 100%. The rate of accumulation, howsoever, follows and depends on the rate of surplus value—to the social capital as well as to each individual capital. The rate of accumulation, as a result of the rate of surplus value is expressed in the following direct dependence:

$$a' = s' \frac{v}{t_p}$$

***

Policy of Taxation

Once the rate of accumulation of the social capital is established, and after the accumulation of capital is realized, the total surplus value for social and state consumption is established which represents the above mentioned *total consumption fund* by both departments filling up with content the total tax on profits, $T_p = It_p + IIt_p$. All people, except the liberal professions, not employed in material production must receive their incomes from the state budget. For this purpose, all enterprises are laid under taxation.

Such is the inevitable role of the state treasure. It requires that a percentage of the mass of surplus value is detached as a tax on profits. In the course of time, however, this percentage tends to zero, i.e., it lessens and dwindles to nothing with the withering away of the state. Except this single tax on profits which has to be proportional but not

155

graduated, all other taxes of the enterprise—a turnover tax, a land-tax, excises, etc., become otiose and without any basis. Yet, the productive workers, as I already noticed, must be free from any taxes on their wages.

Only the fiscal policy of socialism in the modern world may strongly observe the four classic principles of the tax as formulated by Adam Smith—evenness, definiteness, convenience, and profitableness. The fourth principle of the tax, for example, is best observed under simplified and of a small number of taxation laws and the maintenance of a minimum fiscal administration apparatus—this is just what is achieved many times better in a socialist system compared to a capitalist one.

However, Adam Smith's postulate of a state budget amounting to 10 % of the gross national product was observed until the end of the nineteenth century—until the end of the classic capitalism, until the collapse of the free competition. After that, the state as well as the tradition was no longer what it was before. The immersion of the coalescence of the state with the monopolies in the modern highly developed state-monopoly capitalism, the immersion of the étatism in the world capitalist system, the increase of the role of the state in the economy as a real life in acute contrast with the propaganda myth massively imposed by them that this is "market" economy is categorically in evidence in the incessantly growing relative share of the taxes that nationalize more and more large parts of the gross national product in the countries with "western democracy"—if, in 1970, it was between 20 % and 40 % in the states of "market economy," in 1991, it was already between 40 and 60 %[148] (!) when it was started to speak of a still more "market economy," i.e., the passing each other between propaganda and reality nowadays grows and becomes more and more hyperbolic. And the state-monopoly capitalism in the so-called "socialist bloc" (or "communist system") was led to a still higher degree, to its final degree—the state was receiving up to 80 % of the gross national product![149] This state-monopoly capitalism, with its 100 % state-owned property developed a self-denying economic system, a system of the absurdity. On the one hand, it imposed the killing tax on profits amounting up to 80 % and, on the other hand—the mad system of subsidies amounted up to one-third of the common budget expenses![150]

---

[148]. Velcho Stoyanov and Velichko Adamov, *Theory of Finance*, 43-44.

[149]. Stoyanov, et al., *Theory of Finance.*, 8.

[150]. Ibid., 122.

An extremely ineffective economic system in which the state was really a single capitalist—by either hand (through the tax) it takes almost the whole profit of the economic subject that turns out to be not enough for the subject's own development and needs to be subsidized by the other state's hand (like an alms) in order to continue and to complete its extended reproduction.

But out of the antiquated economic forms of the Soviet "communism" and American "market economy," even the newest project in large dimensions of the anarchic-market idea of the neo-liberalism doctrine—the European Union, born in 1993 through blackmail, threats, and by force—is not an exception to its policy of taxation. After twenty-two years, this queer and hurriedly fixed up formation is in front of full collapse and certain disintegration, which will occur between 2017 and 2023. {By the way, I prognosticated the full disintegration of the European Union still in 2002 in the second edition of this book when this collapse was far from any assumption in general and when flowed the Ode to Joy! In 2014 the leaders themselves of this "union" already began to speak about this forthcoming event! In 2015 it was reached to the critical level of Grexit, in 2016 – to real Brexit, the beginning of the end!} This serial absurd system of the capitalism, with its high-handed methods, with its corporate and lobby parasitism, requires increasingly heavier taxes for its existence. This is the serial anti-market, corporative, a state-monopolistic economy, which is represented in its antipode form, and in which the biggest global capital, quite by command and with high-handed methods, in every one of its newly conquered colonies, like Bulgaria for example, indoctrinates from a grandstand, the official public "recognition" that the colony is a "market economy;" an act on its own account that is deeply administrative, but it is perfidiously invented for the colony to fill its menial status amongst the conquerors with calf optimism! Although after 1990, this over-state-owned economic system—the "communist bloc"—collapsed and in Europe, there was enforced the neoliberalism's chaos and anarchy, the tax burden did not fall down at all from the European nations along with their destroyed national states! After more than twenty years of liberalization and deregulation in the European common "market" economy, the taxes upon the nations quite have not disappeared along with the disappearance of their national states! On the contrary, at the alleged market economy, the tendency in years 2011, 2013 and 2015 was a gradual enhancement of the tax burden! Just like a kind of neo-communist state system! As we can see in Table Two, in the old and rich EU members, the income tax is between 40 and 60 %, i.e., it is the same as in 1991, in the same these countries of "market economy!" In this non-market but fully corporate economy the half of the personal incomes are taken away as taxes! And it is without consideration of the indirect taxes! At the same time, the corporate income tax ranges between 20 and 30 % (except in France and Belgium), average 23 %! (Look at Table Three). As it is clearly seen, the tax burden on the persons is heavy and increasing while on the corporations it is two times lighter and decreasing!

Table 2; PERSONAL INCOME TAX RATES in EU, %

	2011	2013	2015		2011	2013	2015
EU 28	38.4	39.4	39.3	**FRANCE**	46.6	50.3	50.3
EA 19	40.6	42.3	42.1	**ITALY**	47.3	47.3	48.9
BELGIUM	53.7	53.8	53.8	**HOLLAND**	52.0	52.0	52.0
DENMARK	55.4	55.6	55.8	**AUSTRIA**	50.0	50.0	50.0
GERMANY	47.5	47.5	47.5	**SWEDEN**	56.6	56.7	57.0
GREECE	49.0	46.0	48.0	**UK**	50.0	45.0	45.0
SPAIN	45.0	52.0	46.0	**PORTUGAL**	50.0	56.5	56.5

151

Table 3; CORPORATE INCOME TAX RATES in EU, %

EU 28	23.0	23.2	22.8	**AUSTRIA**	25.0	25.0	25.0
EA 19	24.4	25.0	24.6	**SWEDEN**	26.3	22.0	22.0
BELGIUM	34.0	34.0	34.0	**UK**	26.0	23.0	20.0
DENMARK	25.0	25.0	23.5	**HOLLAND**	25.0	25.0	25.0

151

Under capitalist mode of production, the revenues in the state budget come mostly from the incomes of physical persons, i.e., from the population—through heavy and hated taxation (in the United States—45–50 % of incomes tax, 30 % of social insurance, 5–6 % of excises)[152] and only 10 % (!) are the revenues from the profits of the corporations—with a high degree that cannot be collected! Under socialist mode of production, this is the opposite case—the state treasury is fulfilled exceptionally from the revenues of the juridical persons, i.e., from the

---

[151]. Source: Eurostat, Taxation trends in the European Union, 2015 edition; http://ec.europa.eu/eurostat

[152]. Stoyanov, et al., *Theory of Finance*, 39.

profits of the enterprises and an insignificant share is borne from the incomes of the population!

The tax on property, widely used in the capitalist system, is, in fact, the second taxation of an income received. And, provided that there is a turnover tax, too, the income is thrice taxed! All that is not only unjust, but it is also superfluous under a socialist mode of production, i.e., except taxes on the income, all taxes are superfluous—both on the property and on the turnover. Besides that, an appreciable part of the income taxes should be taken off, too—the taxes on wages of the industrial workers in the city and in the village. In the socialist society, some taxes on property drop out immediately, such as the land-tax, because there is no ground rent available, while others die out in the course of time, for example, an inhabited house duty, legacy-duty. Immediately in this society drops out a range of other groups of taxes according to the subject to taxation—the anachronistic taxes on the physical person, but also the modern taxes on the sales (the consumption), for example, the tax on turnover and VAT! Together with the tax on the trade, which is a representative of the taxes on a given economic activity, the tax on turnover or VAT may be preserved only during the transition period to socialism, but in its clear form, the socialist mode of production excludes their existence. So, under the developed socialism, only one group of taxes remains available—the income taxes: for physical persons—as a tax on fees, for juridical persons—as a tax on profits.

The tax on profits must be proportional but not graduated, because its percentage rate persists as invariable upon taxation of the income (the profit) of the enterprise. This will say that the ratios between the profits expressed toward their capitals will remain invariable, too, such as they must be under an invariable general rate of profit. So, the part that is taken from the profit under the form of tax for the state will be the same in a relative expression for all participants in the process of expansion of value. In this way, the ratios between the profits expressed toward their invested capitals **before** and **after** their taxation will persist as the same, they will be invariable. This is in full synchrony with the requirement of the same general rate of profit (the equal relation of s to C for all capitals), which is infringed by its ideal form just because of the necessity to detach a part of the profit s as a tax for the state. And the even appropriation of s toward the invested capitals is the requirement for social property of the means of production! So, taxation duty being proportional to its taxation basis is not only equitable, it is economically profitable for **juridical persons** under this economic system. The graduated taxation is more equitable than the proportional in a capitalist system upon taxation of **physical persons**' incomes. But proportional taxation in the conditions of the same general rate of profit is applied to juridical persons due to reasons that have been already explained, while the justice was cleared up earlier—when, how, and why there exists social justice in the socialist system. The graduated taxation should be preserved for physical persons only with so-called free practices. The income taxes should apply just for them, which taxes are absent with respect to the productive workers.

Why, however, is there no turnover tax—gross and net—and excise under socialism?

Because:

1. The turnovers of the capitals are already subordinated to the laws $\mathbf{p'} = \mathbf{const.}$, $\mathbf{S'} = \mathbf{const.}$, and $\dfrac{\mathbf{v}}{\mathbf{c+v}} = \mathbf{const.}$ The number of turnovers of one capital **n** (which enters into the annual rate of surplus value **S'**), in every new annual cycle is equalized in the carrying surplus value with the number of turnovers of all other capitals under the effect of these laws. The sense of the turnover tax within the capitalistic mode of production is precisely that—the capitals of faster turnover to be levied by the state with a higher tax, because the faster turnover under all other equal conditions carries a greater mass of surplus value. But under socialist mode of production, just for this reason the turnovers along with the different technical level of the capitals at every new starting moment with the law $\mathbf{p'} = \mathbf{const.}$ are in harness conjointly for the aim in the society to be produced and appropriated a relatively equal share of the mass of surplus value, i.e., although there are no allowances in this case made in favor of the state, one might say under the condition that their turnover tax in this way, so to say, is already deducted. Continuing the same convention, we can just add that it (the turnover tax or the excise) instead of from the price of the commodity here is already deducted directly from the user's wage (salary), as that is made with the income tax in the same moment with **s'** according to the formula $\mathbf{p'} = \mathbf{n.v.s'/C}$.

So, the turnover tax, and along with it the excise tax, become completely useless;

2. Price coincides with value but does not vary from it. Under capitalistic mode of production, the turnover tax and the excise are indirect taxes, which serve only for additional robbery of the user. They are factors of inflation, levers of the state-monopolistic regulation, which are used as instruments for indirect exploitation in the circulation, because they are included in the price of the commodities, contributing in this manner the increase of the growth of inflation. However, provided that the price coincides with the value, the turnover tax and the excise simply cannot be placed anywhere between the price and the value. That concerns all types of sales taxes, as well.

The arguments that the turnover tax (TT) is completely useless under socialist mode of production are even more intensively applied compared to the value-added tax (VAT)—its refined successor widespread in most contemporary capitalist countries in the world, i.e., the causes rejecting the gross TT reject the net TT, too. It is just the difference between them, which gives the additional reason of even more categorical VAT's rejection. Since the VAT is a tax only on the newly created value, without including also the so-called "previous turnovers," i.e., the value of labor passed, it is represented in a completely pure state in that **n**—the turnover of the variable capital that we currently keep in mind. The turnover of the constant capital—fixed and circulating—is not levied by VAT and this model of the tax is the best illustration of its incompatibility with our system, i.e., VAT in even more pure form than TT proves its untenable nature under the same rate of profit. VAT makes TT useless, while the same rate of profit makes VAT useless. The same rate of profit abolishes simultaneously both the advantages of VAT and the shortcomings of TT, by abolishing both taxes together. The defect of turnover tax—a double levy of certain commodities and no levy of others, this obvious injustice is overcome by value-added tax—**all** commodities are levied! The same rate of profit resolves the question in another way—all commodities not to levy! Besides that, in this manner, it drops out not only the opportunity for speculation through various schemes of drawing of VAT from the state budget, but the entire complexity of the tax credit will be abolished, too—easy and simple in theory, but very difficult to be restored in practice, because the state is easy in taking, but difficult in giving. The advantages of VAT compared to TT are to some extent neutralized by the shortcomings of the excise, concomitant them—if, under the effect of TT, the excise is a different tax in its levying, then, under the effect of VAT, the excise is one of the Three Pillars (excise, duty, turnover) on which this tax is laid because the excise tax, if any exists, serves as a basis of assessment of VAT. So, the hidden justice of VAT shines here—to assess a tax on a tax!

Turnover tax appears at the beginning of the twentieth century, on the eve of the First World War, being imposed in the developed world between the two World Wars as a "child of want or misfortune,"[153] i.e., in reply to the more and more growing appetites of the state—when the State began getting its contemporary meaning of an imperialist state, burying the classical capitalism, i.e., "the more state"—the more taxes! Later, VAT appeared only as a refined, a net turnover tax.

Sales tax, such as turnover tax, VAT, use tax and the like, is a tax on user's expenses, a tax on purchases—a senseless tax! A tax deprived of any sense, because there is something masochistic to pay a tax on purchasing a commodity for personal use—a buyer should be thankful to the seller for latter's good graces to make a deal with him for sale-trade! Instead of it being the opposite. Turnover tax (and VAT) is a new "dish-haki" tax (tooth tax) that the richly fed, unbridled Ottoman wanted at the end of dinner from the scared disenfranchised rayah-host tax for having wasted his teeth! Through the turnover tax, VAT or other sales tax, in relation to the user, the state plays the role of an arch Ottoman sadist! Sales tax is so outrageous that even a toad like Caligula abolished it completely in the Roman Empire! Obviously, the modern world is rotten more than the Roman Empire!

Sales taxes, together with income taxes, are taxes both on incomes and on expenses of the mute society—a proven way to tantalize, to irritate, or to ruin this society! For example, with a tax on wage and with VAT, the income of the worker is twice levied—the first time as an income, the second time—as an expense! The same is with the tax on wage and the tax on interest—twice levy on depositor's income again! A leech system—this is the modern capitalist symbiotic tax and bank system!

Of course, we are speaking of commodities of local production here (and of home trade). In the case of imported commodities, i.e., if we

---

[153]. Stoyanov, et al., *Theory of Finance*, 146.

consider foreign trade, turnover tax (gross or net) and excise tax may be preserved in different economic systems, i.e., at an import of commodities from a capitalist country to a socialist one. But regarding the importation in the case of international or a world socialist system, the aforementioned arguments remain in force, i.e., the commercial relations are preserved without any type of sales taxes because of the two conditions pointed out above. The same applies to customs duties, as well. There are no any indirect taxes under the socialism as a world (or at least international) system—nor customs duties, nor excises, nor turnover taxes—gross and net, nor fiscal monopolies. The existence of indirect taxes is always in contradiction and infringement of the Law of value! The indirect taxes, i.e., the taxes on expenses, are rejected in economic, logical, historical, and ethical aspects. Under international or world socialist system, the now unsolvable problem—"export of indirect taxes" in the international economic relations, drops out because there are no such taxes in this system. The absence of indirect taxes (including customs duties) is an exceptionally important prerequisite for a powerful international and world economic and political integration, much larger than it is at the present time (the European Union, for example), as well as a free movement of commodities and people. Each an economic integration imposes more closely approach to the Law of value when it has been infringed by the economic agents before—an equalization of the taxation systems, a tax unity, abolishing customs duties, etc. However, this is some approximation to the law only, while an exact coincidence with it may occur only when the economic integration is entirely subordinated to this law.

***

Second Form of Social Property

Through the new production relations, every enterprise gets the chance of independent development, without any monopoly expropriating its means—should it be "an organization of highest rank," a mother company or something similar. Precisely this is economic independence, so strongly wished before in our bygone "socialism," with the possibility of self-finance and self-government of each economic subject, so chew on at that time. Precisely this is a free development without hurrahs and the so-called "attacking work," without any alien intervention of upside, outside, and downside, without any patrons and trustees, without any benefactors and charity. And no cent more can go for consumption or for accumulation. Because, if the

163

necessities are an indispensability, the possibilities are not a fortuity! All pecuniary means are quite precisely distributed to their places, thanks to the precise mechanism of the schemes of Marx—this lovely play of the human reflection. Until now, these schemes were considered only to be a theoretic model, simply a scientific abstraction deprived of practical sense. But we know that there is nothing more practical than the good theory. Marx's schemes were impossible until now because they were built on an invariable rate of surplus value—something, which, indeed, is practically impossible for the capital and its reproduction process. But here, there is a way s' to be—to put and to maintain—invariable. And the schemes become a reality.

On the proportions of the extended reproduction, preliminarily established in this way, we can already build a strictly concrete plan—of the enterprise, of the brigade, of the worker. The plan is, in fact, the establishment of these very proportions. There can be a planning only when proportionality is established. The already established proportions are a **guarantee** of the accomplishment of the plan. They are the basis, on which the non-accomplishment of the plan is impossible under normal conditions. Only then it is a real plan, without having to be corrected, "up-dated" continuously after its acceptance—a well-known vicious practice that existed in our country before. Each plan is a plan for expansion of a certain value and it should necessarily establish the proportions at the creation of this value, not admitting contingent additional labor and expenses.

So, the self-government of the workers does not consist of another thing, but of the self-government of their labor time. For this purpose, however, it is necessary to oblige the rate of surplus value to start slumping in accordance with the slump of the rate of profit. That is already the consciously using the technical progress for social but not private development, in favor but not to the detriment of the working class. Only in this way, the technical and scientific progress can be placed at the services of society's good and never directed against it; only when it acts not by the blind force of an elemental process, but as a process that is subordinated to the reasonable activity of the society; only when it is not a result of the work of a handful of elite private laboratories, but of the work of millions of thinking people.

Of course, the process $\dfrac{v}{c+v} = \textbf{const}$ exist until the means of production start to correspond to the labor power under the new, higher productivity of labor—a requirement imposed by the production.

However, limitations are imposed by the market. Will this process exist and for how long, that also depends on the needs of the market for production of the same commodity that is offered until this moment. The accumulation of means of production as an end in itself for the purpose of abruptly increasing the wages, along with a bad study of the market of satisfied or already abating demand of the same commodity is as harmful as the stopped realization of the production of poor quality. A solution may be searched, for example, in the production of another commodity, which is demanded by the market and which, of course, must start to be produced under the conditions of the new productivity of labor—in a way that the regulating process $\dfrac{v}{c+v}=$ **const.** must conclude and that the production starts to be carried out under the next regulating process—$p' =$ **const.**

With the establishment of the process $\dfrac{v}{c+v}=$ **const.** in such critical situations, generated by the abrupt growth in the productivity of labor, it will be observed incessantly and proportionally withering away of certain professions and the appearance of new **for the same workers**, instead of obliging them to trail the yoke of the narrow specialties, hung on them by "the enslaving subordination of the individual to the division of labor"[154] as life-long sentences. The large-scale industry, "in its capitalistic form reproduces the old division of labor with its ossified particularizations"[155] and thus leads to degeneration, to mutilation, to atrophy of the personality and to dullness, to ignorance of the society. That's why, only in this way the changes in a productivity of labor to a higher degree will become without any crises, any stress, any collisions, without polar contradistinction in classes, but at a gradual fusion in a unified profession of a universal worker. It is the single way to carry out the great Renaissance idea, developed further by Marx and Engels, of an all-round personality—as a gradual ascent towards perfection. It is the time when we shall speak not about any separate estate of "scientific worker," but about a worker-scientist! It is hardly then one can be an aim to oneself, but not a means, as Kant wanted. It is hardly then that Plato's ideal could be realized—the time "until philosophers are kings."[156]

---

154. Marx, *Critique of the Gotha Program*, 1:175.
155. Marx, *Capital*, 1:538.
156. Plato, *The Republic,* 216.

The law, $\dfrac{v}{c+v}$ = const., is the third law which does not allow the labor power to be a commodity, to be reduced to the state of a commodity, i.e., to be deprived of any means of production while allowing at the same time the wage to be a self-expanding value. For the wage can increase not only in value at an invariable labor time but also in an increased leisure time at its invariable value. So, except p' = const., the law, $\dfrac{v}{c+v}$ = const., is another form of manifestation of the property of the means of production as **social**. That is just it, which is an obvious, conscious form of social property in critical situations, because the means of production continue to be property of the labor power at any moment, it is not divorced from them, being not alienated even at a time when, otherwise, the capital always does that by violence. The alienation, in general, is characteristic and immanent in the capitalistic production relations and concrete manifested in the production process—by the alienation of the labor power from the means of production, by divorcement of the immediate producers from their implements and objects of work. The property for them becomes "anonymous," "nobody's," as it was found out in our country before. The labor power is divorced, alienated from the means of production, because they are actually of someone else's property, whose—for the workers it is indifferent!

Gorbachev (was he the only one!) otherwise with a wise air exerted himself "to resolve the historical task how to be overcome the alienation of the man from the power, the property, the production, the culture, etc."[157]

It is clear that once being a form of the social property, the law, $\dfrac{v}{c+v}$ = const. represents another expression of social equality, because already there are no "useless" people, thrown out by the production as a technological waste, there are no inferior people, reduced to the status of "objects of small value and short duration"—a kind of account of Capital's accountancy. The higher productivity of labor comes to develop, but not to mutilate the workers. Labor power is placed under equal conditions in relation to the means of production

---

[157]. "Democratization of the Life," *Trud* newspaper, March 1, 1989. Information by Bulgarian Telegraph Agency.

both during normal, invariable conditions of work and in an extreme, variable ones, i.e., in a manner allowing that the property remains social in all cases. That's why I do not enter a contradiction with my assertion exposed in chapter one that the same rate of profit creates social property and the difference from it creates private property. The slump of the individual rate of profit in the given case, which is also a difference from the general rate of profit does not mean at all that any private property is created. Contrariwise, its slump is consciously used thus that not to infringe the social property precisely, but to preserve it in another form. That is such a difference in the rate of profit, the only one in fact, which does not create any private property. The general rate of profit is the same until the slump of the individual rate of profit is imposed, generated by the growth of the organic composition. It rises again later—anew because of the conditions of the organic composition—but not more than a fixed limit: $p' = \text{const}$. This movement of the individual rate of profit is done according to strongly determined laws, but not arbitrarily, i.e., in a way to preserve the same production relations without they are infringed, i.e., the social property of the means of production remains unimpaired even upon a change of the rate of profit! So, the difference here between the individual and the general rate of profit does not give a reason for private appropriation, is not a basis for any private property. A private property is created only in that case of fall of the rate of profit that is accompanied at the same time by respective opposite enhancement of the rate of surplus value. Otherwise, only a difference, resulting not from fall, but from enhancement of the rate of profit **above** the general one, **above $p' = \text{const}$.**, could generate a private property. A rate of profit exceeding the general one, exceeding $p' = \text{const}$., means only one thing—that there is appropriated more surplus value (with certainty by a private way!) than is permitted by the concrete rate of surplus value of the given organic composition in force, i.e., that the rate of surplus value is enhanced more than it is necessary, more than it must be according to the level of the organic composition of capital; it means that more surplus value is appropriated at the cost of the wages, more **s** appropriated at the cost of **v**. So, for the existence of social property, it is necessary that it could not get more than an upper limit is appropriated— the limit of $p' = \text{const}$. The general rate of profit is the utmost limit of the growth of any individual rate of profit. Just like in physics, the velocity of light is **const.** being the utmost limit of all other velocities, so here, the general rate of profit is **const.** being the utmost limit of all other rates of profit.

The individual rate of profit is changed, but in a manner to preserve the same social production relations, through another law already, in another form: $\dfrac{v}{c + v} = $ **const**. According to this law, we obtain:

$$\Delta S' = \Delta p'$$

As it is seen, **S'** not only can rise in a certain case but also can fall in another—in this case, a thing which is completely alien to the capital. "A falling rate of profit does not express a falling rate of surplus value unless the proportion of the value of the constant capital to the quantity of labor power which sets it in motion remains unchanged or the amount of labor power increases in relation to the value of the constant capital."[158] The new moment is that the Law of the tendency of the rate of profit to fall finds its direct realization under socialist mode of production in the law of $\dfrac{v}{c + v} = $ **const**. But in this case, this is not only the general rate of profit which can fall and not only as a tendency, but the individual does, too, and this is done in a regulated way and at a strictly fixed moment only. Its falling is used in order to fall the rate of surplus value. And this fact itself is eloquent enough—s' already loses its significance of being that basic counteracting influence which retains the falling of the rate of profit. The slumping **s'** contributes to, facilitates the lighter slumping of **p'**, and thereby, the introduction of scientific and technical innovations to the production, too, while the rising **s'** retains it—"this reduction is moderated, or checked, by the rise in the rate of surplus value."[159]

We know from Marx that, on the one hand, the rising rate of surplus value at a falling rate of profit causes an acute contradiction between the productive forces and the production relations, creating in this way workers' resistance against the implementation of technical and scientific progress. "The tendency of the rate of profit to fall is bound up with a tendency of the rate of surplus value to rise, hence with a tendency for the rate of labor exploitation to rise."[160]

This was the reason during our "socialism" that all technical and scientific achievements, all innovations were introduced with extreme

---

[158]. Marx, *Capital*, 3:281.
[159]. Ibid., 273.
[160]. Ibid., 279.

difficulties, with Tantalus' torments. By eliminating this reactive factor—the rising **s'**—one of the basic counteracting influences of the free and impetuous implementation of all technical innovations in the production is eliminated, too.

On the other hand, the relative overpopulation, i.e., the unemployment is another factor having a malignant effect on the fall of the rate of profit. Its absence, i.e., the lack of unemployment, under the law $\frac{v}{c + v} = $ **const.**, is transformed into a second cause, contributing to **p'** to fall more quickly.

A third cause, "one of the most important factors checking the tendency of the rate of profit to fall"[161] and thereby, checking the social progress, too, is the depression of wages below the value of labor power. But when the labor power is not a commodity, the wage always corresponds to the value of labor power and in this way, it ceases being another significant factor, too, directed against the falling of the rate of profit. Or, the wage as a self-expanding value contributes to the faster adoption of the novelty, to the faster growing rank of the technical and scientific achievements in the production.

As a reactive factor, the joint-stock capital also drops out, because this fictitious capital as a capital of the speculation simply does not exist, besides all other reasons, because of the fact that there is no monopoly in the system and there cannot be.

Fifth counteracting influence is the foreign trade. The value of commodities in the developed capitalist countries is lower than this one in the poor and underdeveloped countries, because of the higher social productivity of labor, while the prices on the international and the world market are higher than this their national value. In this way, a surplus profit is obtained for the national capital of the economic giants (today's Great Group of the Seven), enhancing in the final reckoning the general rate of profit. The differences in the productivity of labor in the particular countries would not have influenced the general rate of profit in an international or world socialist system, only if these countries work in agreement with the same rate of profit so that, in fact, the difference between foreign and home trade is completely erased and no longer exists.

---

[161]. Marx, *Capital.*, 3:274.

The only factor checking the tendency of the rate of profit to fall can be the cheapening of the constant capital because the productive force of labor leads to that "the value of the constant capital does not increase in the same proportion as its material volume."[162] The increase of the value-composition of the capital is always slower than the increase of its technical-composition having their common influences over the growth of its organic composition.

{By the way, in connection with this subject-matter, a new star of the capitalist propaganda, the serial formal candidate of Nobel Prize appeared who is wreathed in some left mist by the same this propaganda. This economist is noisily sold recently only for that that he is the serial giant of the thought rejecting if not all of Marx then something by Marx—Thomas Piketty "rejects" the Law of the tendency of the rate of profit to fall as fallacious! It looks like Piketty doesn't know that the effect of this objective law was a proven fact during the classic market capitalism in the most developed countries from 1865 to 1895. But in twenty-first century the joint checking influence of aforementioned six counteracting factors in the conditions of the modern state-corporate capitalism is unusually strong, it is stronger than ever—mostly by the incredibly inflated world joint-stock fictitious capital along with the unemployment in disastrous dimensions and the global foreign trade of the multinational capital retain mighty the tendency of the world rate of profit to fall, but not stop it! The modern state-corporate capitalism in no way rejects this law, but just the opposite—proves it, by the simple fact that the organic composition of the social capital in these same countries grew in colossal dimensions and for that reason, the world rate of profit falls observing quite correctly the Law of the tendency of the rate of profit to fall! So, this imitative work *Capital* appears after Marx's original for the second time, but we already know that all great world-historic facts and personages appear, so to speak, twice: the first time as science, the second time as farce. And this is a sufficient reason the Nobel Prize to be awarded!}

In our country and the whole Soviet bloc, technical and scientific progress was slinking with disheartening harrowing of Hell, which was one of the reasons to start to speak and to seek a "new model of socialism." After the crisis of the state monopoly of 1983, an acute need appeared to attach "modern forms to socialism." Indeed, for the

---

[162]. Marx, *Capital*, 3:274.

financial oligarchy of the state-monopoly capital in our parts it was high time that contemporary forms of exploitation were introduced; that the rough, brutal forms of the early capitalism were abandoned and to pass to "self-government" and to "socialist competition" in the economy as well as to "glasnost" and to a new "democracy" in the politics. It was time of a refined and gallant exploitation, all in the spirit of our time, which took no place anyhow still a quarter century later!

But in return, a festival of the Communist church took place in October 1986 in Moscow—all "Communist," "Workers," Christian and "Labor" parties had their council on the royal topic—to examine with concern "the role of the working class in the new conditions of scientific and technical revolution!"[163] Different sermons were pronounced while innocently it was forgotten that Marx envisaged in his day both "the new conditions" of the scientific and technical revolution and the role, which the working class plays in them. Marx had already written that under such conditions to be a man "a productive laborer is . . . not a piece of luck, but a misfortune."[164]

The modern neurotic man placed under these "new conditions," owes his state and his behavior to the contemporary forms of exploitation—more refined, more cultivated, and civilized; exploitation with white gloves and with stiff collars, which is more invisible, but more dangerous. This is perfidy represented like love; exploitation that is more based on relative surplus value and less on absolute one. Still, at the Tenth Congress of the Bulgarian Communist Party in 1970, it was "accounted" and continued to account up to 1989, that the "extensive factors of growth" had been exhausted, and for this reason, a passing to the intensive factors was needed, i.e., the possibilities of the absolute surplus value for the exploitation were exhausted until 1970 and its modern form—the relative surplus value—had to be evoked. But that was not done—until 1989, the working day was continuously prolonged because of "non-fulfillment of the plan" or so-called "working for the holiday"—a practice that was unknown worldwide, except in our country and, who knows, maybe in North Korea, as well.

As it was noticed at the beginning of this chapter, the capitalist production generates as innate an unemployment, furthermore, the

---

[163]. "For Peace and Social Progress," *Trud* newspaper, October 11, 1986. Information by Bulgarian Telegraph Agency.
[164]. Marx, *Capital*, 1:559.

modern high technological capitalist production generates it in colossal dimensions; unemployment, which, according to a European economist, in the next ten years, will be reached until 75 % by the active population. And today, this prognosis startles all the labor market with its black pessimism. But if the people were acquainted well with the economic laws of the capitalism, they would know that under this development of the modern capitalism after twenty-five or thirty years, the unemployment in the advanced states will be not 75 %, but 100 %!

Chapter Four:

The Production Process—A Cycle of Carnot

As various as the world is the variety of its forms, it turns out that in its essence the world is arranged, moved, and directed by the same universal natural laws, which are rather simple, therefore.

Actually, at first sight, it seems that there can be nothing common between two otherwise quite different and so distant sciences—the political economy and the thermodynamics. But during the second reading, it becomes clear that we can vote for accepting certain common principles. Marx and Carnot can scarcely have ever supposed that. The common principles of the two sciences are, however, only one stage to the great unification of all sciences in a General theory of Nature!

So, since the secondary classes in the physics of the thermodynamic systems, we know that to accept a system as such, it is necessary that two conditions must be obligatorily satisfied:

1. The system must be built on an exclusively large number of constructive particles, having chaotic motion;
2. The system must have infinitesimal dimensions, compared to the cosmic objects of the universe.

Any highly developed commodity system with value character, i.e., subordinated to the Law of value, satisfies these two conditions. In other words, any production process, based on large-scale industrial commodity production, represented by its value aspect, could be a "thermodynamic" process. Here, as a constructive particle is represented the basic cell of the value process—the commodity.

The presence of chaotic motion of the constructive particles in occasional and arbitrary directions and magnitudes of their velocities is obligatory for any thermodynamic system in the common case, whereas the directed motion is only a possibility as a special case. Such behavior is presented in the process of expansion of value under the capitalist mode of production—a chaotic motion. Under this mode of production, the commodities have such chaotic motion because of the effect of the Law of anarchy and competition in the production.

We already examined separately each part of the great formula of Marx about the rate of profit as a constant magnitude with its concrete meaning for the socialist production. And since the production process under socialism, as process deprived of exploitation is carried out only under $S' = $ **const.**, it appears the question of how the complete production process would look, provided that the production is always implemented under $S' = $ **const.**, whereupon the wage as a social relation becomes a self-expanding value according to the formula $\Delta v = \Delta(v+s)$.

In thermodynamics, there are three basic parameters, determining in a **qualitative** way the state of a given system: pressure, temperature, and specific volume—**p**, **T**, and **v**. Taken alone, the basic economic indexes in the political economy, being also three—**p′**, **S′**, and $\frac{c+v}{v}$ impose a striking resemblance, which is not only formal—by the resemblance of the symbols, but also by their own contents.

If we examine the process of expansion of value as a "thermodynamic" process, then the "operating body" in this process is the capital as "gasses' mixture" of **c** and **v**, of constant and variable capital, with "volume" (**c+v**). Then its "specific volume" is $\frac{c+v}{v}$. If we examine the production process as a labor process, then the "operating body" is the labor power, but in the production process, it can be seen as a process of expansion of value, it is the total capital (**c+v**), but not only the variable capital **v**. That is why the "pressure" on the "operating body" must be **p′**. Then we have to accept **S′** for its "temperature." Hence, we can establish that **p′** = **const.** represents a "single process," just being an "isobaric" process, **S′** = **const.** is an "isothermal", and $\frac{v}{c+v}$ = **const.** is an "isochoric" process. In this way, the process of expansion of value represents a "polytropic" process and we can represent the entire production process under socialism as a cycle of Carnot.

However, how must the single processes connect in a direct cycle so that the whole production process is possible?

I already scrutinized the succession of the first three processes and explained the need imposing this succession precisely but not as another. And it is as follows:

1. $p' = \text{const.}$

2. $S' = \text{const.}$

3. $\dfrac{v}{c + v} = \text{const.}$

I added that after the third process—$\dfrac{v}{c + v} = \textbf{const.}$, the production process is passed again under $S' = \textbf{const}$. With the latter process the whole cycle is closed, starting again from $p' = \textbf{const.}$, obtaining the look of 1-2-3-4-1. So, in the final analysis, the production on a social scale is always run at a **constant** average rate of surplus value, satisfying the condition $\Delta v = \Delta(v+s)$, which had to be proven.

And to visualize the complete production process as a direct cycle of Carnot, I shall use the **"p-v"** diagram:

Diagram 2

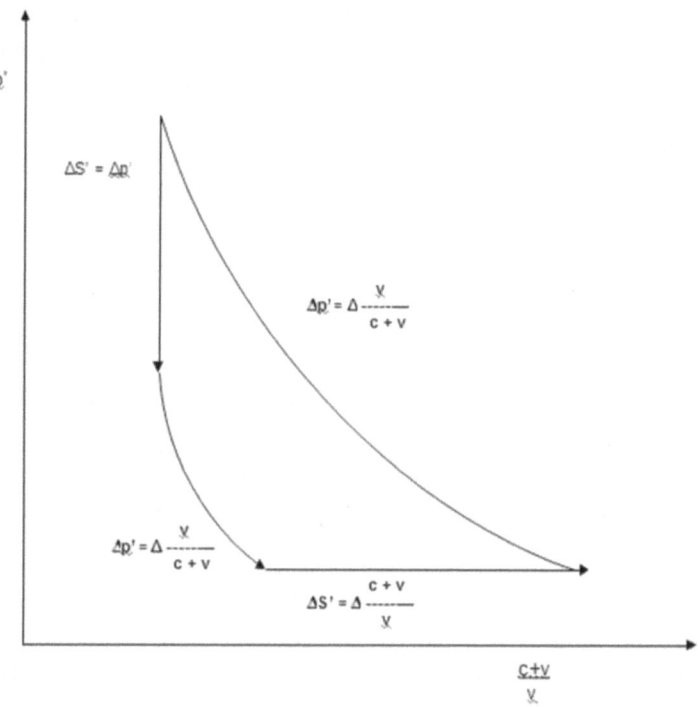

The circular process shows consecutive single processes of the same producer (worker, brigade, enterprise) or parallel simultaneous processes of different producers. In any activity, any process claiming objectivity, it is necessary that an automatism, a clock mechanism is

175

obligatorily present, excluding any subjectivism or, at least, reducing it to the minimum. Such an automatism of the social production can be assured only by its certain repeating cycle, having this look in our case. By this automatic cycle, it is initiated a fully automatic economy independent of exchanges and indexes, independent of the sneeze of some much talked at the present time politician or banker.

It is necessary to note that actually the single processes, as well as the circular process, represent real operational processes of the piston engines of internal combustion than ideal thermodynamic processes of an isolated thermodynamic system. The production based on social property of the means of production represents such an "internal combustion engine," a powerful social engine of expansion of the value, but not a closed and isolated system.

Before and after the process, $S' = $ **const.**, there are two processes— "isobaric" and "isochoric"—during which there is no accomplished work. They serve as **border transitions** of S' in extreme situations. Real work, i.e., real production process, takes place only under $S' = $ **const**. They are two processes, during which the individual S' **moves**— slumps or rises—remaining immobile after that; they are processes where the rate of surplus value is regulated and prepared for its following process, $S' = $ **const.**, which takes place in other, new conditions. In thermodynamics, no work is accomplished during only one process—the isochoric process, while here, the "isobaric" process is the same one. That is a substantial difference between the two sciences.

With respect to the individual capital, the process $p' = $ **const.** is actually a reverse process to the process $\dfrac{v}{c+v} = $ **const.**—the former increases, while the latter decreases the rate of profit p' along with the rate of surplus value S'. And if the process $\dfrac{v}{c+v} = $ **const.** is a process of "condensation" of the labor power towards the means of production, $p' = $ **const.** is a process of "expansion." Just like the process, $S' = $ **const.**, as a second process is a process of "condensation," while as a fourth process it is a process of "expansion." The processes $p' = $ **const.** and $\dfrac{v}{c+v} = $ **const.** are two border states of the production process, when the quantitative accumulations impose qualitative modifications; from this point of view and only from it, they are some auxiliary, some subsidiary processes of the production process, realizing under $S' =$ **const**. These two processes are "phase transitions" to pass from one state to another. At the same time, the different levels of S' that are determined by these processes, represent, so to say, different energy levels for the workers in the works, just like that applies for the electrons in the atom in quantum physics.

Thermodynamics can once again render a priceless favor to the political economy.

We know that the efficiency of a direct cycle is increased when the minimum temperature of the operating body is decreased and the maximum temperature is increased. Or, to enhance the effectiveness of the social production, to increase the efficiency of the social engine, its minimal "temperature," i.e., a rate of surplus value, S'_{min}, should be decreased and the maximum, S'_{max}, should be increased. In other words, that means that like at a Robin Hood's manner the society will obtain the greatest mass of surplus value from guiding branches, high-tech industry for example, but at the same time will be developed and "stimulated" through its relatively more expensive payment the labor power employed in the less developed branches, i.e., with lower organic composition and with slower turnover, as in rural economy, for example.

Chapter Five

The Circulation and Circuit of Capital

Capitalist mode of production is such that there the productive forces are used as a means in a manner that the aim is to expand the value. Socialist mode of production is such that there the value is used as a means in a manner that the aim is to develop the productive forces. The expansion of value is an end in itself of the capital, as Marx says, the motive and the purpose of production; it is the starting and the closing point. "The means—unconditional development of the productive forces of society—comes continually into conflict with the limited purpose, the self-expansion of the existing capital."[165]

The purpose and the means change places under socialism. The expansion of the value is no longer fanaticism, it is not an end in itself, the society does not anymore produce for the production itself, but the purpose is "the full and free development of every individual."[166] The purpose is the continuous and unlimited development of the productive forces and the means of it is the expansion of the value. In other words, the process of self-expansion of value is subordinated to the labor process, while it is the opposite case with the capital—the labor process is subordinated to the self-expanding value process. But when and how the self-expanding value process is able to be subordinated? When does the force of money be able to be mastered, being now already transformed into a fetish?

The almighty power of the money is dethroned only when the root of the capital is cut down—its operation in the production, from where it saps its vital forces and from where it draws energy. Only then the functioning of money as a bribed means is stopped.

The process of transformation of money into capital is done during

---

[165]. Marx, *Capital*, 3:292.
[166]. Ibid., 1:653.

the circulation according to formula **M-C-M'**. Since the labor power does not enter from the production into the circulation as a commodity, still in the first act, **M-C**, the purchase, the link **C** is interrupted, because the labor power is not a commodity anymore under the social property of the means of production. In this way, money cannot be transformed into commodity.

After that, the second act becomes impossible, as well, **C-M'**, the sale, i.e., that the commodity is transformed again into money and especially into grown money. Or, there is no purchase of the labor power at the beginning, so that there will be a need for the sale of this labor power then. So, since the labor power is not a commodity, it is just the latter, which stops the transformation of money into capital. "The change must, therefore, take place in the commodity bought by the first act, **M-C**, but not in its value . . ."[167]

Those words of Marx are heavy evidence that in order for the labor power to not be a commodity, it should not affirm dully that it does not have any value, as the ex-pseudo-science of political economy of socialism did, but to search the alteration within the act of **M-C** when and how its purchase is impossible. And since the labor power is not a commodity, from the formula of the circuit of the **productive** capital, we may work out the formula of the circuit of the social production under socialism in its productive form:

$$MP \searrow \qquad\qquad ----MP \searrow$$
$$\quad Pr \ldots \quad C' -- M' - C(MP) \ldots \qquad Pr'.$$
$$LP \nearrow \qquad\qquad ----LP \nearrow$$

This circuit, as we know from Marx, means a reproduction—"not only production but a periodical reproduction of surplus value,"[168] as well.

The fact that the labor power is not a commodity, that it is outside the circulation, could not be shown in this formula, it could not be directly visualized, but only noted, by specially mentioning which is precisely the commodity—the means of production; that is why I put them into brackets. The labor power, however, we should show as an

---

[167]. Marx, *Capital*, 1:192.
[168]. Ibid., 2:76.

element, as a constitutive part of the production, as one of the factors of the social process of production, because "values enter into the process of production which do not enter into the process of circulation."[169]

In the same way, from the general formula of the circuit of the **commodity**-capital, we work out the formula that will apply to socialism:

$$C' -- M' - C(MP) \ldots \begin{matrix} ——MP \\ \\ ——LP \end{matrix} \Big\rangle \ Pr' \ldots C'(C'') - \text{under extended reproduction}$$

The circuit of the **money** capital under social property is done according to the formula whose general look is modified:

$$M - C(MP) \ldots \begin{matrix} ——MP \\ \\ ——LP \end{matrix} \Big\rangle \ Pr \ldots C' -- M'$$

"As for the process of hoarding, it is common to all commodity production,"[170] i.e., under socialism inclusive. Here also the formation of "the money-accumulation fund serves as a reserve fund for counterbalancing disturbances in the circuit."[171]

This formula, however, does not express the complete process of monetary relations, but its production side only. Since the labor power as a commodity is absent in the circulation sphere, the formula hides some monetary relations—the payment of the labor power, for example. This is so because here the accent is put on the monetary form of the socialist production. Now, the act of **M-LP** does not mean **M-C** anymore, which is the same for the capital—purchase of a commodity of labor power, attraction of a hired worker. On its part, the act, **M-LP**, excludes the act, **LP-M**, the sale of labor power.

In the final analysis, the integrated, the unfolded formula of the circuit of the **industrial** capital under socialism should look like:

---

[169]. Marx, *Capital*, 2:76
[170]. Ibid., 98.
[171]. Ibid., 100.

MP   MP   MP

M-C(MP) ... ⟩Pr... C'-M'. M-C(MP)...⟩Pr... C'-M'. M-C(MP)... ⟩Pr...

LP   LP   LP

So, the act of payment of the labor power cannot be expressed in these formulas, but the formulas themselves show clearly that the labor power is not a commodity, is not liable to exchange, is not subject to commerce, and does not find any place in the stages of the circulation, i.e., the labor power cannot be subject either to purchase nor to sale. In this way, the labor power does not return any more into production as a commodity from the circulation.

Another matter is the payment of the labor power in the circulation itself, of workmen employed in the circulation. How would the salary look in commerce, how should the commercial workmen be paid?

The difficulty comes really from the fact that they do not create, but only realize a value. In other words, they cannot be subordinated to the law, $S' = \mathbf{const.}$, simply because they do not produce a new value that includes the surplus value. Besides that, the commercial workmen are not homogenous in their activities and qualifications, but perform various functions concerning the output marketing. The commercial work related to the immediate marketing of the commodity production is one, while the work related to processing, loading, storage it, for example, is quite different. The workers of load-unload activity, for instance, the same way as the industrial workers, work under some given productivity of labor. And the wages and the productivity of labor in industry are bound in direct dependence by the law of $p' = \mathbf{const}$. Then, accordingly, the service technique, the technical level of the commercial labor, the individual wage is determined as a basic wage. Its increase or decrease may then be bound in direct dependence on either the turnover or the commercial profit with a fixed coefficient to them. The same way as the industrial workers, the scientific and technical progress in the commerce also leads to revolutionary changes in the productivity of labor. That's why, until an accelerated accumulation of means of production is realized, workmen's working time should be respectively decreased, according to the law $\dfrac{v}{c+v} = \textbf{const.}$, as long as it is necessary.

The work of the commercial workmen, directly employed in commodities marketing is organized in another way. Their salaries, the increase or decrease, depends on this marketing only, i.e., on the commodity turnover. Since the salary in the commerce also is established by the value of labor power, the basic salary of the commercial workman cannot be different in this aspect from that one of the industrial worker. However, his concrete movement up or down depends not on the rate of profit or the rate of surplus value, which for this worker there is not, but on the quantity of the costs of circulation as well as on turnover's time. The more the worker cuts down the costs of circulation as well as turnover's time, the more his salary will grow and vice versa. So, it should be most successful, as it has been always, to bind the growth of commercial workman's salary as a percentage of the commodity turnover.

Chapter Six

The Market

In volume III of *Capital*, in chapter 27, as anywhere else actually, in a short analysis in braces, in a space of little more than a page, it is seen through not only the genius but the inimitable scientific modesty of the great Engels—a scientist who is God matched of Marx! There he notices with mastery and accuracy the economic conflict of our time—the abrupt expansion of the industrial production and the inadequate and sluggish response of the market. "What the former turns out in months, can scarcely be absorbed by the latter in years."[172] The objective economic laws of capitalism create such social conditions at which "the extension of the markets cannot keep pace with the extension of production. The collision becomes inevitable."[173] Within the framework of the capitalistic mode of production, the contemporary capital, being a state-monopoly capital, tries to resolve this conflict through state-monopoly regulation of the production and the market through the quantity of commodities produced by several powerful concerns and through the agreement, the regulation of their prices between them. And this is the most evident proof of the bankruptcy of "the old boasted freedom of competition."[174]

The slow extension of the market, its laziness in a profound disruption with the extension of the production is first of all due to the lagging and somewhere even absent solvent demand of the enormous mass of consumers in one country of articles of consumption, as all people of wage labor are, as well as of means of production mostly by the industrial small consumers, i.e., the market narrows by the low incomes of the majority of consumers, resulting from the regulated "incomes policy," on the one hand, as well as by the high centralization of capital in **I** department of the social production, on the other hand. That is why, the production belches produce, but the market cannot consume

---

[172]. Marx, *Capital*, 3:506.
[173]. Engels, *Socialism: Utopian and Scientific*, 1:140.
[174]. Marx, *Capital*, 3:506.

it. That is "a self-dissolving contradiction."[175] But when the demand both of articles of consumption and of means of production become constantly solvent, which is reached through strictly specified economic laws only, the market will be able to consume the entire industrial produce for a much shorter time than that is done under the capitalist mode of production—in terms that are very close to the terms of production, i.e., then the production and the market will be in synchrony and in unity.

> For **the market price** of identical commodities, each, however, produced under different individual circumstances, **to correspond to the market value and not to deviate from it either by rising above or falling below it**, it is necessary that the pressure exerted by different sellers upon one another be sufficient to bring enough commodities to market to fill the social requirements, i.e., a quantity for which society **is capable of paying** the market value.[176]

If the pressure of the competition is slack and the sellers are not able to take out this mass of commodities on the market—the commodities should be sold **above** their market value. If the pressure is too strong, i.e., the mass of the products exceeds these social requirements—the commodities are sold **below** their market value. And Marx adds that under social requirements, it has to understand the solvent social requirements, i.e., the solvent social demand. So, in order for the market price to correspond to the market value, but not to deviate upwards or downwards around it, the mass of commodities on the market must correspond to the social demand. Just this is achieved with the articles of consumption, for example, when on a social scale $\Delta v = \Delta(v+s)$, or more clearly is seen also by the expression after the accumulation $(v+s) = (c+v+s)II$ – the mass of commodities neither exceeds nor lags behind, but coincides with their social demand, i.e., the solvent social necessity, the solvent social demand $(v+s)$, coincides with the mass of commodities on the market $(c+v+s)II$ and the pressure of the sellers is neither stronger nor slacker of the necessary one. And that is the first condition, after Marx, in order for the commodities to be in a position to be sold **at** their values—the market price has to coincide with the market value.

Marx notes "that the 'social demand,' i.e., the factor which regulates the principle of demand," is determined by "the ratio of total surplus

---

[175]. Marx, *Capital*, 3:507.
[176]. Ibid., 212 (bolding is mine—T.B.)

value to wages,"[177] i.e., by the average rate of surplus value, which must be invariable, in order for this social demand to be in a position to coincide with the social supply—the mass of commodities on the market.

Marx teaches us that when supply and demand mutually cover each other, then the market prices coincide with the production prices of the commodities. When the price passes each other with the value, if the demand vastly exceeds the supply, the market price is determined by the commodities produced under the worst conditions. On the contrary, if the supply vastly exceeds the demand, the market price is determined by the commodities produced under optimum conditions. This is why the aim of the same rate of profit is precisely that—to place all producers under the same conditions of production and to make the market price to coincide in this way with the production price, and the supply to concur always to the demand. So, in the general case, the market prices coincide with the production prices, because supply and demand are always covered one by the other. And supply and demand are always covered, because the price and the value always coincide, i.e., the purchase price and the produced value are always the same things.

The market price coincides with the production price of the commodity still because of the fact that with the same rate of profit all production conditions are equalized, i.e., there are no commodities produced in the worst and the best conditions—they are produced under equal conditions, which means that the market value and price are no longer determined by commodities, produced under different, but under the same production conditions, with which the market price coincides with the production one. With the same rate of profit accepted within the production, all conditions under which the commodities are produced are equalized—regarding prices, taxes, turnovers, technical facilities—instead of making them remain under the worst or under the optimum conditions, in this manner, influencing later their market value and their market price.

When the individual value of a given commodity is below the market one, under the average general rate of profit a surplus profit is realized. That is done upon innovations in the production. "A capitalist working with improved but not as yet generally adopted methods of production sells below the market price, but above his individual price of production; his rate of profit rises until competition levels it out . . ."[178]

---

[177]. Marx, *Capital*, 3:213.
[178]. Ibid., 269.

Under the same general rate of profit, the application of new and improved methods of production before they became generally adopted, impose that one sells also at a price different (lower) from the market price, but not higher than its individual production price, because it coincides with its value, expressed in the fact that the rate of profit in this case does not enhance, but remains the same, i.e., there is no surplus profit. The individual production price that is lower than the market price will have guaranteed faster turnover only, until the market price equalizes with it, but nothing more. There is surplus profit for the industrial capitalists when they produce under more favorable conditions than the averages. But by the same rate of profit, the production conditions are equally favorable for all. Then, since all producers work, not only under optimum but under the same conditions it is precisely for that, there does not exist surplus profit to come from the difference between the individual production price and the market price.

The market price of the commodity could be enhanced above the production price, but not beyond the limit of its own produced value (under the capitalistic mode of production). That is why, the market price cannot exceed the production price when the value and the price coincide—there is no the substance (i.e., the value), making possible that the price goes up above it. The price can rise only because and only when there is a value above it. The prices, for example, in the case of inflation, rise because the commodities have value, which they, the prices, gain on. If there was no value above them, the prices could not rise.

The production price is the regulating price around which the market prices fluctuate under the average rate of profit. Under the same rate of profit, the production price is regulating one again but represents also a limit, a maximum price, below and until which could pulsate the market prices. Under the same rate of profit, the market prices could be equal or lower, but never higher than the production prices of the commodities. In only one case, a special case, the market price could exceed the production price—when in the circulation, the merchant has invested additional capital, which must be restored by the price. But that does not mean at all that the price is higher than the value. On the contrary, it coincides with it again.

The market price could be equal or lower than the production price. If the demand exceeds the supply for any length of time and thereby makes the market price higher than the production price for a long time, that means that there is a serious infringement somewhere, a certain disorganization in the whole reproduction process of socialism, having led to passing each other between value and price. In other words, the general rate of profit has ceased to be the same but has transformed into average and socialism has transformed into capitalism!

The reason of the passing each other between value and price is the average rate of profit, i.e., the equalization of the general rate of profit through the competition, i.e., the confirmation as an average magnitude of the various values into an aggregate production price. The passing each other between value and price exists in the case of competition as well as in the case of monopoly, resulting in both cases of the equalization of the profit—more strongly expressed in the first case and less in the second one. Namely, the competition makes this equalization of the values into an average production price, while the monopoly reaches that in another way—the monopoly high price above the value in one case is compensated by a monopoly low price below the value in another case within the created aggregate value. So, in both cases, the prices fluctuate around their values. While through the same general rate of profit, price and value coincide, yet with respect not only to the average composition of the capital, but to any other one. On its part, the unity of price and value establishes a balance, equilibrium between supply and demand, which, in its turn, leads to the coincidence of the market price with the production price. And "the balancing of supply and demand is the equivalent of . . . elimination of the influence of competition."[179] So, **only** the balance, the equilibrium between supply and demand within a free market (i.e., without any monopoly) may eliminate the competition and nothing else, no administrative act. But this equilibrium must be incessantly maintained in order that the competition may be eliminated permanently and forever and along with it, the deviations between value and price will be eliminated, too. The monopoly removes the competition, too, but it does not eliminate the contradictions between value and price, contrariwise, it intensifies them. The monopoly is the bigger from the two evils of capitalism—it is a full negation and trammels of its own mode of production. The monopoly is a bare negation of the competition and it is not a solution of the acute contradictions of capitalism. That is why, the competition is made a cult by the apologists of this system and, as it is always under capitalism, "competition has to shoulder the responsibility of explaining all the meaningless ideas of the economists, whereas it should rather be the

---

[179]. Marx, *Capital*, 3:974.

economists who explain competition."[180] Nowadays, the competition is made a heal-all again by looking for a muzzle for the monopoly, while its restraint is reduced to antimonopoly legislation only without eradicating it at all. But today, as in the past, too, the competition is still understood solely with respect to its positive role as a certain motor of progress, but its negative role is missed, and, namely, that the transfusion of capital from a sphere of production into another as well as within the same sphere goes together with enormous spillage and wasting of social labor and means; with useless and needless expenses and even extravagance of social labor time instead of economizing it; with some stoppage or lag in the development of the productive forces, in spite of their common push ahead as a whole. Namely, this negative side of the competition is abolished by the same general rate of profit, eliminating the competition between the **capitals**. But the competition of the production, i.e., its positive side, is preserved under another form—as a competition of the **labor power**, as a competition for enhancing incomes, and namely—the wages. Just it—the wage— emboldens, stimulates the incessantly and impetuously introduction of new technologies, which bring new and increasingly higher incomes to the workers that put them into motion. While by eliminating the competition between the capitals, the spillage of social labor is stopped, an economy of labor time is realized, which, on its part, gives greater effectiveness of this economic system than the capitalist system does.

The ceaseless aspiration for maximum profit leads to that the different rates of profit are ceaselessly confirmed as an average magnitude in an elemental way by the competition to a general rate of profit, i.e., the general rate of profit as an average one is looking for such a level that, in the final reckoning, the biggest capital only may impose itself in the competition and wishes to impose to all its competitors its own rate of profit, which is no longer average but a monopoly. So, with the development of the concentration and especially of the centralization of the capital, an inevitable bankruptcy of the free competition is reached; the capitalism of the free market is put to an end and through the monopoly capitalism, the state-monopoly capitalism is reached, such the modern capitalism is already one hundred years from the First World War on. So, the competition, glorified and magnified at the average general rate of profit is burdened by inheritance, genetically inclined to its self-denial and crashes. The **elemental** equalization of the

---

[180]. Ibid., 978

different rates of profit into a general rate of profit is just the boomerang of the free competition, which returns to it to kill it. Under the capitalism of the free market, the lure, the bait for the migration of the capital among the various branches of the production is not the value, but the production price, which differs from it. That's why, at their coincidence, which occurs with the same rate of profit only, this migration stops; it becomes useless—should a capital search the price or the value in a given sphere, this is the same thing. Under different rates of profit, the migration of the capital is finally over when the conditions of appropriation of the profit become equalized. While under the same rate of profit, when the conditions of appropriation are initially equalized, the migration of capital is not started at all. This migration, this transfusion of capital is not necessary at all because through the same rate of profit all producers are placed not only in the same conditions, but they are placed in optimum production conditions and that's why searching for maximum benefit in another sphere, in another branch of the production, is not necessary.

At the average general rate of profit, only in the case of capitals of average composition the price coincides with the value of the commodity. "All other capitals, of whatever composition, tend toward this average under pressure of competition."[181] That means, one way or another, there is such a tendency that the production prices become a transformed form of the values. Instead of this being painfully done by the competition and never in a position to get realized, the result is obtained immediately by the same rate of profit. The competition strives for different capitals in their organic composition, but of equal mass, to tear off equal shares from the total mass of surplus value that is produced by the total social capital; it strives for distribution of the entire surplus value proportionally to the mass of the capital. What the competition cannot do, the same rate of profit can do! With which the competition drops out as a necessary force for this purpose, it becomes useless as a factor that regulates both the production and market.

With the competition, why are false impressions created on the surface of the economic life? Because the competition, whose task is to equalize the various rates of profit, by its action incessantly makes the prices deviate from their values and that's why the things are permanently set upside-down, conversely, and "thus everything appears

---

[181]. Marx, *Capital*, 3:204.

reversed in competition,"[182] i.e., it seems as if the value is not determined by the labor time as well as the nature of surplus value as if is not consisting of unpaid surplus labor. Everything comes to its own place with the same general rate of profit after eliminating the influence of the competition in this respect precisely—in determining the general rate of profit. The competition distorts the pictures, Marx says, and says the truth. But the monopoly, on its side, openly replaces or eliminates them.

Since under the same general rate of profit all commodities are produced under equal and optimum conditions, they are sold neither below nor above their individual values but precisely **at** their values. And that is only a preliminary prerequisite, which, if the risk of the market did not exist, would have been absolutely realizable. However, because of the presence of a certain threshold of an unpredictability of the market, the real individual rates of profit will depend on their realization of the market and without being obligatory they are equal, they will endeavor to be equal. After the acceptance of the general rate of profit as equal, each producer is really interested in being equalized to it, to realize his individual rate of profit up to the amount of the general one, after he has the prerequisites for that. The workers themselves are most interested in working at the same rate of profit, because thus and only thus they can receive the possible maximum, but not the possible minimum of their wages related to a given production cycle. The same rate of profit is an aim, a minimum task, which must be accomplished on the market, but not guaranteed rate of profit, which will be surely obtained even if the company had negative economic results. On the contrary, the underdeveloped companies are not encouraged at all by guaranteed rate of profit. It's nothing like that. Any rate of profit must be really marketed under normal economic conditions. Any growth of the individual rate of profit above the general is allowed but which must be immediately equalized with the general rate of profit through an increase in the wage. Nobody forces anybody to have a rate of profit higher than that which it will be able to realize. And it's not to guarantee obtaining profits without any effort. What is guaranteed, what is achieved with the same rate of profit, is the preparation for the sale, for the realization of the commodity of any producer under maximum favorable conditions—created by the prerequisite that just in the price of the commodity is included its realization under the best production conditions.

---

[182]. Ibid., 243.

From here on, if under these optimal conditions, the best possible ones, created in advance, the particular producer does not manage to obtain a rate of profit that is equal to the general one, but lower, he has to reproach only himself, because the profit obtained will not be sufficient for the normal reproduction of the enterprise. If the rate of profit realized is lower than the general one, although a higher rate has been accounted in the price of the commodity that will be a problem for this producer only. So, his aim is to reach the general rate of profit. It is clear that it is possible that there are, in certain similar cases, some temporary deviations, some separate fluctuations between the market price and value, but they should be an exception only—rare and occasional. It is obvious that the market does not exclude the possibility that a difference is able to appear between the rate of profit included in advance at the price of the commodity (the general rate of profit) and this rate of profit, which is realized indeed afterward in the real reproduction process. The market will show not whether it is possible to exist there the same rate of profit but that there not be exist on it an individual rate of profit higher than the general one, accepted for the same in the production. These are contradictions between production and circulation, between industry and market. There is the same rate of profit in the production, but which is in a position to be different (lower) under the influence of the market, *only as an exception*!

If the individual rate of profit under invariable productivity of labor after its sojourn on the market falls below the general one, that means that a part of the surplus value had not been realized, which otherwise had been accounted in the price of the commodity with the general rate of profit but the slow turnover, for example, because of a restricted market, had not restored the whole value of the commodity during the process of its realization. Does that mean that in this case the price (the market one) must fall below the value of the commodity in order that it obtain still some realization and some surplus value? Yes, it's like that, but the loss remains a loss or rather—a missed benefit! It is possible to be compensated by the following faster turnover or by a series of turnovers, which, by creating a greater mass of surplus value, are able to equalize the given rate of profit with the general one. This analysis shows that under invariable productivity of labor, *as an exception*, there could be a **fall** in prices, but a **rise**—not once! A barrier of that is the general rate of profit accepted as the same and constant magnitude by all producers. Under increased productivity of labor, the prices become

191

lower, but they are not lowered, i.e., they coincide with the values of the commodities again, but do not fall below them.

If in the production of a certain commodity produce, there is some advanced capital of 100 units ($C = 85c+15v$) at a general rate of profit of $p' = 20$ % and a rate of surplus value of $s' = 133$ %, that means that this produce must be sold at a price of 120 units. However, if the market did not approve this produce and after a given turnover it was not realized in full, but the value marketed, which was turned back, for example, 115 units, then 5 units of the preliminarily calculated profit are not enough for the further normal reproduction. The amount of 115 restores completely the advanced capital, but the profit in it is not sufficient for the further reproduction, making the real rate of profit slump to 15 %. So, the volume of the commodity produce must include the advanced capital + the profit, which is preliminarily pursued as a goal, because in the contrary case, it would be necessary to seek later a compensation for the missed benefits.

In the given isolated case, the market price could slump below the production price and that means below the value, too. But the opposite case is not possible even as an exception, i.e., a market price above the production price, a market price above the value, because the production price is an utmost price—the general rate of profit is not average in order to seek any compensation in the fluctuations around the value, i.e., there is nothing produced above the value in order so the price can rise above it, in order that the market price can exceed the production price. If, however, in the opposite case, the producer is realized by faster turnover, a commodity produce of 125 units instead of 120, that means that the turnover brought 5 units of newly created value more than the 120 which were normally calculated. Then, these 5 units must be distributed so that the rate of profit must remain the same with the general one, i.e., in order to remain $p' = 20$ %, a part of these $5(v+s)$ must be converted into wages, in our case: $4v$ ($+1s$). And that means that the rate of surplus value enhanced by the turnover must be lowered to such a level that the growth of the wages will keep the rate of profit invariable, after which it, the rate of surplus value, must also remain invariable again. In this case, s' slumps from its enhancement of 167 % to 111 %, i.e., it slumps even lower than its initial level of 133 %. It is clear that if such an enhancement is a single act, then the slumping of s' is also single. It is an additional payment of the labor power, additional wages (26.7%), except the restored already advanced wages of $15v$, which must be re-advanced for the following cycle of the production process. And this 1s could be an additional payment of the management team, of the administrative staff for its successful marketing aiming at the realization of the production. In other words, any improved organization of labor in the production, realizing on the market, under the conditions of invariable productivity of labor, instead of enhancing the rate of profit which remains invariable, enhances the wages through the reverse motion of the rate of surplus value—s' slumps in a manner that the growth Δv detracts the growth $\Delta p'$. Thus, the enhancement of the rate of profit (which can be done by different ways) is always reduced to be invariable and the same rate of profit—just through s'. Any enhancement of the rate of profit in other (capitalist) conditions means here an enhancement of the wages under these (socialist) conditions with keeping p' on the same level. In the contrary case, if these $5(v+s)$ remain as $5s$, as surplus value, they will be appropriated in a private way, with which the rate of profit will enhance but it will not anymore remain the same.

Chapter Seven

The Rent

In spite of the fact that under "socialism" in our country, there was no private landed property, there existed a rent because the owner of the land was the state. The rent is such a tax, which squeezes out the labor power of the agricultural laborer, thus alienating him from the land. The capital as "a perennial pumping-machine of surplus labor"[183] here, in the village, depresses the wage below the value of labor power even more than in the case of an industrial worker.

"A much more general and important fact, however, is the depression of the actual farm laborer's wage below its normal average, so that part of it is deducted to become part of the lease money and thus, in the guise of ground rent, it flows into the pocket of the landlord," (this was the state until 1990 in Bulgaria and USSR) "rather than the laborer."[184]

When the state is an owner of the land, then "rent and taxes coincide,"[185] i.e., the rent is a tax and the tax is a rent. When the state is an owner and lets out on lease "all the land suitable for agriculture . . . there would not be any land not paying rent."[186] Then the landed property ceases to act for the immediate producer as an absolute barrier to his labor and capital, but it continues to act as a relative barrier even after that, Marx says. So, the full state property of land is a relative barrier, while the private property is an absolute barrier for the agricultural production. The absolute barrier of the landed property is the access to the land, the admission to its cultivation by its owner after payment of due tax. That is why both state and private landed property—large and small—appear "as a barrier and hindrance to agriculture."[187] In volume III of *Capital*, in the part of rent, Marx puts under slashing, branding,

---

[183]. Marx, *Capital*, 3:928.
[184]. Ibid., 716.
[185]. Ibid., 893.
[186]. Ibid., 863.
[187]. Ibid., 917.

brilliant criticism, to a computer-precision evaluation, and to a logical sentence the small and large private property of land. The giant Marx! A criticism, evaluation, and sentence that are still of importance today, one hundred and fifty years later, and will be ever of importance until there is capitalism! A dissection of this society and diagnosis that is still valid with the same force now—that is the *Capital*! Every word of his analysis is still topical with the same force today and there is nothing obsolete in it. A nonpareil Marx! *Capital*—this is an eternal book! *Capital* is a capital work, which work did not become a capital, but in which the capital is understood only through the work, it becomes clear that basically of the capital is the work; a capital work separating the capital against the work in the capital-work antinomy! A capital work, which emanates the knowledge that the fate of the capital is decided by the work!

Nowadays, the rent is an anachronism while under social property of the means of production it is an absurdity, it just does not take place. It is like that because the "landed property differs from other kinds of property in that it appears superfluous and harmful at a certain stage of development, even from the point of view of the capitalist mode of production."[188]

The surplus profit—the source of rent in the village—is obtained for the particular industrial (invested in industry or agriculture) or commercial capital, working in conditions that are more favorable than the average. There exist two types of surplus profit: the first, created by the capital functioning in the production and the second, created by a natural force. This surplus profit is abolished by the same rate of profit, at which any difference above it is equalized by an increase of the wage according to the principle of the communicating vessels, which v and s are, i.e., any rate of profit above the general must be lowered to the general rate through enhancement of the wage. Thus, by the abolition of the surplus profit, in the industry there cannot evince the social relation of **capital**, and in the agriculture—the social relation of **rent**, as well.

Under social property of the means of production, there cannot exist ground rent, because there does not exist a surplus profit, which can be transformed into rent. There cannot be a rent because the social property excludes both the private and state landed property and thereby—the monopolization of particular parcels of land. There is simply no owner detached from the land, which receives a rent from the cultivating it

---

[188]. Marx, *Capital*, 3:711.

farmers. Owner and manager are the same juridical person. Just therefore under the social property of the means of production, there cannot exist any price of the land. Not only because the land does not have any value. The land as a means of production cannot be subject to sale-trade; it does not have exchange value. The land does not have any price, because does not exist any rent, which, namely, determines this price through its transformation into capital, bringing incomes to its owner in the form of rate of interest. Under social property, the land does not have exchange value, being the first commodity of all possible, having ceased being a commodity according to both conditions which determine it—value and exchange value.

The rate of profit in the agriculture can and must be the same, but as a basis here, it must be taken under all other equal conditions, the worst land by its fertility (or location) so that the incomes of the agricultural laborers from the lands with the best fertility, which in the common case are higher, to be received in the same manner like the incomes of the industrial workers, which increase unassisted their own productivity of labor. In other words, if from their best lands the agricultural laborers have received marketed produce that is two or three times larger in comparison with those ones employed at the worst lands, that reflects immediately on the increase of their wages in the same way as that would have been done by the workers at any factory, having marketed under equal conditions production of different quantity—the increase of the wage is precisely as much as to preserve the same rate of profit. So, what would have meant differential rent (I or II) in other relations, an income, received by the parasite landowner, now is an income received additionally by the immediate farmer producer.

With the same rate of profit from the richer and more fertile soil, the agricultural laborers will receive higher incomes as wages, but not any differential rent for anyone. At the same rate of profit and the same invested capitals, the production price is the same for the produce received from both the best and the worst soils, no matter what their natural fertility is. The different fertility of the soils at the same price will give different incomes to the agricultural laborers, but nothing more. It is an analogy of the capitals invested in industry, where to the same number of units of capital—to 100 units, for example, different levels of productivity of labor may correspond. However here, in agriculture, the same organic composition, giving the same productivity of labor, can give different produce because of the different fertility of the soils. The same combine-operator with the same harvester combine can harvest for the same time the same parcel with the yield of wheat of 5000 kg per hectare in a geographical region of Bulgaria, say in Dobroudja, but with the yield of 2000 kg per hectare in another region of Bulgaria, in Macedonia, for example! The same productivity of labor gives different results and different incomes! So, this natural inequality could not be compensated at some significant extent except only by more rational agriculture and higher productivity of labor. "So far as the increase in productivity is concerned . . . the increase in absolute fertility of the total area does not eliminate this inequality, but either increases it, leaves it unchanged, or merely reduces it."[189]

If the free importation of given culture is not taken into consideration, "the price of production on the worst soil, . . . is always the one regulating the market price . . ."[190] So, the general rate of profit as element taking part in the formation of the production price is included for this purpose to the cost prices, invested in the worst soil—in order for it to become a regulating market price for all producers of this kind of agricultural commodity. Hence, the production price is constant, if the market price is determined during the given period by the capital, invested in the worst soil.

With decreasing productiveness of successive capital investments of the same parcel, which otherwise would have provided a basis to a differential rent II, the production from the poorest soil becomes useless and for this reason is stopped, making in this way the production price **reduce**, being already determined by another soil, more fertile up to this moment, but accepting since this moment the regulating role of the worst soil. There can be, Marx says, "a **rise in** the price of production and an absolute decrease in productivity only if investments of capital could be made in none but the worst soil."[191] But this case is rather an exception, while the rule is the continual improvement of the natural fertility of the same soil, i.e., an increase of the incomes of the agricultural laborers by intensive cultivation instead of extensive one of the lands. At invariable production prices, the additional wage increases if the agriculture is intensive, but not extensive. There can be a diminution of the additional wage with subsiding of the production price at an invariable productivity of the additional capital investments, in which

---

[189]. Marx, *Capital*, 3:751.
[190]. Ibid., 750.
[191]. Ibid., 773 (bolded by me—T.B.).

case the poorest soil ceases being a soil regulating the market price (see *Capital*, volume III, differential rent II, second case). Everywhere, instead of rent, under the socialist mode of production, it must understand as additional wage for the agricultural laborers. There can be a rise in the price of production in case of decrease of the productivity of the worst soil as well as by a free import of the culture. The increased supply from the better soils can make the production from the worst soil useless and even stop it; then the production price changes, too. It lowers.

Landed property as social but not as private property is no longer "the barrier which does not permit any new investment of capital in hitherto uncultivated . . . land."[192] Contrariwise, the social property of land encourages the careful relation and the good management of both the old and the new capital investments in uncultivated as well as in cultivable lands.

As concerns the absolute rent, there cannot exist such by no means under socialist mode of production, since it is a rent "arising out of the excess of value over the price of production."[193] But such an excess simply is not there at the same rate of profit. Also, there is no landowner alienated from the producer. All of that makes the absolute rent pointless.

By accepting the assumption that the value of commodity passes each other with its production price and that the agriculture has a low organic composition of capital, Marx deduces the absolute rent, at which the agricultural products have a value higher than their production price. That is valid "for that form of rent . . . which can obtain only so long as this assumption holds good."[194] Absolute rent—this is a rent which enters the production price, in contrast to the differential rent, which is rent out of the price. In the capitalist system where the price fluctuates around the value of the commodity, the production price "coincides with its value only by way of exception."[195] What an exception is there, it is a law here! In other words, when the value coincides with the price, the absolute rent no longer holds along with the above assumption. "Wherever this assumption no longer holds, the corresponding form of rent likewise no longer holds."[196] The absolute rent, which is a tax

---

[192]. Marx, *Capital*, 3:860.
[193]. Ibid., 863.
[194]. Ibid., 858.
[195]. Ibid., 856.
[196]. Ibid., 858-859.

added to the price, is superfluous under social property because, firstly, there is no landowner, who receives this tax, and secondly, the price coincides with the value and in this way, even for the agricultural products, the value cannot be higher than their price. The absolute rent leads to a rise in prices of the agricultural products. But when it does not exist, this rise in prices does not exist, either. The lack of absolute rent is a serious cause for the prices of the agricultural commodities to be lower and thereby these commodities—cheaper, in comparison with the case when it exists. The lack of rent in general means that the individual rate of profit is higher than that one if the rent existed. The rent, as a part of the surplus value, does nothing but reduces the share of the profit in it. But when the rent is absent, all the surplus value is expressed in the profit, which remains in the hands of its producers.

The rent—differential and absolute—is a superfluous weight, ballast, which must be thrown in order for the ship of the economy to navigate at higher speed, three feet below the keel. "These two forms of rent are the only normal ones. Apart from them the rent can be based only upon an actual monopoly price, which is determined neither by price of production nor by value of commodities, but by the buyers' needs and ability to pay."[197] So, the third kind of rent—the monopoly rent, "based upon an actual monopoly price,"[198]—also disappear, along with the disappearance of the monopoly as a mode of production.

The social property of the means of production, one of which is the land does not permit the ground rent in any form on the so-called "agricultural lands," i.e., the cultivable lands, as well as on all other natural resources of the land—forests, mines, lakes, and the like. But for one and only kind of construction purposes—the residential ones, the land cannot be social because the construction of private residential buildings supposes its monopolization of parcels. Hence—a rent for the municipality or the citizen as owners, ergo—a price of the land, too, of this land only, the land for housing construction!

As concerns financial rent, the annuity, it is clear that such a rent can exist only in the form of a flow of payment, for example, like payments to sink a credit or similar financial transactions but not as payments whose origin is a joint-stock capital because such one simply does not exist in this system.

---

[197]. Marx, *Capital*, 3:863.
[198]. Ibid., 864.

Chapter Eight

The Credit

The Centralization and Concentration of Capital

When Marx speaks about the role of credit in the capitalist production, he notes clearly that the formation of joint-stock companies, i.e., the centralization of capital creating a monopolization of the production, "it is the abolition of capital as private property within the framework of capitalist production itself."[199] In other words, the monopolization of production is an abolition of capital as private property, but not as **capital**! That is what Lenin and all socialists and communists did not understand until our days. The capital in the form of joint-stock capital "is here directly endowed with the form of social capital . . . as distinct from private capital," (but being howsoever and first of all capital!), "and its undertakings assume the form of social undertakings as distinct from private undertakings."[200] The social undertakings of the joint-stock capital as distinct from private undertakings of the capital, however, quite do not mean **social property** of these undertakings after they are undertakings of the capital! Just here is the key, the nostrum of the comprehension and the delusion about the subject-matter of the property and the capital.

The development of the centralization of capital does not depend at all on the magnitude of the social capital. The question is whether the magnitude of the social capital depends on the centralization? Also no! The magnitude of social capital depends on the accumulation, i.e., on the concentration, but not on the centralization of capital. In spite of the delusion, "progress in centralization does not in any way depend upon a positive growth in the magnitude of social capital. And this is the specific difference between centralization and concentration, the latter being only another name for reproduction on an extended scale."[201] The

---

199. Marx, *Capital*, 3:504.
200. Ibid.
201. Ibid., 1:692.

centralization of capital is a cause of the monopolization of its whole reproduction process—from production to consumption! While the concentration represents the accumulation of capital in the extended reproduction. And if the centralization is a disastrous process for the society, in spite of its initial profits, which can be eliminated, the concentration of capital is an inevitable and vital process for the further development of the social capital and the increase of the social wealth. And if the centralization is a malignant tumor of the developed commodity production, which can be cut off and rejected under social mode of production, the concentration of capital is a vital necessity without which no any highly developed commodity production can pass, i.e., including socialism, too. The concentration—this is the enlargement of the capital through its own means and there is still nothing bad in that. The bad comes with the centralization—this is an enlargement of the capital, but at the expense of another's! So, that is a great delusion, a great error in the theory—the change of poles of evil's origin, and namely, that it comes from the concentration but not from the centralization of capital and hence swarm all misfortunes to socialism as a practice! And the evil for the poor class comes from the capital as essence, firstly, and of its centralization, secondly. Although the concentration really adds oil to the hell fire of both of aforementioned, combined with them. According to the general Law of capitalist accumulation, the concentration of capital is a drowning stone around the neck of the poor only because the social wealth is in private hands and therefore, it accumulates like **capital**, i.e., for the rich. That means the concentration can be an additional, secondary cause, but not a principal one of the impoverishment of the hired class of labor.

The centralization—this is "the attraction of capital by capital."[202] Just this attraction, this gravitation between powerful and weak capitals is mastered and eliminated by the same rate of profit, i.e., the centralization is eliminated. While the concentration, i.e., the consecutive expansion of the production, must remain and cannot but remain. It is possible to pass without centralization of capital, but it is not possible to pass without concentration. It is not possible that there is no concentration under the socialist mode of production, too, because it is not possible that there is no reproduction on an extended scale.

The enormous masses of capital can be obtained either by a

---

[202]. Marx, *Capital*, 1:691.

consecutive and gradual accumulation of a capital by concentration (and there is nothing bad in that under a social mode of production), or by wresting from lots of individual, small, already existing capitals, which are coercively fused into single capital by centralization (in a certain form of monopoly). The centralization is carried out by two ways—either by the violent attraction of broken, bankrupt capitals by one gravitation center, or by the "voluntary" fusion in a joint-stock capital. Both ways lead to monopoly. Both of them are equally unthinkable under socialist mode of production. That is why—because of the monopoly—the centralization is inadmissible as a process under socialism as well as the competition.

On the other hand, the concentration is a too slow process compared to the centralization.

"The masses of capital fused together overnight by centralization reproduce and multiply as the others do, only more rapidly, thereby becoming new and powerful levers in social accumulation. Therefore, when we speak of the progress of social accumulation we tacitly include—today—the effects of centralization."[203]

The centralization finishes off the work of the capitalist accumulation by intensification and acceleration until the Day of Judgment, which has always occurred at the beginning of each crisis. This intense accumulation with the assistance of the centralization carries with itself along with the success and the crash, too, along with the upsurge and the fall, too. And the reason of that is one of "the two most powerful levers of centralization"[204]—the credit, which is a source of the prosperity, but also "one of the most effective vehicles of crises and swindle."[205]

The great benefit for the society from the centralization of capital is the accelerated development of the scientific and technical progress within the narrow capitalist framework.

"The world would still be without railways if it had had to wait until accumulation had got a few individual capitals far enough to be adequate for the construction of a railway."[206]

***

---

[203]. Marx, *Capital*, 1:693.
[204]. Ibid., 692.
[205]. Ibid., 3:695.
[206]. Ibid., 1:693.

The Cooperation

It is clearly, as Marx says, the accumulation is "a very slow procedure compared with centralization."[207] But through the scheme of extended reproduction with increasing rate of accumulation under the socialist mode of production (see chapter three), the accelerated accumulation is already not a very slow procedure but, contrariwise, a fast one enough even in comparison with the centralization, such as is missing under this mode of production. Besides that, nothing prevents the association of some large-scale productions from achieving their common end under socialism, too—in a manner similar to that of the joint-stock capital, but without it being a joint-stock capital, i.e., fictitious, but completely real capital. The joinder of big enterprises may be done in consortiums (in banking, for big construction projects) or under some form of cooperation, but under no form of centralization! The cooperation is one of the best forms of association in the modern world. Perhaps this is the reason for the appearance of the last scientific current in our days of the "co-op capitalism" adherents. According to their conception of the "new capitalism"—this is the cooperative capitalism; it has to be the cooperative capitalism, because this is the "equitable" capitalism, a capitalism of the social justice, after Professor Hurst. She, working in the World Bank, has seen from high that the modern capitalism is bad and therefore, she is at her wit's end and has decided that the co-op capitalism is the solution to the problem "capitalism;" her colleague accepts that the cooperative is a "divine particle," which is the long-hoped-for miracle for saving the sick capitalistic society, giving it more energy. Really, since the modern capitalism is a capitalism of poor quality, the last wave economists are desperately looking for a treatment of its infirmities. For this purpose, they concocted the serial "new" idea for the serial "new" capitalism—this is the idea for saving modern capitalism through a "new" capitalism under the form of "cooperative capitalism." However, this heal-all is not new; about thirty years ago and more, the same idea was to save the then "socialism"—the cooperative as a form of socialism. But this is a divagation in the dark. The cooperative is a subsystem only of the system of capitalism and it is impossible to reform the subsystem at least, and in no case to revolutionize the main system under which laws, it is subordinated. However, "those members of the ruling classes who are intelligent enough to perceive the impossibility

---

[207]. Marx, *Capital*, 1:693.

of continuing the present system—and they are many—have become the obtrusive and full-mouthed apostles of cooperative production."[208] This new wave "obtrusive and full-mouthed apostles of cooperative production," however, obligingly is forgotten the heroic but rueful trials of the great utopian Robert Owen, the knight Robert the Big-heart, during the cooperative capitalism 200 years ago (!), i.e., in times when the cooperative capitalism was much more possible! He was the pioneer of the coop-capitalism who also tried to make it equitable capitalism, but was down and out, and crushed by the whole class bristled against him capitalists. In the conditions of capitalism, he established the first cooperatives—productive and consumer, the first workers' market-places, but he encountered all the united class might of the capitalist system! "Cooperation ever constitutes the fundamental form of the capitalist mode of production, nevertheless the elementary form of cooperation continues to subsist as a particular form of capitalist production side by side with the more developed forms of that mode of production,"[209] as Marx wrote a long time ago. Marx gave a true and precise assessment of the co-operative movement's significance in capitalist conditions but the new wave economists/apostles of this movement ignore it. "We speak of the co-operative movement, especially the co-operative factories raised by the unassisted efforts of a few bold 'hands'. The value of these great social experiments cannot be overrated."[210] The meticulous scientist Marx explained in the best manner that the reason of this impossibility of the co-operative to have its own way with capitalism is the capitalist mode of production itself, and namely, its system of monopoly. Just the monopoly is the main reason that is not allowing the co-operative to get its own way as a principal form of the capitalist system. The great Marx explained that:

> the experience of the period from 1848 to 1864 has proved beyond doubt that **however excellent in principle and however useful in practice, co-operative labor**, if kept within the narrow circle of the casual efforts of private workmen, **will never be able to arrest the growth in geometrical progression of monopoly, to free the masses, nor even to perceptibly lighten the burden of their miseries**. It is perhaps for this very

---

[208]. Marx, *The Civil War in France*, 3:313.

[209]. Marx, *Capital*, 1:375.

[210]. Karl Marx, *Inaugural Address and Provisional Rules of the International Working Men's Association*, 1:316.

reason that plausible noblemen, philanthropic middle-class spouters, and even keep political economists have all at once turned nauseously complimentary to the very co-operative labor system they had vainly tried to nip in the bud by deriding it as the utopia of the dreamer, or stigmatizing it as the sacrilege of the socialist. To save the industrious masses, co-operative labor ought to be developed to national dimensions, and, consequently, to be fostered by national means. Yet the lords of the land and the lords of capital will always use their political privileges for the defense and perpetuation of their economic monopolies. So far from promoting, they will continue to lay every possible impediment in the way of the emancipation of labor.[211]

Thus spoke Marx. Nothing new propounds this new scientific school in our days. For this reason, we'll close this theme with Marx's conclusion that "the co-operative factories . . . reproduce everywhere in their actual organization all the shortcomings of the prevailing system."[212] While the prevailing system is capitalism!

***

The Basic Rate of Interest

Credit is a powerful shield, bearing on itself the capitalistic production, and it is a basis of its social character. "This social character of capital is first promoted and wholly realized through the full development of the credit and banking system . . . It thus does away with the private character of capital and thus contains in itself, but only in itself, the abolition of capital itself."[213] So, the credit, creating the social character of capital, is necessary under the social property of this capital, too. Then, under the same general rate of profit, the basic rate of interest has the tendency of falling with the development of the credit system, which exerts a pressure on it, as Marx expressed himself. Along with that, there must be a **constant** ratio between the interest and the whole profit in order for any producer to be in a position to pay its interest, irrespective whether this one is high or low as per the level of the general rate of profit. Since the competition does not absolutely exert

---

[211]. Marx, *Inaugural Address*, 1:317. (bolded by me—T.B.)

[212]. Marx, *Capital*, 3:509.

[213]. Ibid., 695.

any influence on the magnitude of the interest rate, we are facilitated by this fact, too, although such a competition (between the capitals) simply is missing in our system. The competition, should it exist or not, does not determine the interest rate. "The market rate of interest . . . is directly and immediately determined by the proportion between supply and demand"[214] of money capital.

It is clear, that with $p' = $ **const.**, i.e., when the general rate of profit is invariable, the basic rate of interest will also be invariable, as far as it depends on it for longer periods. Here we must specially remark that the basic interest rate cannot increase by such growth of the average wage, which leaves the general rate of profit invariable. It can go up only by growth of the average wage that depresses the general rate of profit. The raising of the basic rate of interest can come from the raised demand for labor power on a social scale. But when the labor power is not a commodity, there simply are no such fluctuations of the price around its value in order so that they can influence on the basic rate of interest, respectively on its raising. So, the self-expanding wage leads neither to the growth nor to the self-growth of the basic rate of interest, simply because there is no raised demand for money capital as variable capital. The self-expanding wage does not create higher demand for money capital as wage because the general rate of profit remains invariable.

Besides that, the basic rate of interest at an invariable general rate of profit is favorably influenced also by the exempt and light reverse influx of capital because of the invariable value of money and the expansion of the credit. "The ready flow and regularity of the returns, linked with extensive commercial credit . . . prevents the level of the rate of interest from rising."[215]

***

Withering away of Credit

However, at first sight, a queer but fundamental question arises—is the interest necessary at all under socialism? Just like the rent drops out, should not the interest also drop out? It's a question, not without reasons. Something more—curiously enough, there exists the extravagant and naïve anarchical idea, just like the state, the banks and money should be abolished overnight! Unfortunately, the money (and banks) could not be abolished, they could only wither away.

---

[214]. Marx, *Capital*, 3:425
[215]. Ibid., 565.

So, since the property is social, would not that mean that the loan of money to invest in the extended reproduction should be free of interest, as in a special case of a preferential loan, like the credit of the Islamic banks, for example! In other words, loan and return of the principal only, but not to pay any interest? Or, is the social property basis of such a loan—"equitable" and not usurer's? It is not. The reason is that the social property is not a state one, but it is not anybody's property, too. It is a concrete property of a certain juridical person and it is only for this reason that it is social because the general rate of profit is the same for the entire society, i.e., the property is social only because during a production activity based on one's own (but not loaned) means, the realized rate of profit remains in the same relationship with all other producers in the society, in the same relations of appropriation. But since the economic life imposes various situations in the reproduction process, not infrequently it occurs to resort to the use of another's, but not one's own pecuniary means as **money** capital, although the property of the means of production as **industrial** capital in an appointed way is social. It is social, but not common! And in order to encourage the loan in such cases, there is no other way except through the interest and the rate of interest! It cannot do without interest and it cannot do without encouraging through it the supply of money when in the society there is an objective demand for such one. Without the existence of the interest and the rate of interest, it is impossible to develop the credit, too, which represents the most modern form of payment and which will have a more and more significant role in the development of the society by ousting all other out-of-date forms of the commodity-money relations. Credit, which is an evidence of the might of a certain society and which will become Atlas of the future, doing single-handedly the mountains of the large-scale industry in mega and Giga dimensions, cannot do without interest and a rate of interest. Actually, if inside an economy 100 % of the firms work only with their own pecuniary means, there is no and there cannot be interest, $i = 0$, because all the profit remains for their own use. This is in the last reckoning of the aim and when that occurs, the interest will be needless, it will drop out by itself from the mode of living and the mode of production.

Finally, there is no doubt that the credit system will serve as a powerful lever during the transition from the capitalist mode of production to the mode of production of associated labor; but only as one element in connection with another great organic revolutions of the mode of production itself. On the other hand, the illusions concerning the miraculous power of the credit and banking system, in the socialist sense, arise from a complete lack of familiarity with the capitalist mode of production and the credit system as one of its forms. As soon as the means of production cease being transformed into capital (which also includes the abolition of private property in land), credit as such no longer has any meaning.[216]

As Marx mentions, the credit will be necessary for the transition period to the mode of production of associated labor, after which "credit as such no longer has any meaning." In other words, the credit will be necessary in the beginning of the socialist mode of production and for a long time after that—until 100 % of all economic objects started to work only with their own pecuniary means. And if the market was not existing with its inevitable deformations reflecting on the realization of the product, which realization determines the state, the image of every enterprise, i.e., if there would exist the production only without a market, as that is in the communist mode of production, the credit would have dropped out still on the first day of the socialism. But since the circulation exists, since the market admits the probability to be located on it not only profitable, but even such losing companies, especially during the early stage of socialism, the credit remains necessary until the economic conditions impose its dropping out by itself. That means a dropping out of the interest and the rate of interest, too. Then the profit will not be in a position to divide anymore, because the rent, firstly, and the interest, after that will be forgotten as concepts. This difference between rent and interest and their different withering away in the course of time, in spite of the similarity of their contents, comes from the difference between industrial capital and money capital, whose manifestations they are. The withering away of the credit means that the sphere of circulation will be more and more restricted relatively, but expanding absolutely, i.e., the relative share of the sphere of circulation will reduce compared to the share of the production sphere, in spite of its own colossal absolute development took alone. In this way, the withering away of the credit will be a consequence of the withering away of all factors, which interrupt the production and impose getting a loan until the realization of already produced production. That means

---

[216]. Marx, *Capital*, 3:695-696.

that the seasonal character of any production will wither away, in particular by the rural economy and the rural economy itself will wither away with the development of the biotechnologies. The market, in the retail trade as well as in the wholesale trade, will be more and more erased and disappear in its current form, and more and more will be modified itself into a market of the order, as a market working increasingly to order and in this manner will be mastered and completely ceased its elemental character and entropy, its indeterminateness and chaos, the uncertainty and the fear, which it hides for any producer. The use of cash money, i.e., the paper money on hand will be completely ousted just like the paper money had ousted the metal money before. That can be done only during an exclusive high development of the credit and precisely then, when not only one rich minority, but when all the society, when each one of its citizens has a bank current account to effect his payments, then the "cheques become the sole circulating medium."[217] Within a rich society without division in classes, with perfectly developed credit system, the only money to circulate in the currency will be the checks and the debit cards. And probably the debit cards will be the last tangible shape of money before its final cremation.

By the way, it seems this process of a paper money shift has already started since 2009. Although its contentious existence, the new electronic currency BTC (Bitcoin) for five or six years only, is already making great strides in the world obsessing earnest elbow-rooms in the United States, Germany, India, and elsewhere. The governments in the mentioned states closely watch this currency because for the present, it exists chiefly as a currency of the jobbery, as a pyramid scheme and money laundering, but in the near future it could be an equipollent means of payment of the big business if it assumes after law regulations all the world commodity circulation.

---

[217]. Marx, *Capital*, 3:469.

Chapter Nine

The Commodity of Labor Power

Capital represents a process of expansion of value. And just because it is a **process**, because it is a movement of self-expanding value, we may follow up this movement, in which the containing in itself value labor power is proven to be a commodity and has the behavior of a commodity. The self-expanding value is capital only because the labor power is a commodity, only when it is forced to behave as a commodity, i.e., the behavior of the labor power determines whether the social relation of expansion of the value will be capital or not. And the labor power becomes a commodity in the production, though it is realized as such during the circulation. Within the circulation, we cannot understand at all the nature of the commodity and the mechanism of transformation of the labor power into a commodity. That happens in the production only. That's why, it was not occasionally that Marx started his investigation from the process of production first, dedicating to it the entire first volume of *Capital*. The labor power as a commodity is an **essence** in the production process, while it is a **phenomenon** in the process of circulation. The nature of the commodity and of the capital may be examined and understood only when they are followed where they originate—in the production. This is the reason that I also investigate the production process first—where the labor power may and must cease being a commodity.

We have already seen that under social property of the means of production is not only a single process but also the entire circular production process excludes the labor power as a commodity, regardless of the fact that this happens at every single process taken alone. The second condition in order for the labor power to be a commodity—to be deprived of the means of production—becomes invalid with the laws p' = const. and $\dfrac{v}{c + v}$ = const., through which the means of production

210

become social property. Besides that, these laws keep invariable the rate of surplus value, which, on its part, in the production process does not anymore treat the labor power into commodity form.

Until the "reconstruction" (perestroika), the theory that was thinking itself as Marxist admitted that the labor power was excluded from the commodity world. But it was all; **how, when,** and **why**—these were not explained. Along with this, the obvious fact was pointed out that the wage (and the labor power with it, as well!) enters the commodity-based relations! What a banal humor! The impotence of this "political economy" of socialism consisted of the impossibility to explain its own assertions. It took decades of the formal science to grind into the theorist heads the scientific paradigm that the labor power under socialism was not a commodity. But why? This was neither telling nor was proving by somebody. This "political economy" of socialism was a fabricated school subject, but not the science of political economy at all.

During the "reconstruction," just the opposite happened; the theorists went to the other pole. Separate voices were heard, which insisted on admitting that the labor power was a commodity under socialism (!) too, in order to pass to the so-called "market economy" or "market socialism." Indeed, under Soviet "socialism" until 1990, this was objectively like that—the labor power was a commodity; which only proves that this was not socialism. Just that, however, all economists at present also accept it as its eternal status, i.e., they do not see that the labor power could not be a commodity.

The labor power becomes a commodity not as much with the production and the appropriation of surplus value, as with the deduction from its wage, with the continuous depression of the wage below the value of labor power. Because the surplus value is subject to a private or social appropriation, but the deduction from the wage is a specific capitalistic law only, i.e., the relation of the surplus labor to the necessary labor is what makes the labor power a commodity. The labor power is produced in the form of a commodity during the production process because of the uncontrolled effect of the factor s'—rate of surplus value. Just it is the reason for squeezing more and more value from the value containing the labor power itself, transforming it into a capital-value. So, because of the chaotic effect of s', the wage never corresponds to the value of labor power, varying always around it as a price of this labor power. The labor power is a commodity when the rate of surplus value is a variable magnitude. But when it is fixed as a

211

constant magnitude, when it is established as **const.**, then the relation between surplus labor and necessary labor does not change, i.e., its influence on the labor power does not change, too. In other words, the value that is taken away from the new value created by the labor power remains invariable in the course of time. And this will say that the growth of the wage always concurs exactly to the growth of the value of labor power. The value of labor power decreases relatively, but continuously increases absolutely in the course of time and if to this objective increase does not correspond to the same degree an increase in the wage, too, then the wage lags behind, depressing below the value of labor power, by which its normal reproduction is disturbed. That is why, the wage as a money equivalent of the value of labor power must always grow respectively to the same extent with the growth of the value of labor power. The value of labor power grows continuously with the growth of the average wage, not because the socially necessary labor time grows, but because the social productive force of labor grows. It, the productivity of labor, continuously shortens the necessary labor time, but allows more and more commodities—means of existence—to enter and to form the value of labor power with their steady cheapening, which commodities become accessible only by the steady increase of the average wage at the extent of increase in the social productivity of labor. Thus, the increase of the average wage always corresponds to the increase of the value of labor power. When the wage corresponds to the value of labor power, it practically corresponds to the necessary labor time that the variable rate of surplus value endeavors always to shorten. Because the value of labor power—this is the value of the means of existence, corresponding to the necessary labor time of the average worker. While the fixing of the rate of surplus value as a constant magnitude persists just the necessary labor time of the worker, i.e., the time that is necessary for the normal reproduction of worker's labor power. But when it is stolen by the necessary labor time in order to increase the surplus labor time "through deduction from the wage,"[218] then it—the wage—depresses below the value of labor power, which, namely, transforms it into a commodity.

So, since the labor power does not go out of the production as a commodity, it does not enter the circulation like such one, too, i.e., it is not subject of sale-trade. When the owner of labor power is not an

---

[218]. Marx, *Capital*, 1:741.

owner of means of production, as well, then he is deprived of the possibility to sell commodities because he does not have any means for the production of such commodities. The lack of his own means of production forces the worker, the owner of the labor power, to sell the only commodity he has—his own labor power. But under the social property of the means of production, when the worker possesses his own means of production, the necessity that his labor power is purchased drops out, i.e., the act **M-C** drops out. This first act—the non-purchase act, makes the second act—the sale, the act **C-M**, impossible too. Since there is no purchase, there cannot be a sale. In this way, the entire process of sale-trade of the labor power, **M-C-M′**, becomes null and void. Thus, the labor power remains out of circulation; it is excluded from the market. The labor power is no longer subject to exchange, which means that it does not have any exchange value. The exchange value is a sufficient condition for the product to be a commodity, even though it does not have any value. If the product has a value but is not subject to exchange, then it is not a commodity. The product may have no value, but if it is being subject to exchange, then it will be a commodity—for example, the land under capitalism. In order for the product to drop out as a commodity, it must drop out in **both** conditions, as the sufficient, as well as the necessary one—both the exchange value and the value. While in order for the labor power to drop out as a commodity, it is necessary only the sufficient condition to drop out—the exchange value. This is like that because the labor power is a specific commodity, a special commodity.

The labor power under socialism does not have a value! It was like that the scientific thought that made believe us until recently—the labor power does not have a value because it does not have a price! And it does not have a price because it is not a commodity. And it is not a commodity because it does not have a value! And so on—in a magic circle. The labor power does not have a value—by this trick only, by this stunt only, Marx's political economy is turned into a bourgeois one, i.e., set upside-down. This trick was born from the miserable logic that since the labor power should not be a commodity under socialism, the wage should not be a price of this commodity. And since it does not have a price, it does not have a value, too! That's ready! The trick is done and the naïfs believe in it. And what is this labor power reproduced with, what does the workman live on? Is it possible that the means of existence does not have any value? Is it possible that the quantities of commodities that compose these means of existence and which determine the value of labor power does not have any value? It looks like it lives on air only, on photosynthesis!

Really, with this scandalously low wage, with this "wretchedly small, a starvation pittance,"[219] the labor power was so cheap in our country that, according to the above "theory," it had almost no value. The state monopoly of the capital in Bulgaria (and USSR) extracted colossal, astronomical profits sponged on the flagrantly cheap, but, in return, highly skilled labor power that had been sold and purchased dirt-cheap. That is why, it was not accidental the fact that for forty-five years of "socialism," the number of the millionaires in Bulgaria in 1990 was over fifteen times (!) higher than in 1944, i.e., before the "socialism!" They were a product only of those economic laws that dominated in our country and our system during that time—the capitalist laws. These same men, "communists," continued to rule for years until today simply by replacing "socialism" that was already unprofitable for them, with "democracy," in which they had to legalize the grab money, transforming it into private capitals.

The wage in our country was (and still is!) actually social relief for poor people, which wage was not objectively bound to the quantity of labor that the labor power put in, i.e., not bound at all to what was fundamental law of prosperity, as the former "political economy" of socialism taught us. The wage was a monopoly low price of the labor power, a price far below its value. Bulgaria had (and still continues to have in the early twenty-first century!) a colonially cheap labor power—in insulting contrast and for a mockery with its quality and qualification. The labor time was almost completely composed of surplus labor time, while the necessary was reduced near to zero.

"Surplus labor in general, as labor performed over and above the given requirements, must always remain. In the capitalist as well as in the slave system, etc., it merely assumes an antagonistic form and is supplemented by complete idleness of a stratum of society."[220]

Under the socialism the labor power has a value but is not a commodity—it does not have an exchange value. Each commodity has two-fold character; each commodity has a value and an exchange value. Each commodity has a value, while the value of labor power could not

---

[219]. Marx, *Value, Price and Profit*, 7:63.
[220]. Marx, *Capital*, 3:925.

be a commodity. Wage as a transformed expression of the value is no longer a price of labor power. Wage is equivalent to the value of labor power, which always coincides with it. Labor power does not have a price, not because it does not have a value, but because it does not have an exchange value, because it is not at all subject to sale-trade. Wage is not a price of labor power anymore, but it is anew a transformed form of the value of this labor power. It is only when the wage corresponds to the value of labor power, only then it fits the possibilities and satisfies the necessities of the worker.

Labor power is no longer purchased with a variable capital, spent for wage, although it is a variable magnitude again. The commodity of labor power acts as variable capital "only in the hands of the buyer, the capitalist."[221] But when the buyer, i.e., the capitalist, is absent, neither the labor power is a commodity, nor does it act as variable capital. As a value, money advanced for payment of labor power is "only potential variable capital."[222] So, money for paying the labor power is only a potentiality, only a possibility for variable capital, which could not happen.

It is possible, however, to arise the following misunderstanding, which may incite the thought to delusions. We are speaking of the fact that since the wage always coincides with the value of labor power, does not this mean the same way as all other commodities under socialism, the labor power is also sold and purchased always **at** its value, i.e., that the labor power is commodity again whose price—the wage—as any other price, simply always coincides with its value. That could be an artful ruse of the speculative mind only. For the above impression could be created upon a superficial observation only. Really, because of the participation of the labor power in the commodity-money relations, that looks like that at first sight. Such an apparent impression is created because of the fact that the labor power has value, which fact would have given a sufficient reason the labor power to have exchange value, too, that coincides with it in our case. However, what factor imposes the labor power to have exchange value expressing in the wage? In other words, in what conditions only the labor power reaches the market as a commodity; when and why it is present in the circulation; what imposes that the labor power appears on the labor market, where it can be assessed as a commodity in money having the form of wage?

---

[221]. Marx, *Capital*, 2:495.
[222]. Ibid., 497.

Such conditions are imposed by the production. A production process on capitalist basis always takes away the means of production from the immediate producer. And only then does the labor power become a commodity, which appears on the market. The labor power reaches the circulation as a commodity only when the worker is deprived of the means of production, which deprives him of the means of existence, too. Then, in order to provide them, in order to purchase these means of existence from the market, the worker is forced to sell on this market only what he has—his labor power, by exchanging it against the commodities that are necessary to his existence. And he may get them only through his wage that is given him by the capitalist. That is why, in this case, the wage represents an exchange value of the labor power—it is the value by which one commodity—the labor power, is exchanged against other commodities—the means of existence.

However, the entire reproduction process under the socialist mode of production repudiates the possibility that the labor power lapses, even for a moment only, into the status of a commodity, since the labor power possesses means of production at every given moment. With the entire economic mechanism, "the produced conditions of labor and the products of labor in general"[223] are no longer withstand to the immediate producers as **capital**. Labor power provides its means of existence without exchanging itself as a commodity to them. It purchases commodities without having to sell itself as a commodity. That is why the wage no longer represents exchange value of the labor power— because its value is no longer assessed on the market, as exchanged against another value. Thus, under just determined conditions only, mentioned above, the labor power, which is located in the ocean of the commodity relations, could not be a commodity. Under social property, it is not a commodity, although the same way as when it is a commodity, it is a value again, which produces a higher value.

Workers' wage could be a self-expanding value. But a question arises—how will the non-workers' payment look? What will be the incomes of the people of intellectual work—in administration, in education, in health services? Liberal professions and arts represent a special difficulty . . .

It is clear that where it is possible, the income in the form of salary— mostly in education and health services—will be a salary for the time of

---

[223]. Marx, *Capital*, 1:626.

service, but not payment by the piece, which means that its magnitude should be determined mainly by the intensiveness of the working time, its duration being the same. The profit tax is just for that taken by the state—in order to support namely this part of the society that is not employed in productive labor. In the opposite case, it would be superfluous. The salary of these social groups is determined by the law $p' = \text{const.}$, too, more precisely, it is equalized to the respective kind of high intellectual labor, let's say, engineering labor so that the salary (or the fee) could not exceed the annual wage of an engineering worker at $p' = \text{const.}$ This is done in order to not violate the social equality. There is no tax on wage for the productive workers, but there must be a tax on fees for the free practices in order to regulate the incomes in favor of the social equality and social justice. Because an artist does not employ more creativity and ideas, respectively labor, in his working time than an engineer-constructor. An evidence of that is the genial Leonardo da Vinci who had gathered both of them in himself. It is widely known that he had been a great engineer first, but next a great artist!

However, a casus arises here—if a writer or a musician, for example, sells millions of copies of his or her hit work, and thus gets proceeds many, many times over the annual maximum of incomes in the society, then what next? In this case, he or she has three options to spend the proceeds: as income, capital or endowment—singly or together. If the author decides to spend the proceeds as income, he or she has a legal right to maximum annual income not only in the current year but in some next year, too, under respective tax limitations, of course. But if the author decides to be useful to the society, he or she can invest the proceeds as capital, but only as a sponsor or grantor, never as an owner!

Concerning the production administration, the clerks in the enterprises, their payment will be done immediately from the profit of the enterprise according to a preliminarily concluded contract between them and the board of workers, but not the board of directors. They have the full freedom of equal rights contracting without any restrictions. After concluding this contract, neither party may impose prerogatives to the other—the workers undertake to produce certain commodity production, while the administration undertakes to market it. So, the responsibility at the completion of a production cycle is always direct and personal and should be searched at the exit of the "black box," i.e., according to the work was done by every participant at the end of the cycle.

Chapter Ten

The Inflation

Labor power under the socialism is not a commodity that is sold and purchased at its value, although this seemingly looks like that. But the fact that the wage coincides always with the value of labor power as well as the price with the value of the commodity means something else. It is hardly now that an exact and full conformity is gotten between prices and wages, which conformity namely excludes any possibility for the existence of the phenomenon of **inflation**—because the price and the wage always fit, exactly reflect the value, the former—of the commodity, the latter—of the labor power. They are an exact copy, a photo, real images of the value, but not crooked ones by the awry mirror of the competition or the monopoly. The source of the inflation of contemporary capitalism, a result of the state-monopolistic regulation, is precisely this—that the price and the wage have detached not only and not so much from the gold (paper-credit money), but from that of the value. The passing each other between value and price of all commodities, including the commodity of labor power is a necessary condition to the appearance of inflation; it is a *condicio sine qua non*, existing even under pre-monopoly capitalism. The sufficient condition—it is the intervention of the monopolies and the state in the reproduction process so that this passing each other degenerates into a conflict.

Still Marx subjects to a ruinous criticism the principles of the "monetary school" about the absolute erroneousness of the theory and its baneful practice in England in the middle of the nineteenth century. But until our days, as well, the inflation is interpreted by this school with the unreal and imaginary "principle of the money circulation," although today's English bankers, after once burning their fingers, do not try anymore to introduce for a second time the banking act of 1844. But since the "moderate inflation" is an advantageous, profitable thing to the large-scale capital under state-monopoly capitalism, in the theory, sundry paid agents can be freely exerted in eloquence to interpret the inflation, while in practice omnifarious ways are searched for its perpetuation. Today also, Lord Overstone's descendants on both sides of the ocean continue to expound that the commodities are "too dear because" there is "too much money in the country."[224] Even to these latter days in the same stupid, but surely intentional (!) manner, the value of commodity is still confused with . . . the value of money! That the price of commodity is one thing, but the price of money (the interest rate) another, completely different thing—this primer truth scarcely requires to be commented on, if on its cross it had not built a whole system of lies and delusions. Each professor of that academic elite (Milton Friedman, for example,) as an ex-student has been congested in his mind, and grinding this candid lie by heart, he is multiplying it later from the stature of his post on generations of new young proselytes with smoothed brains, whose aim is the career! A science is made like that!

The modern monetary school during all the twentieth century was the same as the old one without any development! Just like in the nineteenth century Lord Overstone's vacancy, Milton Friedman in the twentieth century still continues to expound "that the price level is determined by how much money there is—how many pieces of paper of various denominations."[225] That is the monetarism! It's a childish-minded "explanation" if it was not intentional manipulation and utter vacuity! Many generations of modern economists reiterate in a trance until now Milton Friedman's "central thesis: that inflation is always and everywhere a *monetary* phenomenon."[226] This mental castration runs like a red thread through all the monetarism and is deeply underlying in the impotence of the whole contemporary economic science, which is amputated against any scientical interpretation of the phenomenon of inflation. What does it mean that the inflation is a monetary phenomenon? According to this spurious guru, "*inflation is always and everywhere a monetary phenomenon* in the sense that it arises and could arise solely when the quantity of money grows faster than the production."[227] This is sheer nonsense, sheer metaphysics! This is calling out the phlogiston back in the theory but this time in the economics of the twentieth century instead of the chemistry of the eighteenth. But this dogma as a Pope's or Bolshevik's infallibility is grounded on the whole modern economic creed especially after 1990; this wrong conception is beyond

---

[224]. Marx, *Capital*, 3:636.
[225]. Milton Friedman, *Money Mischief*, 41.
[226]. Friedman, *Money Mischief*, 12.
[227]. Ibid., 64-65.

any doubt but the deluded Friedman presumptuously fancies that "there is no any other so undeniable affirmation in the economy."[228] Because this affirmation is a rather flat fraud! It is obviously that Friedman has never heard about the Law of money circulation, nor that he knew what the money represents as a whole. Albeit he knows, of course, the famous Irving Fisher's "equation of exchange" which describes in an incomplete way the social demand for money. Indeed, what can we say about a scientist who in 1992, just 125 years after the appearance of *Capital*'s first volume still continued to ask, "what determines the particular item that will be used as money,"[229] and being continued has no "answer to that simple question."[230] Friedman has never heard about the five functions of money and hence bound up with them various economic phenomena. That is why, this monetary colossus on clay legs interprets the objective economic laws by a void of sense subjectivism. As per him, after 1971 any relation between money and commodities had broken off, and because of that, from then on the monetary mass depends on "the bureaucratic needs of the authorities, the personal beliefs and values of the persons in charge, current or presumed developments in the economy, the political pressures to which the authorities are subject, and so on," and so on "in endless detail."[231] This was in a Friedman essay full of idiocies in which he failed to add the sunrise and sunset, as well as slugs' sexual life as reasons for the existing monetary mass! As for the broken off relation between money and commodities: by the gone off gold in 1971 and the transformation of the US dollar into paper money there is not broken off the relation between money and commodities but the relation between commodity circulation and money circulation and it is not from 1971 and not from President Nixon but a long time before with the appearance of the developed credit. But for Friedman, the money has its own parallel life toward ours and out of any objective economic laws.

Trying to explain the inflation, Friedman introduces the divine outset—helicopter in the heaven! *Deus ex machina!* Great, this is a science! This is how the inflation appears—"one day a helicopter flies over our hypothetical long-stationary community and drops additional

---

[228]. Friedman, *Money Mischief*, 222.

[229]. Ibid., 26.

[230]. Ibid.

[231]. Ibid., 30.

money from the sky equals to the amount already in circulation . . ."[232] A Nobel laureate born and bred! And then we learn that all people, just each individual is picked up his or her cash balances. After the imaginary increase of the cash balances, it follows the people to relieve of this burden: "the tries of the people to reduce their cash balances will mean simply further inflation of prices and incomes."[233] In other words, after drawing the savings out from the banks and vanishing them, the people reduce their cash balances (obviously, Friedman has in mind only physical, but never juridical persons, too!) and this operation after some absurd logic inflates the prices! A unique interpretation of the inflation for ignoramuses! But at the same time, for some unknown reason and unknown way, after reducing their cash these same people are happy because . . . their incomes are inflated, too! This is schizophrenia! This is a serious infringement of the mental processes, confused thinking, and false beliefs! Because Friedman gives an imbecilic explanation of the inflation at which "money rains down from heaven,"[234] cash money, of course, because there is no any other! This is a rather low intellectual level, rather low—just scribbles, scribbles from the cave!

For all this monetary inanity and the like, Milton Friedman received the 1976 Nobel Prize! A product of the capitalist propaganda, this father of the contemporary monetary school, however, has a quite rudimentary knowledge about the commodity and money. Friedman, in all his monetary approach, treats money's functioning always only as income and never as capital! But actually, the principal movement is the transformation of the money into capital. The transformation of the money into income is secondary and concomitant movement of the first one in which just the capital is the author of inflation. The capital but not the income is the cause of inflation! Besides that, there not exist for Friedman juridical persons, the companies, for him, the sole perpetrator of the inflation are the physical persons, the consumers. This is, namely, the main Friedman's monetary conception—the consumption, that the consumption is the determinative in the modern economy. According to this Nobel Prize winner, "accumulating an asset requires saving, that is, abstaining from consumption."[235] That means that the accumulation of capital is due to capitalist's thrift and he increases his fortune only by . . .

---

[232]. Friedman, *Money Mischief*, 42.

[233]. Ibid., 48.

[234]. Ibid., 47.

[235]. Ibid., 37

asceticism, by abstaining from consumption! That ascetic samaritan, "that queer saint, that knight of the woeful countenance, the capitalist 'abstainer'"[236] is a hero by the bourgeois mythology for a long time ago. This is not a new conception and the normal man wonders how is possible such naïve interpretations by the eighteenth and nineteenth centuries to be disseminated and force in the twentieth and twenty-first centuries! Something more—this nonsense is devoured, imbibed by thousands of modern economists without any criticism down the years until now! The abstaining from consumption, however, except as a "cause" for the accumulation of capital, is recommended as a monetary "cure," "the single cure against inflation"[237]—the reduction of the growth of the money mass through "fortunate abstaining."[238] Fortunate abstaining—this is the formula, this is the final aim! The rest is a movement! Fortunate abstaining—fortune for the rich, abstaining—for the poor! Fortunate abstaining—money fetishism for the former, commodity voyeurism for the latter!

Being far beyond the real comprehension about the contemporary world economic system in its two main forms, Friedman draws startling inferences—probably discoveries for himself. The first shocking conclusion is that "inflation is not a capitalist phenomenon!"[239] After this fundamental discovery, Friedman throws the public into confusion through the insight of genius: "But inflation is not a communist phenomenon, either!"[240] Then this colossus of the monetary thought dumbfounds us with his last fundamental inference: "In the contemporary world the inflation is a printed phenomenon!"[241] Great! It is the same as the printed of newspapers, postcards, and comic strips!

The contemporary monetary school just like its predecessor by the nineteenth century gives a smattering of the real economy. Monetarism is sciolism. In monetarism, all is upside down—the value is fiction, the fiction is value! Monetary theory is a whey, an insipid mess, a speculation in the science which by all five money's functions, is interested in the most stupid and false manner with one function only—the function as a medium of circulation, which is a full maiming of the subject-matter, a

---

[236]. Marx, *Capital*, 1:660

[237]. Friedman, *Money Mischief*, 243.

[238]. Ibid., 253.

[239]. Ibid., 221.

[240]. Ibid.

[241]. Ibid.

fully maimed interpretation not only of the inflation but of money's nature as a whole!

The contemporary economic science not infrequently eschews calling political economy the more that it is not such itself. The contemporary economic science from Keynes's time on quite consciously has broken off all relations with the classical political economy, by erasing any trace there and wringing any notion of the genesis of the profit and the production relation capital-labor. The contemporary economic science is already occupied only with the most inoffensive field for it—the money capital, that which is seen only on the surface of the economic life. Finances, credit, interest rates, securities—this is its credo today. But after Marx, the bourgeois political economy cannot do anything other. Keynes tried that but failed. The monetarists with Friedman at the head did the same. The contemporary economic science Marx would have called a vulgar political economy. It is quite obvious that after Marx the bourgeois political economy is not able to bear an economist by the rank of Smith and Ricardo but produces in a mass such ones who spew only lies and delusions. Keynes is one of them. Obviously, because of a lack of better turbid whey, the academic circles selected his. Almost a century until now, many generations of economists were educated in the abstract and otiose Keynesian ISLM model and its derivatives, which are not able to expound at all the real economic processes in the modern world. Only under the hypnotic influence of the interest and money one can write and tens of thousands after him to reiterate in a trance the economical Surahs of Keynes's Quran!

Inflation as a phenomenon is observed because of an acute or chronic infringement of the Law of money circulation. This law, just like any other law of capitalism, exists therefore in order to be infringed! In this system, it is more profitable to infringe the laws than to observe them, like Marx already commented. The same is valid with regard to the inflation and the Law of money circulation—it is more profitable infringe it, the law, in Keynes's manner in order for it, the inflation, to exist as an additional source of oligarchic richness.

According to the Law of money circulation, the quantity of money in circulation is determined in opposite dependence on the velocity of the turnovers of the monetary unit—the more the velocity is higher, the more the mass of money necessary in circulation is smaller and vice versa, i.e., at a slowed up turnover of the money, its mass increases. And this lag of its turnover is caused mostly by the rise in prices of the commodities. "The erroneous opinion that it is, on the contrary, prices that are determined by the quantity of the circulating medium"[242] was refuted still by Marx, some one hundred and fifty years ago!

In order for the quantity of money in circulation to increase, that means that the velocity of circulation is slowed up and low. But it is only a consequence of the effect of other causes—the monopolies and the state at the contemporary stage—on two functions of the money: as a means of payment and as a medium of circulation so that the result is delay of the payments of credit as well as in cash, in the wholesale trade as well as in the retail trade. The artificial intervention of the state and of the monopolies in the economic laws causes a lasting infringement and deformations of the Law of money circulation, so that firstly, there is a rise in prices of the commodities and after that, on this basis, the quantity of money in circulation is increased, too. But not the opposite! The rise in prices is a cause but not an effect of the increased mass of money in circulation. And a principal part in the rise in prices has the credit when it marks a drop, i.e., at a time of crisis.

"In periods of predominant credit, the velocity of the circulation of money increases faster than commodity-prices, whereas in times of declining credit commodity-prices drop slower than the velocity of circulation."[243]

The structural relation of two of money's functions plays a significant role in the existence of the phenomenon of inflation—the functions as a means of payment and as a medium of circulation.

"Should circulation as a means of payment increase at a higher rate than it decreases as a means of purchase, the aggregate circulation would increase, although the money serving as a means of purchase would decrease considerably in quantity."[244]

And vice versa, in a crisis, the decrease in the circulation of money as a means of payment leads to decrease also both of the aggregate circulation of money and its circulation as a means of purchase, which would lead to a considerable increase in the quantity of the latter, i.e., as an increased and devalued mass of money in circulation for the general public.

So, inflation is due not to the "printing of money" because of wage-

---

[242]. Marx, *Capital*, 1:146.
[243]. Ibid., 3:518.
[244]. Ibid.,530.

rise, as it is hammered into the heads of millions of working people in a naïve and demagogic manner, as it is suggested in a Jesuit manner to the general public, but it mostly is due to the imposing increase of the circulation of money as a means of payment, whose function in its relative share prevails far above its function as a purchasing means, an increase due, especially and mostly at a time of crisis, to the difficulties and to the delay of the payments of enormous financial transactions. This exclusive exceeding of the function a means of payment over the function a means of purchase, expresses the great share of the credit operations of big business in front of strongly restricted and reducing consumption of means of existence with money in cash by the millions of small depositors—the workers, and proves to be the most significant factor of the inflation *seen from its purely monetary side*, however, itself being an effect of the activity of the monopolies and the state, but not a cause. This lack of balance between the two functions of money is slightly expressed at a time of thriving but being particularly strong at a time of crisis.

"And this actually occurs in certain periods of crisis, namely, when credit collapses completely and when not only commodities and securities are unsaleable but bills of exchange are undiscountable and nothing counts anymore but money payment, or, as the merchant puts it, cash."[245]

Namely, because of the existence of the function a means of payment, it appears an inevitable passing each other between the quantity of money in circulation and the quantity of commodities in circulation. If the credit did not exist, that would not have been like that but it would have seemed much simpler and clear—as a medium of circulation, money would have always corresponded exactly to all commodities in circulation. But that means that the human civilization would have remained forever on the same primitive level of development. However, with the function a means of payment, which is a function of money of the highly developed commodity economy, the direct relationships between money circulation and commodity circulation are dissolved and "the quantity of money current and the mass of commodities circulating during a given period . . . no longer correspond. Money that represents commodities long withdrawn from circulation, continues to be current. Commodities circulate, whose equivalent in money will not appear on the scene until some future day. Moreover, the debts contracted each

---

[245]. Marx, *Capital*, 3:530.

day and the payments falling due on the same day, are quite incommensurable quantities."[246]

The passing each other between commodity circulation and money circulation is the first prerequisite for a possible general rise in prices, under determined conditions, i.e., a potential factor in inflation. But that's all—it is only a potential one. While the passing each other between value and price is the other such factor—fundamental and determinative. Because, even if there is a discrepancy between commodity circulation and money circulation, if there does not exist a passing each other between value and price, there will not be inflation!

In the contemporary, highly developed, capitalistic production, credit has reached such dimensions, such a development that in comparison with its manifestation of the money as a means of payment, money's function as a medium of circulation is an unimportant magnitude. And precisely for that, this function—a means of payment, because of its relatively outweigh in the money functions, is a paramount potential factor for inflation, but not the cash money in circulation, which has minimum importance and influence on it, i.e., manifold more the credit within the wholesale trade is a possible pump for inflation than the sales in the retail trade. The printing of bonds, but not the "printing of money" because of wage-rise; the business on account transactions, but not the cash money as a whole! It is very interesting what explanation would given the economists of monetary school, Friedman's successors, after twenty or thirty years when the cash money will fully disappear?!

For whom is, however, intended this theory with its naïve explanation of the inflation as "printing of money" because of wage-rise?—For the poor, to make them suggest that their miserable incomes are to blame for their later back vanishing like Balzac's shagreen skin, that their relatively decreasing wages and salaries are the cause of the absolute increased commodity prices! The share of the wage (salary) compared to the other incomes at the capitalist society—profit, rent, and interest— as well as compared to the total capital, is so small that it would not have deserved any attention at all, if it, the wage, was not especially branded as the fatal source of the inflation. Even if the wage had some influence on the inflation, it would certainly have occupied the last place there! It is not the printing of money for wages and salaries, but the printing of shares and bonds for the stock exchange that is the modern

---

[246]. Marx, *Capital*, 1:163.

pump of inflation; not the wage, but the share capital is the genuine source of inflation; not the real wage, but the fictitious capital, not the worker on the street, but the stock-jobber in Wall-street who generates night and day inflation.

The passing each other between value and price exists also at the market, pre-monopolistic capitalism. But because of domination of the gold standard and even more because of the absence of monopolies as a basic mode of production, as well as the role of the state far from that which it currently has, there is no inflation or it is a sporadic phenomenon only. On the contrary, the statistics gives us a continuous drop in the general price level in the most developed capitalist states Great Britain and United States in the second half of the nineteenth century, thirty whole years—between 1865 and 1895.[247] The appearance of the monopolistic capitalism from that time on radically changes the things while putting an end to the free competition, whose end coincides with the appearance of paper money or rather monopolistic capitalism itself introduces it and imposes as a more profitable mean for itself. The banknotes were not devalued at the pre-monopolistic, classic capitalism of the nineteenth century, because they had a gold guarantee, too, except that one by the credit. At the time of the monopolistic capitalism in the beginning of the twentieth century, the gold standard was abolished and the banknotes were not exchanged anymore against gold, while becoming in this manner more and considerably more than the real needs of commodity circulation. Thus, the banknotes were transformed into paper money and their overflow into the circulation—into inflation.

Today, when the gold standard was abrogated long ago, opening the way of the domination of paper money, the role of world money instead of gold is played by the currency of the most powerful economy—at the border between two centuries and two ages, it is the American dollar. But the depreciation of money in great dimensions follows the same scheme as formerly. At the time of great crises, there is always a reflux of gold (currently, in the shape of US dollars) from the given country to abroad. The internal currency remains without the respective gold holding at the central bank and instead of being retrenched, overflows with its nullity the channels of the circulation. The power of money as a purchasing means slumps, being a result of its acute deficit as a means of payment. The feverish demand for money as a means of payment,

---

[247]. Friedman, *Money Mischief*, 133.

parallel to its extremely restricted supply, increases the basic rate of interest until superlunary heights because of the abrupt cheapening of money, in whose value is already measured less, a much less number of commodities. Then "the quantity of paper money issued,"[248] if it is really replacing a commodity-value measured out in gold that is two times less, then the price of this commodity-value will be respectively two times higher. This scenario of crisis in a time of peace was illustrated in colors and manifold played in Bulgaria from 1990 to 1997—during the seven-year Night of Walpurgis (combined with the Bartholomew's), when the plunder of the rich was the despair of the poor—an infinite! (This plunder in this endless night is ominously repeated until now— 2016! Using absolutely the same scheme, which razed the whole bank system in Bulgaria in 1996, eighteen years later, in 2014, was robbed with 3 billion US dollars Corporate Commercial Bank, one of the mightiest Bulgarian banks until this moment. The helplessness and the lawlessness in the society are just disheartening!)

The inflation, which on the surface of the economic life manifests as a rise in prices of the commodities with the simultaneous diminution of the purchasing power of the money, is only an external manifestation of the monopolization of the reproduction process. That is why, during the pre-monopolistic capitalism, the inflation is an occasional phenomenon, only a keen fit at a time of crisis, while in the contemporary age, it is a chronic disease of a dying organism. Initially, the monopoly was a brief solution of the keen contradictions of the capitalism, one of which is the passing each other between value and price. This is not a contradiction between I and III volumes of *Capital*, not a contradiction in Marx's theory, but a contradiction within the capitalistic mode of production. And initially, the monopoly was its temporary measure precisely at the time of crisis. The monopoly stops the automatic mechanism of free determination of the prices by the competition. In this manner—through the monopoly prices, the big capital gains and survives, while the small capital loses and perishes. After the end of the crisis, however, the monopoly becomes superfluous; it becomes already chains for the free development of the productive forces. But until the monopoly functions, the prices are determined not by the average (the general) rate of profit as market prices, but by a strongly increased monopoly rate of profit as monopoly prices. During the classic capitalism, the general price level of the commodities is determined by the general (average) rate of profit.

---

[248]. Marx, *Capital*, 1:151.

Because of its tendency of falling, the general price level evinces also a tendency of falling. That is why, under pre-monopolistic capitalism, there is always inflation just and only at a time of crisis, after which the free competition imposes even a tendency of certain falling of the general price level as a result of the tendency of falling of the general rate of profit. But during the monopolistic capitalism and especially during the state-monopolistic capitalism, the influence of the general (average) rate of profit is stopped for the purpose of extracting monopoly excess profits through monopoly prices. If these prices are monopoly high, they are initially increased—as a cause. And if they are in force for a rather long time, as it was in Eastern Europe, in particular in the USSR and Bulgaria—monopoly low prices for series of commodities that were retained artificially, they are later increased because that becomes necessary—the socially necessary expenses impose that. This general rise in prices is possible, only because there is a reserve, an excess above the monopoly low production prices of the total value produced, allowing in this manner for the prices to gain on their total value—the cause is precisely the passing each other between value and price of all commodities.

Nowadays, since already a hundred years, inflation has become chronic. Chronic inflation is immanent only to the state-monopoly capitalism, because it is a product of the state-monopoly property, a product of the contemporary centralization and concentration of capital. The market mechanism of the free competition never leads to the rise in prices, even on the contrary, while the state-monopoly does it always, because of the artificial regulation of the market precisely through its prices. The automatism of the market pricing is ousted by the regulated state-monopoly pricing.

The monopolies are one of the paramount factors of chronic inflation. The independent and objective determination of prices by the free competition is ousted by negotiation, agreement of the prices between powerful monopolistic groups and unions. Thus, because of the artificial intervention in the economic processes, the monopolies lasting violate and deform the effect of the objective economic laws of the capitalist commodity production, which leads to a durable, long-lasting, chronic crisis of the capitalist reproduction, whose outer manifestation is the inflation. For this reason, the interpretation of inflation is not found only in the peculiarities of the monetary system, of the money circulation, of the specificity of the paper-credit money as a cause, but they are only an effect of the functioning of the whole economic system of the monopoly capitalism, and as for chronic inflation—of the state-monopoly capitalism. Inflation is generated as essence by the overall reproduction process of the monopolistic capital with its exploitation, by the mode of production, exchange, and distribution. Inflation is only a form of unjust distribution of the national income, i.e., a form of social injustice in the capitalist society. In other words, inflation is a form of exploitation in this society—it is a hidden, secondary, indirect, and additional exploitation in the circulation, except the overt, primary, direct, and basic exploitation in the production. Inflation is one of the levers of the state-monopoly regulation, which regulation is a basis of the humane "incomes policy"—a regulation of the incomes in favor of the rich, in favor of the monopolistic financial oligarchy, of the state-monopolistic Establishment. Inflation is an insolent and hypocritical way of robbery of the working class and the society in general, it is a form of the relative impoverishment of the working class—the case when $\Delta v < \Delta(v+s)$. The wage-price "spiral" is invented by errand ideologists in justification of the additional capitalist exploitation in the circulation. Such a scurrilous advice of "moderate inflation" was given by Keynes for the first time and echoed by Friedman—the rise in prices continuously to outstrip the rise in wages but to affirm constantly the opposite: for the purpose, firstly, to credit the budget deficit of the state and secondly, to regulate the conflict capital-wage labor.

Just Keynes in direct text wrote that the inflation is a convenient and profitable way for a robbery of the real wages of the workers without they are able to resist! The philistine Keynes saw that the united clan of the capitalists is much more powerful against the working class with joint actions through a centralized rise in prices, i.e., through state regulated inflation, than through the reduction, the cutting down of the nominal wages by every individual capitalist of his workers! "Whilst workers will usually resist a reduction of money-wages, it is not their practice to withdraw their labor whenever there is a rise in the price of wage-goods."[249] Keynes's frank cynicism is praised as a higher science already a century without being decisively repulsed! His collection of scrawls, however, serves as a textbook for the capitalist class on how to cope with the working class. Quite impudently, Keynes advises his rich patrons, promoters, sponsors, and supporters that for the workers:

---

[249]. John Maynard Keynes, *The General Theory of Employment, Interest, and Money*, 18.

It would be impracticable to resist every reduction of real wages, due to a change in the purchasing power of money which affects all workers alike; and in fact reductions of real wages arising in this way are not, as a rule, resisted unless they proceed to an extreme degree.[250]

In other words, for untroubled trample on worker and workless, Keynes recommends "moderate inflation," and Friedman reiterated this conjuration later. But in contrast to Friedman, Keynes unabashedly acknowledges the purpose of the inflation—easy, fast, and sure enrichment of the capitalist class through additional robbery of the other class, the working one—not in the works only but in the shop also!

That is why, a reproduction process based on social property of the means of production, deprived of exploitation, a process with equal rights relations in the production and distribution, repudiates the possibility of inflation. This reproduction process creates that social relation of the wage as a self-expanding value, which precisely establishes the equilibrium between prices and wages, not admitting such a rise in prices, which means a cut of wages, i.e., inflation. The uninterrupted growth of the wage as a self-expanding value means uninterrupted growth of the purchasing capacity of the working class, of the large masses of the population, which, on its part, excludes the depreciation of money.

Besides that, during this reproduction process, during these production relations a monopoly cannot appear and develop, however large, however powerful a given company is, because it is forced to appropriate surplus value toward its capital with the same degree as the smallest and the weakest company. The **property** does not allow the big business to absorb the small one, i.e., the latter will never be able to fall in bankruptcy because of the gravitation of the former. The social property neutralizes this gravitation precisely, the centralization of the capital. Only the competition of the private property creates the centralization of the capital which leads to the monopoly, i.e., the monopoly is born from the private property, although swallows it then, just like Zeus—his father.

The other paramount factor for the existence of chronic inflation is the state with its intervention in the activity of the monopolies through its continuously growing unproductive expenses. As a usual practice in

---

[250]. Keynes, *The General Theory of Employment, Interest, and Money*, 24

our days, following Keynes, the deficit of the state budget is chronic, constant, mostly due to the avalanche of the increasing parasitism and militarization of the economy. And both the budget deficit is a speculative affair for financing the parasitic structures in the society and the national debt is a known medieval means for "management of the state's property by the Bourse and in the interests of the Bourse,"[251] widely applied still since the dawn of the developed capitalism, i.e., since the beginning of the 19th century, for fast, facile and sure profits of secret and open world bankers' families. "At their birth the great banks, decorated with national titles, were only associations of private speculators…"[252] The enrichment of this world financial oligarchy, of this world class of persons of independent means, is due to the fact that in every country the national debt, the "government bonds form the most important subject of speculation and the Bourse is the chief market for the investment of capital … in an unproductive way."[253] Therefore, in such a country the ruling class is a deeply corrupted breed of scoundrels, because "in such a country a countless number of people from all bourgeois or semi-bourgeois classes must have an interest in the state debt, in the Bourse gamblings, in finance."[254] This debt circumrotation is invariable already hundreds of years; the new is only the engulfment of more and more new states with their state debts. But once it exists, the system remains "the same: constant increase in the debts, masking of the deficit."[255] Thus "each generation leaves behind another more deeply in debt—each new generation begins under more unfavorable and more aggravating conditions…"[256] "Thus the villainies of the Venetian thieving system"[257] as a source of the national debts and the world credit system led to "the modern doctrine that a nation becomes the richer the more deeply it is in debt"[258] and this doctrine is steady in full. "Public credit becomes the *credo* of capital."[259] The capital conquers new lands precisely by means of the public credit. As Marx notes, "the public debt becomes one of the most powerful levers of primitive

---

[251]. Marx, *The Class Struggles in France, 1848 to 1850*, 3:113.

[252]. Marx, *Capital*, 1:823

[253]. Marx, *The Class Struggles in France, 1848 to 1850*, 3:114.

[254]. Ibid.

[255]. Ibid.,117

[256]. Ibid.,121

[257]. Marx, *Capital*, 1:824

[258]. Ibid., 822

[259]. Ibid.

accumulation"[260] of the capital, i.e., from the primitive accumulation until our days the Venetian thieving system remains the same! It says that capitalism and national debt are synonyms of this very social system. "National debts, i.e., the alienation of the state—whether despotic, constitutional or republican—marked with its stamp the capitalistic era."[261] In other words, the national debt has given rise to modern capitalism. Because precisely "the national debt has given rise to joint-stock companies, to dealings in negotiable effects of all kinds, and to agiotage, in a word to stock-exchange gambling and the modern bankocracy."[262] The subject-matter of the national debts and the modern bankocracy in the first two decades of the twenty-first century is especially topical, is a problem of the present day since there is neither a country in the world that is not a subject to political and economic bondage through heavy state loans by this very bankocracy. And the more developed is a nation the heavier is its national debt—quite according to its modern doctrine … from the nineteenth century! This concerns especially the killing indebtedness of the United States and the European Union as well as China.

So, the big capital and the state, and their products—the joint-stock capital and the national debt, i.e., the modern bankocracy, are precisely the modern factors of inflation! The "printing of money" as if takes its rise from the nothing! "The state creditors actually give nothing away, for the sum lent is transformed into public bonds, easily negotiable, which go on functioning in their hands just as so much hard as cash would."[263] Here is the mysterious origin of the inflation—the bonds, the negotiable effects emitted by the state, which functions on the market flush with the cash! In the final reckoning, the state creditors, this "class of lazy annuitants,"[264] are financial alligators "to whom a good part of every national loan renders the service of a capital fallen from heaven."[265](!)

However, the national debt must be guaranteed. How? By taxes, of course!

As the national debt finds its support in the public revenue, which must cover the yearly payments for interest, &c., the

---

[260]. Marx, *Capital,* 1:822
[261]. Ibid.
[262]. Ibid., 823
[263]. Ibid., 822
[264]. Ibid.
[265]. Ibid., 823

modern system of taxation was the necessary **complement** of the system of national loans. The loans enable the government to meet extraordinary expenses, without the tax-payers feeling it immediately, but they necessitate, as a consequence, increased taxes. On the other hand, the raising of taxation caused by the accumulation of debts contracted one after another, compels the government **always to have recourse to new loans** for new extraordinary expenses. Modern fiscality, whose pivot is formed by **taxes on the most necessary means of subsistence** (thereby increasing their price), thus contains within itself the germ of automatic progression. **Overtaxation is not an incident, but rather a principle**. In Holland, therefore, where this system was first inaugurated, the great patriot, DeWitt, has in his "Maxims" extolled it as the best system for making the wage laborer submissive, frugal, industrious, and overburdened with labor.[266]

The permanent increasing national debt, which has currently become a tedious annoyance only for any Cabinet, is a feature characteristic of increasingly growing parasitism, leading to putrefaction of this system. But in a withering away state, this cause for chronic inflation—the state expenditures—simply drops out. Because, instead of continuously seeking different ways to cover its expenditures, including an emission of new paper money, such a state will reduce continuously these expenditures themselves. By decreasing the unproductive expenses, by not admitting a national debt as well as a budget deficit, by reduction of the state orders, by the unburdened until its maximum tax policy, the withering away state will favorably influence the stability of the monetary unit, i.e., the state will also drop out as a factor for the appearance of inflation.

So, the basic cause for inflation under state-monopolistic capitalism is the artificial raising of the general rate of profit—by the monopolies—with the so-called "premeditated rate of profit," as well as by the state—in the nationalized branches and productions, for the purpose of increasing the revenues to the state budget. In other words, the fundamental authors of the chronic inflation are two—the monopolies and the state. During socialism, inflation cannot exist, because, firstly, there is no ground for

---

[266]. Marx, *Capital*, 1:824 (bolded text is mine—T.B.)

development of the monopoly, since the general rate of profit is **const.** and cannot be raised. This law—$p' = $ **const.**—does not admit the monopoly, since it does not admit the private property of the means of production before, not admitting in this way further the centralization of capital and the capital as such. And secondly—the state is withering away, i.e., a permanent process is realized of reduction of the unproductive expenses.

However, under capitalistic production relations, both factors with their mutual effect separate, detach the price from the actual value of the commodity, creating a contradiction and even a tension between them. The contradiction between value and price leads to a disturbance of the reproduction of the capital, which is expressed the best at the time of crisis. This contradiction, slighter during the classic capitalism and especially strong during the state-monopoly capitalism, leads to deformations of the relation between commodities and money, between the general price level and the mass of money in circulation—a contradiction generating inflation. But when the price coincides with the value, when price and value are in harmony, in correspondence, this contradiction just drops out and along with it—the phenomenon of inflation, too. The lack of inflation exerts an extremely favorable influence on the stability of the monetary unit, of the incomes, of the capital, of the safety of the investments. Provided that chronic inflation misses, there would be no continual rise in prices of the means of production, i.e., at an invariable value of money, the constant capital does not become more expensive and then the same value-composition of the capital will not express a different organic composition or the same organic composition will not be expressed in different value-composition and thereby, a different productivity of labor. On the contrary. But that is done again only upon the coincidence of value and price, achieved by the same general rate of profit.

Chapter Eleven

The So-Called
"Payment of Labor"

This is a term that comes from the pre-Marxist political economy, yet, and has widely entered also into daily use. This is a jargon, but not a scientific language. The "payment of labor"—a beloved hit of the bourgeois folklore, led formerly to an impasse in the theory, confusion, and insoluble contradictions that Marx cut up with (his) labor power. Only just Marx introduced the laborer with his labor power as a figure in the political economy and even as a determinant figure. Only then as a fundamental category, together with the capital, was imposed the wage, too. And if the crisis in the social sciences was recognized today again and especially in the political economy, this is still due to the very same reason—that what is paid? The labor! But not the labor power!

This delusion led to divagation and stumbles in the labyrinths of the bourgeois political economy of all theorists of that time and of our days. Because with the "payment of labor" the nature of the capital and its process of exploitation is veiled, is dimmed, representing it in its transformed form, and "this confusion of the theorists best illustrates the utter incapacity of the practical capitalist, blinded by competition as he is, and incapable of penetrating its phenomena, to recognize the inner essence and inner structure of this process behind its outer appearance."[267]

The contemporary, already "socialist," thought "under the warm summer showers of state socialism"[268] fabricated this falsification by promoting it to the rank of law that applies for socialism—as a "Law of payment according to the quantity and quality of labor." So, the above puzzle got even the form of law in our days! However, there is no such a law in the political economy of socialism, neither such socialism, yet!

Firstly, payment according to the quality of labor—this is a crown

---

[267]. Marx, *Capital*, 3:198.
[268]. Ibid., 2:16.

of academic ignorance. For the value of a commodity is determined only by the quantity of socially necessary labor containing in it. The value of a commodity, from which ostensibly depends on worker's payment under the form of wage, is not determined by the quality of labor, i.e., by the concrete labor, but only by the quantity of labor, by the abstract labor. The quality of labor, i.e., the concrete labor, determines not value, but **use value** of the commodity, from which, however, the worker is not paid because this value does not take any part in the process of producing and expansion of the value.

Secondly, as far as the payment according to the quantity of labor is concerned, we must underline especially that the labor is only a function of the labor power, because of which not the labor is paid, but the labor power of the worker, not the function, but its owner, its bearer. The worker really puts a certain quantity of labor for the production of a given commodity. His payment, however, is not for this quantity of labor that he puts now, but as a part of **passed** labor, of another labor done before him. Just because of that the capital is a production relation of domination of dead labor over living labor. The passed labor is that with which worker's labor power is purchased and advanced as a potential power having the respective habits and abilities to put a determined quantity of labor according to a production quota established previously by the capitalist. So, not the labor, but the labor power of the worker is paid as an aggregate of knowledge, skills, habits, etc., i.e., as a supplied by the worker commodity! "Wages, therefore, are not a share of the worker in the commodities produced by himself. Wages are that part of already existing commodities with which the capitalist buys a certain amount of productive labor power."[269] I would like to recommend here to the ex-state professors, being market luminaries now, to consult Dr. Marx with respect to this question (and not this one only!) because he had resolved it long ago. To such unenlightened theorists, otherwise "Marxists" until recently, and political weathercocks now, I'm obliged to tell that the struggle against the capital begins as a struggle with the *Capital*!

Nowadays, like in Marx's time, too, the wage looks deceitful and is seemingly accepted as "a certain quantity of money that is paid for a certain quantity of labor,"[270] i.e., as a price of labor—both by the general public and the academic science. Although Marx had already warned us

[269]. Marx, *Wage Labor and Capital*, 7:23.
[270]. Marx, *Capital*, 1:588.

Todor Bombov

that the "classical political economy borrowed from every-day life the category 'price of labor' without further criticism."[271]

"It is not labor which has a value. As an activity which creates values it can no more have any special value than gravity can have any special weight, heat any special temperature, electricity any special strength of the current. It is not labor which is bought and sold as a commodity, but labor *power*,"[272] i.e., labor does not have a value and labor does not have a price in order to be paid. "Labor is the substance, and the immanent measure of value, but has itself no value."[273] This coloring of payment of labor comes from the "fact" that the labor power allegedly did not have any value under socialism. Not the labor is the commodity that the worker sells in order for it to have any value and price. The "payment of labor" leads to value of labor and price of labor; because the payment of the value of each commodity is done at the price of this commodity—the labor in our case. But "the value of labor is only an irrational expression for the value of labor power."[274] And also the "'price of labor' is just as irrational as a yellow logarithm."[275] "In the expression 'value of labor,' the idea of value is not only completely obliterated, but actually reversed. It is an expression as imaginary as the value of the earth."[276]

The wage represents a passed labor, by which the present living labor is advanced. The capitalist does not pay for worker's work under given productivity of labor but by reason that the worker works for him in general. This is precisely the content of the so-called "wage fund" (or "labor fund")—the worker is paid with money obtained from realized passed labor, but not according to the quantity of labor put by him at the present moment. It is paid not the labor put by the worker now, but by another worker's labor put before. The labor power, but not the labor is what made by the worker a potential commodity. The labor power, but not the labor is what the worker sells as a commodity against payment. That is why, under socialist production relations, too, we have to proceed not from payment of labor, but from payment of labor power when we study the conditions of when and how it ceases to be a

---

271. Marx, *Capital*, 1:591.
272. Ibid., 2:24.
273. Ibid., 1:590.
274. Ibid., 593.
275. Ibid., 3:924.
276. Ibid., 1:590.

commodity. Unfortunately, the dominating opinion, the official thought was and is the profoundly rooted "payment of labor," which was entangled both before and now the political economy "into inextricable confusion and contradiction, while it offered to the vulgar economists a secure basis of operations for their shallowness, which on principle worships appearances only."[277]

This "law" negates itself by its own systems of payment implemented in various periods of sharpening of the economic contradictions in our country. So, for example, the grading system is a negation of "payment according to the quantity of labor." The grade is a subjective assessment of the wage based on the professional experience but not on the quantity of labor put in and on the productivity of labor. A young worker with a lower grade may produce more value in a given time, all other conditions being equal, but to get a lower wage than an older worker having a higher grade, i.e., more quantity of labor is paid less! In other words, the "law" is not valid but is fabricated because its manifestation—the grading system—does not correspond to it and it cannot apply as law.

If the grade represents a payment not according to the quantity of labor put in, where for an equal quantity of labor different wages are paid, the situation with the "factor of labor participation" (FLP), which displaced the grade, was not better since the subjectivism was led to a still higher degree. If the grade is permanent, the FLP is variable subjectivism—assessed every month. Here it was paid not according to the quantity of labor in this "new" system, but according to the obedience, according to the submission.

And the so-called "skill ranks"—apprentices, journeymen, and masters—were the last mousy strain of our economic thought until 1989 to give birth to a mountain, representing an attempt to implementation of the caste differences, quite remote from any payment according to the labor. Contrariwise, this was a payment according to the points won. The extreme subjectivism of this lottery system with Masonic suspicion led to countless "infringements," which was the reason to suspend it in many places. In short, at these three "socialist" wage systems, the payment was for worker's skills, knowledge, and knack, i.e., as payment of a commodity of labor power, but not according to the quantity of labor put by him in the commodity's production.

---

[277]. Marx, *Capital,* 1:592.

The need to revive our agonizing rural economy evoked to existence a "new" form of payment—the piecework—that was loudly advertised in the late 1980s of the twentieth century and was discovered with gunshots by our great Marxist coryphées. But let's listen to Marx's opinion in this subject-matter:

> But the wider scope that piece-wage gives to individuality tends to develop on the one hand that individuality and with it the sense of liberty, independence, and self-control (i.e., "self-management") of the laborers, and on the other, their competition one with another. Piece-work has, therefore, a tendency, while raising individual wages above the average, to lower this average itself.[278]

Just because there was "payment of labor" in our country, but not payment of the labor power, in the conditions of the absolute state-monopoly capitalism the so-called "wage leveling" appeared. The wage leveling that is possible in this form of capitalism only on the surface of the economic life seems as getting an equal wage for a different duration of the labor time, different intensiveness, and different productivity of labor, an equal wage for different tension in the labor process. But this is the phenomenon only. Wage leveling actually represents a monopoly low price of the commodity of labor power. Besides that, it is a constant price of the labor power, despite its growing value. Or, the wage leveling is an artificially retained, permanent, monopoly low price of labor power for extracting monopoly profits. The monopoly, and in particular the absolute monopoly of the state does not allow the market mechanism to actuate, under which the price of the commodity of labor power—the wage—is to be influenced and determined by the competition. The monopoly low price of the commodity of labor power, together with the monopoly high prices of plenty of other commodities—dwellings, household electronics, vehicles, etc.—provided to the financial party oligarchy in our country, which was the owner of both the state and monopolies amalgamated **enormous** and **secure** excess profits. On the one hand, the costs of purchase of labor power—the variable capital—were insignificant, while, on the other hand, the revenues were guaranteed and high, since, because of the monopoly, this labor power had no right to choice and was forced to pay at monopoly high prices for a part of its necessary means of subsistence. This scissors of the

---

[278]. Marx, *Capital*, 1:611, (added in brackets is mine—T.B.).

monopoly prices allowed really shameless profits to be sapped. This difference between the monopoly low purchasing price of the labor power and the monopoly high selling prices of a number of other commodities provided maximum monopoly profits to a handful of party-state ruling top.

So, the wage leveling is not a feature, immanent to the socialist mode of production, but to the egalitarian capitalism, to the utter form of the state-monopoly capitalism where the price of labor power stays totally far below its value.

If the aforementioned "law" was in force and worker's payment was according to the quantity and quality of labor, then at that "socialist" time, we would not have been led to desperation from the quality of our commodities for the home market to which national party conferences were dedicated (!) and to say nothing of their quantity—an eternal deficit!

The infantile economic thought was interlacing and stumbling in its own dogmas—eliminating some of them, they were replaced with new ones. For example, it "broke off" theoretically with the wage leveling replacing it with "stimulation of labor"—another product of the "payment of labor."

The bonuses were one of the forms of "stimulation." They were prizes for worker's "good service," introduced to "stimulate" him to corvée to the state. The bonuses for the worker were the lure in the trap only, a candy for good children, a wile for faster pumping of surplus labor, something that was usually only a big official's privilege. Accepting such stimulators gave the state capitalists good profits and the workers poor health. "Stimulation of labor" is doping without control.

From the "payment of labor" was generated the economic category of "real incomes," intentionally introduced to distract worker's attention from his basic place where his labor was squeezed in order to transform his entire life into labor time. Since the wage from the basic work position was not enough, the worker was forced to make incomes from "external activity." "Real incomes" are a legalization of the speculation, the jobbery, and lead after themselves to the so-called "unearned incomes." Category of "real incomes" skillfully hides the essence of the capitalist exploitation as well as belittles the importance of the wage (salary). The so-called "real incomes" are actually a metamorphosis of the well-known "earned incomes," which, in spite of being criticized by

Marx (as Lassalle's "proceeds of labor"), had stably spread in our days, as well. In its turn, the latter generates the term of "unearned incomes." We have to emphasize here that every member of the socialist society must live on nothing but one's own wage (salary) only and no other "real incomes." (About the incomes of the liberal professions see chapter nine.) The wage (salary) is the only **real** and the only **earned** (work-based) income. For the one who lives on "real incomes," does not, in any case, live on *real* (!) wage. The sources of incomes under the capitalist mode of production are three—**capital**, whose income is profit (interest), **labor**, whose income is wage (salary), and **land**, whose income is rent. So, within the category of "real incomes," if the incomes do not come as a wage (salary) only, i.e., from labor, they are either from capital as profit (interest) or from land as rent, as well as from speculations or crimes. But in any case, they do not come from labor only or even from any labor at all. (The interest on workers' savings in banks under socialism represents secondary income from the source labor but not from capital!). These "real incomes" were a direct legalization of jobbery and acquisitiveness. This was the reason that there existed a second market—a speculative, black market, running in parallel with the official one. Two such incompatible, mutually exclusive concepts cannot exist in the political economy of socialism—real wages and "real incomes." "Real incomes" create and justify the conditions of transformation of money into capital. Drug business and prostitution could also quite legally enter this income bracket—they claim to be "real incomes," too. "Real incomes" were a real ground for the appearance and development of the business small owner who was later transformed into small capitalist by the same ruling big financial oligarchy.

The so-called "payment of labor" is a concept of the pre-Marxian political economy, which only Marx's labor theory of value could reject as theoretically unsubstantiated. That is why, in their impotence against his iron arguments and facts, specially hired "denouncers" of Marx's theory of value resort not to attempt an elenchus of this theory in essence, in detail according to structure and concepts, but writing big fables and calumnies, a priori, because in this way it is easier, crossing it off whole at once. Just like that, with naked words. Such a scrubby critic of Marx's theory of value, the essence of the Marxism, is Karl Popper. This one is such a jackstraw, that he deserves no attention at all if he was not so totally printed and so often republished for more than seventy years now. This fact allowed him to irradiate the heads of millions of people, unprepared in the matter, with his hollow effusions, by which he aired his disregard and disparagement **without any proof** to the theory of value of Marx. (Product of this irradiation is one of his showed clones—George Soros, the "philanthropist," Jabba the Hutt of the modern world's economy and politics, who is only a secondary source of Popper's philosophical interference). It is obvious that Popper was either with low intelligence, not understanding anything, a layman, who was occupied with activity extrinsic to him, speculating on Marx's creative work, or he was an arch-rogue in the science that was boosted into a position in the society by his likes. Marx's theory of value is, according to his opinion, "one of its rather unimportant parts"[279] of his creative works; it is "a redundant part of Marxism,"[280] which Popper vituperates even as "the Marxist creed!"[281] In his manipulative malice for debasement of Marxism, this creator of similar science slops lies like a gypsy the ready dupes that "the value theory turns out to be a completely redundant part of Marx's theory of exploitation."[282] Quite as a vile swindler, Popper libels Marx even in plagiarism by Smith and Ricardo! This is a mean way to refute Marx's theory. Engels a long time ago wrote "that the criticism of the Marxian system cannot consist of a refutation . . . but merely in a further development."[283] He again, quite exactly explained what represented this sort of theorists—that "in our eventful time, just as in the sixteenth century, pure theorists on social affairs are found only on the side of reaction and for this reason they are not even theorists in the full sense of the word, but simply apologists of reaction."[284] One just wastes his time to answer the local invective of a dwarfish for the science mind! It's beyond any doubt—his history has no meaning.

---

[279]. Karl Popper, *The Open Society and Its Enemies*, 2:185.
[280]. Ibid.
[281]. Ibid.
[282]. Ibid.,191.
[283]. Marx, *Capital*, 3:1010.
[284]. Ibid., 8.

Chapter Twelve

Withering away of the Commodity and Money

The materialistic comprehension of social justice and social equality has its concrete economic meaning. The social equality finds its content in the social property of the means of production, while the social justice—in the production process that is deprived of any exploitation of man by man as well as of man by state, which allows justice in the distribution relations. The production process under the social property of the means of production represents a process of social justice, which in its border transitions is represented by two forms of social equality.

We cannot speak of social justice in a society when social inequality reigns in it. In such a society, it always turns out that the distribution processes are infringed. Actually, they have never been in order. The capitalist distribution relations are always infringed, which allows in the capitalist society to be always found out "deformations," "negative phenomena," and other similar pearls from the lexicon of the bourgeois mind.

Socialism is a society of social equality and social justice, but still equality and justice on **commodity-based** relations. Only under communist society could we speak of equality and justice in their absolute sense—when nothing will be purchased and sold, when neither the equality nor the justice would have been based on **money**, as it is under socialism. That is why, the question arises—how the transition from commodity-based to non-commodity-based production relations would look like, from one mode of production to qualitatively another, a new mode of production, from socialism to communism? This is a question that has never been scrutinized until now, but which is the most interesting and very important question of the political economy. When and how will the commodity drop out and will lose its features? When and how will the product cease being a commodity? How will the commodity-based relations wither away? And what about money?

244

For this purpose, we should remember the two-fold character of the commodity.

Two characteristic conditions determine the commodity: **necessary**—a value, and **sufficient**—an exchange value. The necessary condition in order to be a product commodity is that it has to have a value, i.e., a quantity of human labor embodied in it, and the sufficient condition is that it is intended to exchange, but not for one's own personal use only.

The withering away of the commodity according to the necessary condition—**the production**—is historically predestined by the objective course of the general rate of profit to fall, i.e., by the universal economic, almost natural, process of the continuous growth of the social productivity of labor, by the gradual but certain extinction of human labor in the production of the commodity, by the fact that $\dfrac{v}{c+v} \to 0$. In that moment when the equation $\dfrac{v}{c+v} = 0$ is satisfied for the overall social production in all branches of the world economy, i.e., when the living labor in the production of the social product is extinct in full, the value will wither away. Because there will be no **labor** in the production which, namely, creates the value. According to the Law of value, only the labor may create any value. Therefore, along with the withering away of the labor, the value withers away, too.

The withering away of the value means that the production process will cease manifesting itself not only as a process of producing and expansion of value, but as a labor process, too. The human labor will be such that it will no longer create any value because it will be outside the production process, it will no longer participate in the manufacture of the product. Labor process will not be a production process. Just therefore the production process will exist neither as a labor process, nor as a process of producing and expansion of value. That means that the production process, once having been fully released from human labor, from the presence of the man in it, will continue being fulfilled by **self-reproducing** means of production.

Nowadays, it is a worldwide practice to follow the line of the smallest resistance—since the production continuously throws away more and more "redundant" people, as a result of the objective law in it $\dfrac{v}{c+v} \to 0$, the solution is that they are settled in the circulation, in the services sector and the commerce as well as at sinecure positions in the state and support of enormous mass of unemployed people on relief. All these practices, but especially the last two of them, retard the development of the productive forces and the production itself unleashing the parasitism in the society as a result of the modern bourgeois policy of so-called "social (welfare) state" intended for a class peace under capitalism. And the last vogue's scream now is the revival of the old idea of "unconditional basic income"—another state policy of support of the poor alive and lazy! Although it must be there, in the circulation, the employment tends to zero, too. Because if this objective process is not directed, even though it becomes $\dfrac{v}{c + v} = 0$, even though no labor will be put into the product, if there is an exchange, if there exists a circulation, then the product will be a commodity, too, as soon as it is intended for sale-trade. Indeed, it will not have any value, but it will be a commodity yet. Simply the commodity will be quite modified. Commodity-based relations will again dominate in the society, although they will be no longer value-based relations. The exchange and its reflection—the State—will remain, but maybe not for a long time. The Capital will lead to self-destruction, to a ruin of the civilization because of its own contradictions—no matter if it will be by the outburst of social conflict, of a world war, or as social leukemia—through moral degradation, degeneration, and consumers' corruption. That is why the withering away of the exchange is of vital importance for the society.

The withering away of the commodity according to the sufficient condition—**the exchange**—is determined also by the objective course of the growing productivity of labor, but the withering away of the *exchange value* must go together with the withering away of the *value* and must coincide with it at the same time. Here, precisely here is proved at its best the requirement of coincidence of value and exchange value, here—at the Exodus. Only through the same rate of profit under the socialist mode of production may this be done—because value and exchange value of the commodity coincide preliminarily much before this moment. And it's in no other case. Only then, value and exchange value may wither away simultaneously, to drop out in the very same moment. In that moment when for the overall social production in all branches of the world economy the time of circulation is reduced to zero, $t_{circ} = 0$, i.e., when the production process becomes a process at which is worked only to order, but not for the market, which thus, on its part, becomes extinct as necessary, and the payment is made upon the delivery of the product in producer's own means of production, i.e., in nature, but not in value, then the exchange vanishes, dissolves, dwindles to nothing into distribution! Only then the product, having already nullified both its conditions, ceases existing as a **commodity**! This is the end of commodities' being and along with it of their universal equivalent form—the **money**, too! In this very moment the production relations cease being commodity-based, they become communist. This is such a high development of the productive forces when they themselves will erase the characteristic features of the commodity. That means a full fusion of Man and Nature! It's a complete unity of the animate nature, Shambhala, a joint metabolism of the living planet Earth. Such a technological circumrotation will be reached when society and nature will represent one organism, when the means of production will be an organized, although not reasonable matter, while the labor power will be the gray substance, the brain of this matter.

The production process will not be fulfilled by the direct, immediate participation of the labor power in it. The labor will be radically different, unrecognizable modified, a cybernetic work in full, while the production process will be realized by self-reproducing means of production. So, the production process will run as a natural, but not as a social process. The exchange, dissolved in distribution, will vanish and the product will drop out in its wrapping of a commodity. The distribution will be a stream of products, a direct motion of articles of consumption—for the person, and means of production—for the production process. Such a distribution means that the goods from all the springs of social wealth only then will "flow more abundantly,"[285] as a high-water stream, as a **blood** in living organism. Blood bedewing the brain—the human society, in which every human will work as a neuron according to the great principle: *from each according to his possibilities, to each according to his necessities.*[286]

It is highly probable that the production process will run as an **adiabatic** process, i.e., in constant entropy, without any evolvement of heat. Compared to the "isothermal" production process of socialism, it will have a much higher efficiency, a much higher effectiveness. And Engels is proven to be right when considers that from the entire political economy only the concept of effectiveness will remain!

---

[285]. Marx, *Critique of the Gotha Program*, 1:175.
[286]. Ibid.

Why, however, for construction of the economic laws of the socialism we proceed from the economic laws of a more distant in the time classic capitalism, but not from those ones of the contemporary capitalism? And why just after Marx?

For, firstly, they are laws of the developed commodity production.

For, secondly, the contemporary state-monopoly capitalism is only an effect, a result of just that, free capitalism, its ambivalent modification, a morally degrading variation but not any completely new organization of the society, implanted at once and from on high. Contemporary capitalism cannot be a basis for looking for laws of socialism because it is only a derivative of the classic capitalism. Contemporary corporative capitalism is an exceptional prosperity of the monopoly law and of the monopoly capitalism with the imposing assistance of the state, which, however—the monopoly system and the state—are both the most poisonous scorpions in the garden of socialism and which are developed only on the basis of the classic capitalism of the private property and free market. That is why, by eliminating the prerequisites of the classic capitalism the prerequisites of the contemporary capitalism are eliminated, too, of the capitalism as a whole, of any capitalism in general! So, by rejecting entirely today's capitalism as a social organization and proposal for socialism, we have to return to its first origin, to its first image, to its causes, to its genesis. And there the best interpretation is done by Marx!

Since socialism is a transition period between two radically different, opposed in every respect, economic systems, it contains in itself the characteristic features of each of them—both of capitalism and of communism. Socialism, from the point of view of the commodity-based relations, of the value-based laws, is a special case, at that—a borderline case, and a higher phase of capitalism, but as an economic formation of social property of the means of production, as a society of social equality and justice—a lower phase of communism! It's a lower phase for communism—because of its commodity-based relations, a higher phase for capitalism—because of its humanism.

Communism is a quite different, quite unknown mode of production and mode of life compared to today's ones. Really, from the stage of our time, it is very difficult to see that, it is difficult to believe in it, because everything looks like fantastic nature, utopia, or hallucination. After today's crash of socialism as an experiment—still more.

But it will be like that!

Is not true that the satellite, the laser, the computer, the atom, the smartphone as means of production and communication were not fantastic nature, utopia, reverie even for such great minds like Marx and Engels, which are distant from us at approximately one hundred and fifty years? The world is changed in such a way that today's reality is an illusion, a science fiction for yesterday's tomorrow. "The paradise" is not situated beyond space but beyond time! Because:

The human life

will be an endless upsurge

upwards! upwards!

The earth will be a paradise,

it will be![287]

VIVAT SCIENTIA![288]

---

[287]. Geo Milev, *September* (poem), 26.
[288]. Long live the Science! (Lat.)

New Communist Manifesto

The Contemporary Epoch

The contemporary epoch is a *crisis of the spirit.*[289] This was the indirect definition given by the most eminent ideologist of the modern "industrial society," of the modern capitalism—Zbigniew Brzezinski. The "Prophet" Brzezinski had predicted the fall of the "communist" system. This was not any particular difficulty for a lettered specialist in political science. The subject-matter was to see what would follow afterward. And it was this very blindness about "afterward" which led to the *crisis of the spirit.* There is nothing to be seen "afterward," after "the communism." This was the opinion of the great strategists of the imperialism.

Nowadays, in the beginning of a new century and a new millennium, when the so-called "communist system" had collapsed and a quarter of a century later is already forgotten, when the new prospects to the free development of the capitalist economic system were opened, it was suddenly proven that these gentlemen public prosecutors of the world did not have any ideological (to understand philosophical) adversary. The sorrow that they miss (and as per they—that will still miss) an ideological adversary brings the need for unraveling the infirmities of their own capitalist system, which some its apologists even no longer call it capitalist, but classify, by various euphemisms, the fabricated by them new stages of development of the contemporary dying society. But nobody can suggest any way out. And since it is impossible (and dangerous) to these strategists to be more deeply penetrated below the surface of the things, it is inevitable and normal to reach to a *crisis of the spirit*.

It is true—that leading spirit, **spiritus rector**, which directs any human activity and which is immanent to the free human person, is no longer present. The free spirit in free flight remained to haunt in the

---

[289]. Zbigniew Brzezinski, *The Grand Chessboard*, 241.

glorious historical time. The contemporary consumers' society insists more and more on the consumption and less on the spirit. What Marx was illegally accused by the public prosecutors of the capitalist system—vulgar (and combative) materialism, is actually just the image of this system.

Today, we live in a world changed by new industrial technologies, a world transfigured if compared to the last 150 years, when communism as a doctrine had started mightily to invade the minds and the hearts of millions of people. That is why nowadays some prominent apologists of capitalism want to convince us that the communist idea is dead, that communism is inadaptable and archaic to our time, the new time, and that capitalism, although modified, is the eternal and the best system. Nothing like that, gentlemen! This delusion is on your account!

What, in fact, has changed over the last 150 years? The world! But not the Capital!

Today, in the second decade of the twenty-first century, we live in the epoch of information technologies and electronics, of atomic energy, and cosmic flights. The sooty and grease-stained worker from the smoking factories is almost in the past. We can already see the iron-muscled proletarian, stand-up against black walls only on the old placards. Hard and exhausting labor withers more and more away, transforming into more attractive and lighter work. But this is not a merit of the Capital. This is due to the technical progress, to the science, to the education, and to the continuous workers' struggle for a better life. Labor becomes lighter, but remains **hired**! Physical labor yields the place more and more to the intellectual work but in both cases, it is hired! What does this matter for the Capital if its accumulation is done not by much sweat, as formerly, but by many nerves, as nowadays? This is only what has changed for 150 years: the form, the visible form of robbery of the labor—less sweat, more nerves; mental work instead of manual labor; intensive labor instead of extensive; compound labor instead of simple. But the nature of the robbery—the suction of surplus value—remains the same as it was 150 years ago. Worker's labor power is a commodity that he is compelled to sell just as he did 150 years ago. The capital-labor relation remains the same as 150 years ago. Labor is hired, but not free! Labor is hired—when and where it existed! The unemployment in the contemporary advanced capitalist countries has assumed alarming proportions and it threatens to reach after thirty years 100 % by the fit for work population! The exploitation is no longer exploitation of the black corns, but of the white gloves. But it is the same by its contents both within the early industrial society and in the so-called "post-industrial" society. The exploitation may already be not only rough, but fine also, not barbarian, but civilized, but it still exists!

Today our weakness (and superiority) in comparison with the people of the nineteenth century, after Goncourt's words, "is that they were living on the eve of all hopes, while we do in the day after their wreck!"[290]

Within the contemporary crisis, which is the deepest in the development of Marxism, we are witnesses of the decline, of the inhumation of one idea—the idea of communism. A specter is haunting Europe! Still as specter! Today, it continues to adopt by lots of people that communism is only a beautiful fiction, a fiction from the nineteenth century. Today, it continues to adopt by lots of people that that perfect society without violence and injustice, that world without commodity-based relations, the world without money and without wars, is a utopia only. But this is not true. Communism is not utopia! Communism will be a reality! But the gradient toward it is named socialism.

Why, however, from being the ideal of the poor, socialism transmuted into a guillotine of the grocers? Why from a "brilliant future" did it become an obscure past?

Since the Marxist, i.e., the scientific, truth of it was transmuted into a lucrative demagogy through the canonizing of it as a state religion. However, any demagogy crumbles one day—even if it has been a religion.

Socialism has collapsed with rumble because, in fact, it had never really existed! Its false nature just like a termite pillar, internally eaten, was ready to grind into dust upon a most delicate exterior touch. For a very long time, socialism was ceased to be a science and was turned back into utopia. Because of that, it had never existed in practice, too. But if the recent utopia had been called socialism that does not give reason for socialism to be called utopia!

The contemporary epoch—since the Great October Socialist Revolution to our days—is an epoch of turbulent political events, whose scale and power were unknown during all the human history. This is an epoch of the strongest until now deepening of the general crisis of

---

[290]. Edmond de and Jules de Goncourt, *Diary*, 296.

capitalism and entering upon the final its stage, having its expression in extreme conflicts of class, race, religion, and nation. This is an epoch when the state-monopolistic capitalism in the so-called "socialist" system reached to its extreme and possibly final form in the utmost degree of monopolization of the property—the complete, the absolute fusion of the state and the monopoly capital, with concentration and centralization of capital unknown to that time that led to the fusion of the industrial, banking, and trade capital in one and only center directed by an unimportant in number but a powerful financial oligarchy. This is an epoch in which, after the dissolution of this political system, the imperialist neo-liberal doctrine led to the last repartition of the world markets and spheres of influence. This occurred when the multinational capital trampling on all kinds national barriers did away with the national states in Europe ensnaring them in a shapeless feudatory formation and in the same time created unipolar world despite Putin's circles efforts in the last decade to redress the former influence and political parity of Russia. This is an epoch in which the monopoly structure of the world imperialism from the beginning of the twentieth century grown in its end and in the beginning of the twenty-first century into the oligopoly structure of a mega-imperialism, i.e., imperialism raised to several powers! The mega-imperialism in two of its manifestations—militarism and parasitism, already in mega-dimensions—nowadays stifles even the last attempts at a free development of the humanity. But thereby, it only creates the conditions and prerequisites for a forthcoming new Great Socialist Revolution, for a radical change of the contemporary capitalist society, for revolutionary conversion of capitalism into socialism!

In this epoch neither the wars decreased, nor the weapons did. On the contrary, militarism shot up with a new mortal force as if the 50 millions of victims of the Second World War were not sufficient. Actually, that was just the state-monopoly capital, which gave the economic base of fascism which touched off this monstrous war. Nowadays, this is always the state-monopoly capital, which creates and develops new strategies to wage local wars instead of world ones; for the rich North and West opposite the poor South and East; for the triumph of the violence, hardened by the Corps of Peace! This contemporary neo-colonialism must ensure new markets and marionette regimes in the poor corners on the earth where to carry out a quiet and obstacle-free export of capitals; and nuclear garbage, too.

After the dissolution of the "communist" empire USSR in 1991, only one great power remained—the world empire of the USA, the other Evil Empire, as world gendarme and enforcer to establish peace. Then even the epitaph of "communism" stated so—a New World Order! The New World Order meant the end of the ideological bipolar world divided between "Communism" and "Democracy." But for the general public, this was a great delusion that they were two different social systems. On the contrary, this was one capitalist system in two forms. Then why was this delusion convenient for both sides facing each other at the ideological frontline? Eh, well, for an easy control of the masses—from both sides of the line. For an easy manipulation of the public spirit from both sides of the barricade, that was the most convenient formula—communism! The ones were attacking "communism," the others were defending it. Thus, the masses were obeying—each one with own masters shaping its own part of the world in its own image. Meanwhile, the formula was worn out by use and had to be changed. Simply from the 1980s on, the civilization was attacked by the predatory things of the century, the society from both sides of the line started to be not interested at all in the spirit of communism, too! So, like Pascal correctly noted, "it is natural for the mind to believe, and for the will to love; so that, for want of true objects, they must attach themselves to false."[291] What are the results of today's NWO—to speak of high ideals today? Quite to the contrary—of low passions only! Ideals? Empty words!

***

The Socialism

History, Theory, Practice

Before decapitating the king in London, nobody had been able to believe this was possible. Before decapitating the "communism" in Europe, nobody had been able to believe this was possible. But that happened—in both cases. To the spectators, history always gives surprises. The king in London and the "communism" in Europe were dethroned without glory. Without the king being able to reach Europe, nor the "communism"—London! The common point, in this case, is not the king and Europe but the communism and London. It's named Karl Marx.

Since the end of the twentieth century, we live at a time when again

---

[291]. Blaise Pascal, *Thoughts*, 79

a flood of verbal mud, dirty foam waves flooded the name and the memory of this scientist of genius and brilliant philosopher. Marx—one of the Seven Wise Men of all times does not deserve such a destiny!

In 1830, on Paris' barricades, the working class appeared with much blood for the first time at the political stage as an independent force. During the next decades of the century, its miseries did not touch at their end, neither its striving for freedom found peace. Half a century later, in 1886, the American worker obtained, with blood again, the right of each worker to hold his head proudly and its body straight. Out of the dark and hard workdays, he gained one day of the year for his own luminous holiday—the First of May. A second century already, this Easter of the working class is celebrated with the flying flags. Really, only the most luminous dates in the human history can establish such a secular tradition. But it looks like this holiday, together with the reduced working day, remain the most significant successes until now within its long age-old struggle against the Capital.

To describe the existing system, Marx and Engels appeared. They gave the scientific explanation of the existing economic system and traced the trajectory of the future—the socialism. Marx and Engels were the first who pointed out, like Lenin notes later, that the working class with its claims was a necessary product of the contemporary economic system; that just it was and is the driving force of the future new economic system—the socialism; that socialism and free labor are equivalent concepts and they are possible only if based on a social property of the means of production.

The continuation was not late. Lenin appeared with his Bolshevik party, with the determination to upturn socialism into reality. The Great October Socialist Revolution came in the name of a radical change in the status of the working class, for socialism, but it did not succeed to put into practice its project. On the contrary, its flags and ideas were used for oppression just of the working class and for contradistinction between two imperialist systems. It placed the beginning of a despotic political system, but not in the favor, just the contrary, to the detriment of the working class and the wage labor, known nowadays as totalitarianism. Totalitarianism—this was not socialism. Socialism is with a human face! And no one else!

Actually, in 1968 in Czechoslovakia, Dubcek requested, "socialism with a human face!" And he won the sympathies during the Spring of Prague. Then, just like all the others, he was maybe thinking that **this** was socialism. The delusion, which had invaded not only his person there and then, is still living in all minds here and now. Why? Because socialism cannot have another face, but human! If this face is not human, that means this is not socialism! Still, Oscar Wilde had written "that no Authoritarian Socialism will do,"[292] when was seeking a place for the soul of man under socialism. Still, he rejected such "an industrial-barrack system, or a system of economic tyranny."[293] Still he rejected such an "authority, by bribing people to conform, produces a very gross kind of over-fed barbarism amongst us."[294] Unfortunately, Wilde was one of the few thinking people until now, who understood that "the true perfection of man lies, not in what man has, but in what man is!"[295] Without accusing him of communism, he could understand "that man thought that the important thing was to have, and did not know that the important thing is to be."[296] He was the first who wrote socialism with a capital letter, precisely because the soul of man under Socialism had to find peace and Individualism.

Socialism—this was the lie of the century, the lie of the twentieth century! A lie that has been repeated one hundred times is adopted as truth! This Goebbels's axiom had its absolute confirmation about socialism. Moreover—one hundred times by one hundred per day, during forty-five years for East Europe, and for the USSR this was for seventy-five years, adopted as truth by millions of people, which still cannot shake off this lie—the past was socialism for them.

The current historical situation after 1990 is not a restoration of capitalism. For socialism did not ever exist. The danger of false socialism was foreseen still by the classics of this doctrine. And despite everything, socialism was visited us in the twentieth century precisely such—as false, which is a proof in itself that this was not socialism. The so-called "real socialism" was a virtual reality, whose fraudulent nature showed up quickly and easily—immediately after its overthrow as a state religion, which was no longer profitable for the priests of this system. Socialism was not socialism. It was ordinary capitalism—of state, monopolistic, state-monopolistic. The so-called "world socialist system" was actually a state-monopolistic capitalism—more of state and more

---

[292]. Oscar Wilde, *The Soul of Man under Socialism*, 3:236.

[293]. Ibid.

[294]. Ibid., 243.

[295]. Ibid., 237.

[296]. Ibid.

monopolistic of any other at any time. The "world socialist system" was a state-monopolistic capitalism in its supreme form with a full, absolute degree and therefore—utmost, degree of socialization of the means of production, with an extreme degree of monopolization of the property by a single owner—the state. Such an utmost degree of socialization, such an extreme degree of monopolization of the means of production means an over-centralization of capital in the hands of a single master, the state-capitalist. Marx had a long time ago written that "in any given branch of industry centralization would reach its extreme limit if all the individual capitals invested in it were fused into a single capital. In a given society the limit would be reached only when the entire social capital was united in the hands of either a single capitalist or a single capitalist company."[297]

Such a socialization of the means of production, with kept old production relations of the capital created that absolute monopoly, which cemented the entire economic and social life and enclosed this system with "iron curtains." The old production relations in this sham socialism meant again, in the same way, the transformation of the money into capital, i.e., that the labor power was a commodity again, such as it had been always under capitalism until this moment. This was an unknown precedent in the history of capitalism originated from the Soviet Union and copied by its satellites—an over-concentration and over-centralization of capital, allowing a financial oligarchy to have an unlimited power of the analogy of the feudal absolutism.

Socialism suffered a fiasco as an experiment because of two basic reasons.

Firstly, because of deep delusion, that the economic laws of socialism were revealed, while, in fact, all economic processes were subordinated to capitalist laws. Marx's political economy was replaced by the constricted bourgeois political economy, repudiated by Marx himself a long time ago, with its narrow-minded "payment of labor." After Marx having categorically and utmost clearly explained that it was not the labor but the labor power, which was the commodity to be sold by the worker against payment, it should not come down back again to the level of this—pre-Marxian—political economy, but it should be explained when and how in the commodity world the commodity of labor power

---

[297]. Marx, *Capital*, 1:692

ceases being a commodity and hence, when and how it ceases the transformation of the money into capital.

Along with that, the inveterate thinking raised the indestructible dogma that the state property is a social one. The state property is not social! Ever since the state exists in the society, the state property has not ever been social! How does the state property become social—that is the question! That is what had to be cleared up.

Secondly, because of the intentional renunciation and no applying of the principles of Marxism concerning the state. This especially brutal attempt was carried out against the underlying principles of socialism about the state—those five guiding principles, which are mandatory as measures for the destruction of the old state and for the construction of the new, the socialist state. It was exclusively easy on the capitalist base of the social production to distort, to vitiate the principles of the scientific socialism, i.e., those principles of orthodox Marxism, which build up socialism as a political system, all those postulates of Marxism about the state, which since Lenin's death until our days were brutally crushed down and forgotten. These are five underlying principles, directed against the place hunting, the lawlessness, the waste, and the corruption in the state, against the feudal inviolability of the privileges and the arbitrariness of the autocracy—against all that, which had been so deeply penetrated like leprosy in our rueful reality. These five principles provide the socialist contents of the state as a class state, but not as a people's state, what it was proclaimed in all countries of "the world socialism". The *people's state*, which was under slashing criticism by Marx, Engels, and Lenin is an ideal state, a utopian and impossible state within the class society, in which, no matter if we want this or not—we live; a nonsense in the scientific explanation of the essence of the state, but an exclusively convenient illusion for any ruling plutocracy for the purpose of easy manipulation of the society, having its expression in the "solidarity of the people," the "unity of the nation," etc., for forming class peace and class collaboration.

During all the time of ex-socialism's existence, but hitherto, as well, the worldwide economic opinion and popular fallacy is that socialism—this is state's intervention into the economy. Hence, "more socialism" means more state's intervention! Nothing like this! Socialism is a market economy, but without private property! Socialism is a market economy without state's regulation. Socialism is a market economy more than any other, even the most market capitalist economy! Socialism—this is the free market analyzed by Marx cleared up from any state's intervention and regulation. Something that is absent even in the most developed and "free" market of today's capitalism. One of the purposes of the socialism is the emancipation of the economy just from any ward and regulation from the state, not only restraint but the full removal of the étatism in the economy. Socialism is not private property; it is not state property, as well. Socialism is something completely different—an antipode both of the private and of the state property. Socialism is social property and only of the means of production, but not of anything else— women, dwellings, or chewing gum, for example!

The aim of socialism, the proper aim, as the great British man had truly perceived it, is to "reconstruct society on such a basis that **poverty will be impossible!**"[298] Indeed, as distinct from Christianity, which is a doctrine to relief the poverty only, Marx's socialism is a doctrine to abolish the poverty in general. Something more—Marxism is the only **scientific** ideology that defends the poor. Another matter is that in the same way as the Christianity did, it was promoted to the rank of being established church for defending the rich!

Laying up a fortune is a weight, a duty that one has to be continuously a slave of. That is why still after the words of the genius of Albion, the rich (not only the poor!) are interested in the abolition of the private property and their emancipation from the excessive duties through establishing socialism. Just socialism incarnates really the idea of the civil society, which is so insistently propagated in our days, because entirely under it—the socialism—the guiding policy in the society is the withering away of the state, i.e., development of the civil society and the permanent dwindling to nothing of the state compulsion and bureaucracy. Only under socialism "as a natural result, the State must give up all idea of government!"[299] Only under socialism is Rousseau's *social contract* feasible.

Many years ago, Lenin wrote that Marx and Engels were the first to expound in their works that socialism was not a fiction of dreamers but ultimate aim and necessary result from the development of the productive forces in the contemporary society. Socialism is not a fiction. Socialism is not utopia. Socialism is a science, at that is an exact science. A

---

[298]. Wilde, *The Soul of Man under Socialism*, 3:232, (bolded text is mine— T.B.).
[299]. Ibid., 242.

science, whose principal task is to explain how becomes the change of the society from one its state—of bestial animosity, to another—of soaring of the human spirit.

Is the socialism possible in practice in the modern high technologically world?

It is not only possible, it is not only a completely feasible reality, but more than anything else, it is high time the socialism to put in practice just in today's highly developed but already dying and in a death agony capitalist world. In order to implement the socialism in practice, however, it is necessary to accomplish a radical turn, a radical change in the economic and politic status quo in the present capitalist system. And this radical turn in the whole mode of production involves the implementation, at least in the most developed countries, of the following fundamental measures:

1. Demolition and abolition of the monopolies and the contemporary corporative capitalism in general through the establishment of a social property of the means of production, which is completely feasible reality even in the conditions of the developed commodity production, however strange this may seem to anybody! It is possible such an economic mechanism of the social reproduction which ceases the effect of the capitalist economic laws in such a way that the labor power ceases being a commodity, and the process of expansion of value stops creating the social relation of capital.

2. Repudiation in whole of the contemporary capitalist model of a criminal economy in its two basic manifestations—the share capital and the offshore zones. Share capital is a fictitious capital, a capital of speculation, and just it engenders the criminal bargains of all kinds. Just the share capital—shares, bonds, securities (corporate and state)—is the root of the evil in the modern world. Share capital is an unreal, inexistent concretely capital, which, being printed on expensive paper, exceeds thousands of times in value the real capital in the material reproduction and is annually pumped as a colossal balloon; in this way, the share capital becomes a source of all contemporary local and world financial and debt crises. Stock exchanges, the Wall Street mostly, are those boils and tumors in the economy that must be weeded in order to turn it back to the initial position of normally functioning world economy. That means an emancipation of the society also from the baneful coalescence of the state with the share capital in the process of abolition of the share capital itself as immanent of the capitalist mode of

production. That means an abolition of the modern economic slavery of the nations through incessant floating of national debts by the modern multinational inquisitors and assassins—the banks, whose feeding navel string for this purpose is precisely the share capital. In this connection, the offshore zones and centers are established, and just with that end in view—the brigandish plunder from each point of the world to be hidden away in a safe place! They are depots of the organized criminality—all the world profiteering and criminal business remain intangible there. They are treasure islands where are buried the money-bags under close guard by their bands after the pirate forays and plunders over the serial big bank or a destroyed state.

3. Repudiation of the contemporary capitalist system of exploitation with its private and state corporative property, system that is based on wage labor and generating unemployment in alarming proportions. Repudiation of the contemporary rapacious tax system which is a serving subsystem of the exploiting system of the national debts providing the excess profits of a world financial oligarchy; replacement of this tax system with a new one—equitable and effective, which is not allowing double and triple taxation both of physical and juridical persons as the present taxation is.

4. Repudiation of all forms of parasitism. The modern capitalist state buys its class tranquility from the poor by starving the class contradictions using a doctrine it invented itself, the so-called *welfare state,* i.e., by using the high growth of unemployment, the modern capitalist state especially breeds parasites that it pays in order that they do not mutineer against it! In West Europe after the Second World War already the third generation grows and reproduces on the dole and reliefs only! So-called *welfare state* (or *social state*) is a policy of class peace and class collaboration. Labor is a right when there is an expressed free will for it, but labor is a liability when there is a scornful refusal of it. Just this had ever in mind Marx and Engels in their Communist Manifesto when they wrote about "equal liability of all to labor,"[300] i.e., that in a new society the former nabobs have to give up their scornful idleness and parasitical life on the labor of the enormous mass of supporting them paupers.

5. Freedom of labor, social equality and social justice in their concrete economic and politic dimensions. Social equality and social justice are attainable solely in the social and economic formation socialism and its higher stage communism.

---

[300]. Marx & Engels, *Manifesto of the Communist Party* , 1:59

6. Inauguration of direct democracy in all spheres of the social and political life. That means inauguration of a new electoral system, repudiation of the so-called *free* electoral system and acceptance of the *mandate* system under which every elected person is responsible in front of his or her electors *at any time*! That means still inauguration of this mandate electoral system in all spheres of the social life but not only in the representative state structures, i.e., in the economy, in the education, in the health services, in the forensic system. This, in fact, is the most democratic system ever possible in the contemporary society with sophisticated mutual relations and connections.

7. The working men have a country! Today's mixing of nations and cultures occurs in a forcible and inadmissible way under the specious pretext for allegedly free movement of capital, goods, services, and people, on the one hand, and under the guise of refugees owing to unleashing local wars, on the other hand, just like the wars were recently in North Africa and the Near East. Actually, we are speaking of a perfect organized criminal traffic of people on a world scale with ultimate effect a substitution of the native population of each one of states with an endless influx of immigrants. One of the results of this loathsome trade in people is precisely an overthrow of the resistance of the native population in everyone national state against the arbitrary of the national and mostly of the multinational capital and the achievement of class peace with other means. Thus, for example, in the European Union, in a short time was built a new Tower of Babel, which is soon coming to be pulled down. The break of this deadlock is the establishment of a New World Order by nations with equal rights and with mutual respect between them. Marx and Engels have never envisaged the internationalism in a different way. "A sincere international collaboration of the European nations is possible only if each of these nations is fully autonomous in its own house."[301] The break of this deadlock is a world socialism which will make an end of the militarism and all wars in the world! In the modern world order of trusts' and banks' arbitrary rule called *globalism* the nations are forced to endure their torments but this slavery will not be continued still a long time. "No nation will put up with production conducted by trusts, with so barefaced an exploitation of the community by a small band of dividend-mongers."[302] It is now high time for all the nations to liberate

[301]. Marx & Engels, *Manifesto of the Communist Party,* 1:32
[302]. Engels, *Socialism: Utopian and Scientific,* 1:142

themselves from this global trusts' oligarchy through a New World Order—a world Socialism!

The ultimate aim of Marxism is the creation of a classless society on a world scale, a society called Communism—super developed cosmic civilization by free people. That means a new qualitative leap in the organization of all the earth civilization—without states, without money, and without all the evil on the Earth. Only then on it will establish the Kingdom of Heaven, the Kingdom of Perpetual Peace and Love where the men will be the gods themselves!

Let it be socialism! It is possible now! All over the world! A New World Order! Let it be!

The slogan of the New Times in the twenty-first century is:
FREE LABOR, EQUALITY, JUSTICE!

References to Book Two and Manifesto

(All quoted material is from texts in the Bulgarian language.)

Brzezinski, Zbigniew. *The Grand Chessboard: American Primacy and Its Geostrategic Imperatives,* Sofia: Obsidian, 1998.

Engels, Friedrich. *Socialism: Utopian and Scientific*, vol. 1 of *Selected Works* of K. Marx & F. Engels, Second complementary edition in 10 volumes. Sofia: Partizdat, 1985.

Friedman, Milton. *Money Mischief*: *Episodes in Monetary History*, Sofia: Damian Yakov, 1994.

Goncourt, Edmond de and Jules de. *Diary*, Sofia: Narodna Kultura, 1982.

Keynes, John Maynard. *The General Theory of Employment, Interest and Money*, Sofia: Hristo Botev, 1993.

Lenin, Vladimir Illyich. *On the So-called Market Question*. vol. 1 of *Complete Works*, Second complementary edition in 55 volumes, Sofia: Partizdat, 1979-1982.

Marx, Karl. *Capital,* vol. I, II and III, Sofia: Partizdat, 1988, 1989, and 1990.

———. *The Civil War in France*. vol. 3 of *Selected Works* of K. Marx & F. Engels, Sofia: Partizdat, 1984.

———. *The Class Struggles in France, 1848-1850*, vol. 3 of *Selected Works* of K. Marx & F. Engels, Sofia: Partizdat, 1984.

———. *Critique of the Gotha Program*. vol. 1 of *Selected Works* of K. Marx & F. Engels, Sofia: Partizdat, 1984.

———. *Inaugural Address and Provisional Rules of the International Working Men's Association*, vol. 1 of *Selected Works* of K. Marx & F. Engels, Sofia: Partizdat, 1984.

———. *Manifesto of the Communist Party*, vol. 1 of *Selected Works* of K. Marx & F. Engels. Sofia: Partizdat, 1984.

————. *Wage Labor and Capital*. vol. 7 of *Selected Works* of K. Marx & F. Engels, Sofia: Partizdat, 1985.

————. *Value, Price and Profit*. vol. 7 of *Selected Works* of K. Marx & F. Engels, Sofia: Partizdat, 1985.

Milev, Geo. *September* (poem), Sofia: Septemvry, 1983.

Pascal, Blaise. *Thoughts*, Sofia: Naouka & Izkustvo, 1987.

Plato. *The Republic,* 2nd ed. Sofia: Naouka & Izkustvo, 1981.

Popper, Karl. *The Open Society and Its Enemies*, in 2 volumes, vol. 2: *The High Tide of Prophesy: Hegel, Marx, and the Aftermath.* Sofia: Otvoreno obshtestvo & Zlatorog, 1995.

Stoyanov, Velcho & Adamov, Velichko. *Theory of Finance*, Varna: Galactica, 1991.

Trendafilov, Toncho, et al., *Political Economy* (Short Course), Sofia: Partizdat, 1977.

Wilde, Oscar. *The Soul of Man Under Socialism*: *Selected Works*, in 3 volumes, Sofia: Narodna Kultura, 1984.